THE LANDSCAPE OF ROMAN BRITAIN

Ken Dark &
Petra Dark

SUTTON PUBLISHING

First published in 1997 by Sutton Publishing Limited
Phoenix Mill · Thrupp · Stroud · Gloucestershire · GL5 2BU

This edition first published in 1998 by Sutton Publishing Limited

A catalogue record for this book is available from the British Library

ISBN 0 7509 1874 8

Cover illustration: Reconstruction of the Roman Port, Caister on Sea*, by Alan Sorrel (1904–74) (Norfolk Museums Service/Bridgeman Art Library, London/New York)*

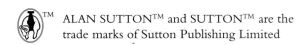
ALAN SUTTON™ and SUTTON™ are the trade marks of Sutton Publishing Limited

Typeset in 10/13pt Bembo Mono.
Typesetting and origination by
Sutton Publishing Limited.
Printed in Great Britain by
Butler & Tanner, Frome, Somerset.

THE
LANDSCAPE
OF ROMAN
BRITAIN

Textual and artistic depiction of part of the Romano-British landscape: the command of the Count of the Saxon Shore from the Notitia Dignitatum. *(Reproduced by permission of the Bodleian Library, Oxford. MS. Canon. Misc. 378, fol. 153v.)*

CONTENTS

PREFACE

Since the early 1960s, increasing attention has been given to 'landscape archaeology' – the archaeological study of the built and natural environment beyond the confines of a single site. Large numbers of archaeological sites have been recognized, and many excavated, and these have been related to their natural surroundings and to local topography. Such research has been assisted by the growth of 'rescue archaeology' – fieldwork ahead of development (such as road construction) and destruction (for instance, by quarrying) – and by new techniques of site discovery, notably aerial photography and geophysical survey. Consequently, the number of archaeological sites of all periods that are known, and that have been excavated, has increased considerably in the last few decades.

Among the most frequently discovered, and excavated, sites are those of the Roman period. The quantity of archaeological material for Roman Britain now probably exceeds that available for any equivalent period of time before the Middle Ages. Simultaneously, increased study of soils, sediments and biological remains by environmental archaeologists has provided a vast amount of new information about the climate, plants, animals and natural features of Britain in the Roman period. Much of this data has only recently become available, and has the potential to provide an increasingly focused picture of the Roman environment.

Despite this wealth of new research, there has been no synthesis that incorporates both 'natural' and 'archaeological' aspects to provide an overall picture of the Romano-British landscape. The various types of biological evidence have seldom been examined together in detail, while the main archaeological syntheses have either been partial (mostly relating to a single type of site or small locality) or are more than a decade old: that is, pre-dating the publication of much of the relevant material. In this book we aim to combine the results of recent archaeological and environmental research to provide a picture of the nature, origins, and end of the landscape of Roman Britain.

We thank Dr Richard Hingley for commenting on an earlier draft of the text. All drawings are by Petra Dark unless otherwise indicated. Sources of other illustrations are acknowledged in the figure captions.

CHAPTER 1

INTRODUCTION

THE ROMAN LANDSCAPE TODAY

It is commonplace to see the modern British landscape as the outcome of historical processes operating over long periods of time, but most studies of landscape archaeology have concentrated on the medieval origins of this landscape. Beneath the overlay of modern and medieval fields, villages and churches there are, however, other – and older – landscapes, which archaeology is beginning to reveal. Currently, perhaps, the most fully evidenced of these is the Romano-British landscape.

The landscape of Roman Britain is at once both present and distant from the modern observer. Roman remains are found in almost every part of England and Wales, yet they belong to a distant millennium. In this earlier landscape, much is strange to us today, yet much seems immediately comprehensible to the observer. To understand why this is so, we must understand the paradoxical character of Roman Britain.

This was a world in which a townswoman in London might sit in her centrally heated living-room reading a letter from her soldier son, and where an upwardly mobile businessman might get a new house built in the country in order to impress his neighbours, while the shopkeepers 'down the road' lived above their premises. It was a world in which all of them paid taxes, and could, in theory, appeal to the law courts if something went wrong.

Yet Roman Britain was also a place with less familiar aspects. Before the Roman Conquest, the Britons had been tribal peoples, with polygamous kindreds, and now-lost myths and folklore. They had been taken into a pagan empire, established by force and without our values or beliefs about human rights or individual liberty. This was an empire in which slaves were held, gladiators fought to the death and – in the earlier part of the Roman period – people were executed for failing to worship a 'god emperor'.

Yet what seems to us today a land of contrasts was a single society, in a sense a single place, in the past. All these aspects of that society were played out in the landscape. In this landscape, as in Romano-British society, there was much that is easily comprehended by someone living in the twentieth century, but much that seems puzzling, even bizarre.

As in the familiar landscapes of today, there were towns, both large and small, and farms and villages in the countryside surrounding them. There were manufacturing centres and military establishments, and areas that were more or less built-up or economically developed. Between these places, roads formed a network of communication, and ships provided longer-distance travel between Britain and other parts of the Roman Empire. As today, generally speaking, the towns were more technologically advanced, and had a greater range of services and businesses, than the country. Likewise, army bases tended to be located either in border regions or close to major political centres, as again we might expect.

There were, however, sites in this landscape that were unlike those of today. The 'Roman villa' must be among the most well known of all Roman monuments, but has no exact modern British counterpart. Although some villas might be seen as stately homes for the rich and aristocratic, as we shall see later, most were not like this. Instead, they were often prosperous high-status farms, with architecture that symbolized their status and associations with the Roman world. It is easy to be so impressed by the most elaborate examples, with their fine mosaics and complex plans, as to lose sight of this fact, but, at the same time, they were not the kind of homes owned by the majority of farmers.

The Romano-British landscape also contained many temples. These would be even less familiar to most modern people. To comprehend them at all, we need to avoid seeing them as in any way similar to churches. Romano-British temples were not designed to serve communities, or even families, by providing places for collective acts of worship. They were not places of burial and were, therefore, not surrounded by cemeteries. Nor were most settlements provided with their own temple. Instead, with the possible exception of a few small cults, such as Mithraism, temples were the settings for rituals performed by priests alone. The surrounding zone, the *temenos*, was kept ritually 'pure' by excluding adult burial, although the bodies of (probably sacrificed) infants have been found at such sites.[1] Non-priestly worshippers visited these temples for a specific reason or on a festival day, as devotees seeking to make offerings. The evidence left by these people in the form of 'curse tablets' (texts inscribed on lead) shows that what they sought was frequently revenge or profit rather than religious understanding.

Villas and temples show a few of the ways in which the landscape, society, culture, religion and economy of Roman Britain were inextricably connected. To try to understand one, we must attempt to comprehend the others. Thus, in this book the landscape will be analysed as a source for Romano-British society and economy, politics and culture, with the hope of clarifying current interpretations of Roman Britain. To achieve this, a range of sources must be employed.

SOURCES FOR THE ROMANO-BRITISH LANDSCAPE

TEXTS AND INSCRIPTIONS

There is no detailed written account of the Romano-British landscape, so it is only in an indirect fashion that written sources – such as the *Notitia Dignitatum* – provide us with relevant information. For instance, there is much general topographical information in texts relating to Roman Britain, and the names of specific places sometimes reveal details of the contemporary landscape (e.g. *Pontis* 'bridge') or even hint at their function (e.g. *Salinae* 'salt-works')[2]. A smaller number of written sources, such as Caesar's *Gallic Wars* and Tacitus' *Agricola*, provide details of the names of specific rivers, hills and other landscape features, but this information is incidental to the purpose of these works.

Similarly, there are no known Roman-period descriptions of the buildings that lay in the Roman landscape. For instance, there is no written description of a Romano-British villa, although such descriptions do survive for villas in other parts of the Roman Empire, even in Gaul (approximately modern France).[3] Nor are there estate maps or financial records from any civilian site in Roman Britain, although fragments of military accounts have been found at Vindolanda on Hadrian's Wall.[4] This scant written testimony can be supplemented by the detailed local information provided by Roman inscriptions.[5] Some of these were both parts of, and give specific information about, the Romano-British landscape, such as milestones,[6] although, again, the information that they provide is very localized.

As evidence for a particular place, inscriptions can assist in landscape reconstruction in several ways. Some enable us to interpret categories of sites, because they identify the function (fort, temple, etc.) of types of site that we can recognize on archaeological grounds alone by the recurrence of similar features and finds. If that type of site can be associated with inscriptions telling us the function of some of its constituent sites, then it can be argued that all sites in this archaeological category are to be interpreted similarly, although such arguments must be applied critically.

It is on this basis that we recognize some sites as temples, others as towns, and others as forts, even where there are no such inscriptions. This is a crucial point because it enables large numbers of Romano-British sites to be assigned basic functional interpretations on strong logical grounds. Sadly, we cannot apply such arguments to every site or even every category of site, because many types of site did not, it seems, ever have associated inscriptions.

Inscriptions can also help to elucidate the social and economic system within which these sites operated, because they include references to social positions and customs, and to economic activities, such as the professions of those commemorated. Inscribed altars and curse tablets show us the religious beliefs of Romano-British pagans, and occasionally Christian inscriptions are found that attest to the Church in Roman Britain.

The relevance of written sources and inscriptions from elsewhere in the Roman Empire as a source for the study of Roman Britain has been a controversial issue among archaeologists in recent years. It can be argued that what happened in, for instance, Roman Italy or Egypt need not have much significance for understanding Roman Britain, although a stronger case can be made for evidence from the north-west Roman provinces, such as Gaul.

Alternatively, and even more controversially, some archaeologists have tried to use post-Roman (but British) written evidence as a guide to understanding Roman Britain. Smith and others have suggested that the 'kin group' and 'extended family' (similar to post-medieval Scottish clans) found in medieval 'Celtic' societies (such as that attested to in the thirteenth-century Welsh laws) help us to interpret Romano-British settlements.[7] In their view, civilian settlements in Roman Britain accommodated large family groups of this sort. This is not an approach that will be employed here, but the reasons why it is of doubtful utility will be discussed at greater length in chapter 3.

Consequently, while inscriptions and other written material are of central importance in reconstructing the political and economic history of Roman Britain – they provide vital evidence of its society, economy, culture and religions, and they enable us to recognize named individuals, population groups and places – they are of little use in the reconstruction of the details of the Romano-British landscape, except as a supplement to (and guide for interpreting) archaeological sources.

ARTISTIC REPRESENTATIONS

There are few artistic depictions of the Romano-British landscape, mostly graffiti showing structures, as at Hucclecote villa, but also the representation of Hadrian's Wall on the Rudge Cup. While figures, plants and animals (and occasionally buildings) can be found in the semi-formal and formal art of Roman Britain, it is hard to be sure that these are depictions of British reality rather than stereotypes derived from wider imperial artistic fashions.[8]

Fragment of wall plaster from the villa at Hucclecote, Gloucestershire, with graffito of a building façade

Romano-British art is, therefore, not very helpful as a means of reconstructing the Romano-British landscape. The limited usefulness of this, and of the textual evidence, means that our key sources are from the natural sciences (especially in the form of environmental archaeology) and archaeology. These are the principal sources on which this book is based.

ENVIRONMENTAL ARCHAEOLOGY

Environmental archaeology is the study of past human environments, involving the analysis of a range of biological remains, soils and sediments. Environmental archaeologists have usually worked on material from individual archaeological sites, but there are now moves towards greater use of sources from the surrounding landscape – 'off-site' environmental archaeology.

Beginning with the 'on-site' evidence, the most direct 'environmental' information about Romano-British agriculture comes from the remains of crops and domesticated livestock. Use of natural resources may also be indicated by the remains of wild plants and animals on the site, although it is not always possible to tell whether these arrived by accident or design. Such biological evidence is generally scarce, because plant remains decay quickly under normal British soil conditions and bones seldom survive in acidic soils. Plant remains may, however, be better preserved if they are charred or waterlogged. Evidence of crop processing and of the storage of foodstuffs is thus most often found at settlement sites in the form of charred grain, while waterlogged material may occur in wells and ditches at the same sites. Occasionally, wooden structures have survived due to waterlogging, such as the waterfronts of Roman London.[9] Animal remains, including those of insects and parasites, can be preserved in a similar way, while bones and snail shells can survive on sites with dry calcareous soils, as in chalkland areas.

This evidence needs special methods of collection. While the recovery of large pieces of wood and of bones from archaeological sites is usually straightforward, smaller plant and animal remains present the excavator with more problems. Seeds, shells, and the bones of small mammals, are usually extracted by fine-sieving large quantities of soil. Charred seeds and other small charred plant remains float in water and can be separated from the soil quite simply: soil likely to contain such remains is mixed with a large amount of water in a container, the sediment is allowed to settle and then the charred material floating on the surface is skimmed off. In a similar way the remains of beetles can be floated out of soil by mixing the sample with paraffin. It is possible to recover even smaller plant and animal remains (including pollen grains and parasite eggs), but this requires chemical preparation of small samples of soil or sediment in a laboratory (see below).

Interpretation of plant and animal remains recovered from Romano-British sites is complicated by several factors. For example, the widespread trade of agricultural products in the Roman Empire means that the presence of a particular species at a site does not necessarily indicate that it originated locally. Such problems may mean that much of the biological evidence from archaeological sites tells us more about diet, plant and animal husbandry, and the processing of agricultural produce than about the surrounding environment. For example, examination of animal bones can reveal evidence of age, disease, and cause of death, as well as the way in which the carcass was butchered for meat. The presence of mollusc shells may reflect their inclusion in the diet also. Oysters were consumed in abundance in Roman Britain, and not only at sites close to the sea.

The remains of some native snails can provide information about the local environment, because different species tend to be specific in their requirements for shade and moisture. These molluscs may enable the environmental archaeologist to tell if the surroundings were open or wooded. Insect remains can provide more detailed information about the environment, as some feed on specific plants. Analysis of insect remains can also give an impression of how people lived, such as the cleanliness of their houses.

In addition to the evidence provided by studying animal bones, human skeletal remains can provide information about diet, nutrition and the health of the human population. However, this is again of limited use in reconstructing Romano-British agriculture, because of the movement of foodstuffs and people between regions.

Biological remains found during the course of archaeological excavation can, therefore, tell us much about agricultural activities, diet, and the range of plants and animals involved in these. Generally, however, biological remains from archaeological sites do not give much indication of what the surrounding countryside was like, since most would have been brought to the site where they were found, whether deliberately or not, from an unknown distance away. For reconstructing the broader landscape we must employ off-site evidence, particularly the technique of pollen analysis.

POLLEN ANALYSIS

Pollen analysis is the main technique for identifying the general character of past vegetation and for studying the way in which it changed over time. Any sufferer from hay fever will be painfully aware of the large quantities of microscopic pollen grains released into the atmosphere by many plants. If they land in waterlogged areas, the pollen grains become incorporated into the sediment and are preserved. Archaeological features, such as ditches and wells, often contain pollen preserved in this way, as well as the larger plant and animal remains mentioned above. However, such deposits tend to have accumulated over short periods, and have often been disturbed by human activity, such as ditch-cleaning. So, off-site sources, especially lake sediments and peat bogs, provide the best deposits for pollen analysis because they have often been undisturbed for thousands of years. Thus, they enable us to monitor long-term changes in the landscape, such as variations in the extent of woodland, grassland and arable land.

To sample these deposits, two methods are employed: cores are removed from lake beds, while peat bogs can be sampled from open sections. Once a sequence of deposits has been obtained, small quantities of sediment (about 1 cc) are removed at intervals and treated by a variety of chemicals to remove as much as possible of the sediment matrix, leaving a residue rich in pollen (1 cc of sediment can contain tens of thousands of pollen grains). Specialist examination with a microscope enables identification of these pollen grains by comparison with modern reference specimens, although the level to which identification is possible varies: some trees (such as pine) and a few herbs (such as ribwort plantain) can be identified to species level, but most herbs can only be identified to groups, such as grasses or members of the daisy family.[10]

For each sample about five hundred pollen grains are identified and counted. Each type is then expressed as a proportion of the total pollen count in each sample, and the results are plotted as a pollen diagram, which shows the way in which the pollen composition of the deposit changes through time. As with archaeological evidence, interpretation of the pollen diagram involves consideration of many factors, such as the different amount of pollen produced by different plants, the variable preservation between species, and the area of vegetation represented. A detailed knowledge of modern plant ecology is required, and often also of geology and sedimentology. This may be why most professional pollen analysts train first as biologists rather than as archaeologists.

Again, as with archaeological evidence, all these types of biological evidence must be dated if they are to be of use in reconstructing the Roman landscape. On archaeological sites, biological remains often occur in the same layers as datable finds, such as coins and pottery. If timbers are present, tree-ring dating (dendrochronology) can be employed. Many on-site sequences do not, however, have such datable finds and off-site deposits almost never do, in which case radiocarbon dating can be used.

RADIOCARBON DATING

Radiocarbon dating can be applied to a range of biological materials, including bone, wood and charcoal. It is also possible to radiocarbon date lake sediments and peat deposits directly. Alternatively, individual plant remains, such as seeds, may be collected from the deposits for a type of radiocarbon dating called accelerator mass spectrometry (AMS), which can be used for much smaller samples than 'conventional' dating.

Even with such dating methods it is often difficult to relate 'events' in a pollen sequence (such as evidence for woodland clearance) to activity connected with the occupants of a particular archaeological site, because there may have been several sites within the 'pollen catchment' of the lake or peat bog. In other words, the pollen record provides an integrated picture of vegetational change in the surroundings.

It must also be remembered that radiocarbon dating does not yield usable dates directly – the results have to be calibrated to produce dates in true calendar years.

Calibrating radiocarbon dates

Radiocarbon dates are conventionally published in the form of uncalibrated radiocarbon years Before Present (BP), Present being taken as AD 1950. Conversion of these dates to calendar dates requires calibration because past fluctuations in the level of carbon-14 in the atmosphere (on which the method is based) mean that radiocarbon years are not strictly equivalent to calendar years. Calibration curves, enabling the conversion of dates from a BP format to calendar years, have been produced by radiocarbon dating wood samples of known age (dated by dendrochronology). Although several calibration curves have been produced, the most recent and most reliable is that published by Stuiver and Pearson.[11] Calibrated radiocarbon dates are conventionally cited as 'cal. AD' to distinguish them from true historical dates, and this convention will be followed here.

To show why calibration matters, and is worth discussing here, let us take an example. A radiocarbon date centred on 1660 BP would be equivalent to AD 290 if radiocarbon years were the same as calendar years (i.e. 1950−1660 = 290), but calibration shows the true date in calendar years to be centred on AD 410. The radiocarbon date, therefore, provides an over-estimate of the age of the sample in this case, which could have serious implications for the understanding of where the event fitted into Romano-British history.

Calibration of a radiocarbon date does not necessarily produce a single calibrated age. This is because the calibration curve is not consistently a straight line but contains 'wiggles' and flat areas or 'plateaux' where change in calendar age is not matched by changes in radiocarbon age. Thus, calibration may substantially increase the timespan represented by a radiocarbon date. For example, a radiocarbon date centred on 1580 BP can be related to the calibration curve by drawing a line that intersects a plateau lasting from AD 450 to AD 530 in calendar years. Furthermore, the error term (i.e. the figure following the +/− after the original radiocarbon date) should also be calibrated in order to give the full possible chronological range of the date. Radiocarbon dating, therefore, always provides an age range for a sample rather than a single date, even after calibration. This fact is of critical importance when attempts are made to correlate different sources of information for a given period.

ARCHAEOLOGICAL SOURCES

Archaeological data might seem to provide an immediately accessible source for the Romano-British landscape. This is partly true in that much archaeological information is available, and the methods of archaeological fieldwork are well-established in Britain. There are, however, problems that must be discussed before attempting to use the vast array of relevant archaeological data.

PROBLEMS WITH EXCAVATED DATA

The principal difficulties in reconstructing the Romano-British landscape are in assessing which sites were, or were not, contemporary with each other, and in dating field systems and minor landscape features.

Excellent dating 'tools' are available to the archaeologist working on Roman Britain – coins, closely datable pottery types, dendrochronology, radiocarbon dating and (often) clear stratigraphical sequences recovered in excavations – and these methods have the potential to enable us to date excavated Romano-British sites very closely.[12] Yet chronological problems do occur. 'Residuality' (the survival of disused objects in later layers) and 'curation' (the continuation in use of valued artefacts) affect the archaeological use of almost all closely datable Romano-British finds.[13] So, a coin of AD 300 need not have been deposited in AD 300 or even AD 350. In coin hoards we find that coins a century or more old were still apparently in use, so that a site with coins apparently dating it to AD 300 might belong to that date, or it might be much later.

These problems combine with the usual difficulties imposed by *terminus post quem* dating: a layer containing a well-sealed artefact may be of that date or later, but we cannot tell (on these grounds alone) how much later. In practice, this means that even excavated sites can seldom be dated to 'brackets' closer than half-centuries, and often only to broad periods within the Roman period, such as first–third century (or early Roman) or third–fifth century (late Roman). Such dating problems mean that contemporary sites, in archaeological terms, may not have been historically contemporary at all. For instance, a group of sites with a date range of AD 100–300 could include sites in use from AD 100 to 150 and those in use from 200 to 300 with no chronological overlap of usage between them. This renders distributions of Roman-period sites, without closer dating, depictions of archaeological data rather than Roman settlement patterns.

Greater precision is sometimes possible at individual sites. For instance, large numbers of well-sealed and closely datable finds come from some villas, where they are found in association with clear-cut sequences of walls and floors.[14] At such sites, therefore, accurately dated structural sequences can be reconstructed as a result of excavation, but the sequences of buildings, enclosures, roads, etc. at most sites cannot be closely dated in this way. This is sometimes overcome by a combination of dating methods, but usually it is not possible to be more exact than to attribute many civilian non-villa rural sites to the earlier or later Roman period. Where few datable objects are recovered, or dating rests on radiocarbon or archaeomagnetic dates, even these broad date ranges may be too narrow. It may only be possible to say that a site is 'probably Romano-British' and no more.

In northern and western Britain, few datable artefacts were in use at most sites during the Roman period, and the form of farmsteads was remarkably unchanging for centuries: from before the Roman period until long after it. In these areas, thin soils and poorly defined stratification often also affect the chances of accurate dating.

In all areas, minor landscape features, such as field-banks and trackways, were seldom places where many datable objects were likely to be deposited. As people did not usually live, or dispose of rubbish, in such places, the discovery of coins, datable metalwork, ceramics and even charcoal (datable by radiocarbon) is rare. Comparison of the form of such features and those more adequately dated may permit the conclusion that they are probably Romano-British, but this is only dating at the very broadest level. Consequently, although we can assign a large number of settlements, temples, forts and roads to the Roman period, we cannot date anywhere near so many field systems or other minor elements of Romano-British topography.

There are also problems of association between finds and landscape features. For example, it is illogical to date a set of field boundaries to the Roman period simply because Roman pottery has been found in the associated ploughsoil. Such pottery could be residual, or it could derive from miscellaneous Romano-British activity at, or near, the site.

Partial excavation further complicates this picture, so that the excavated evidence from a site may relate to only part of a complex plan, or zoned pattern of activity areas, within its total extent.[15] All excavated data are samples of much larger totalities, and, even if a site is completely excavated, we still have to ask questions about its surrounding landscape.

Yet more problems arise in the interpretation of artefact distributions. Objects seldom occur in the positions in which they were once used, and patterns of rubbish disposal and tipping (for instance in disused buildings) can be demonstrated or assumed at many sites. Sites may have been deliberately cleared or dismantled when disused, and structures may have been systematically demolished.[16] The collapse of buildings through age, and the salvage and re-use of 'good' timbers, tiles, etc. in other structures (not necessarily either on the same site or in the Roman period) complicates this.

Subsequently, natural factors usually play a large part in modifying – in practice, reducing – the available data over a period of time. The action of rain, decay, plant growth and of animals living or scavenging among the remains of a disused site can damage, destroy and move artefacts and structural evidence. The data from even well-excavated sites, examined with the latest archaeological methods, are a mere trace of what was once there, and no more than a partial (usually small) sample of such a trace.

These problems have major implications for our ability to reconstruct the Romano-British landscape. Most known sites have not been excavated recently, and many not at all. The majority of excavated sites were either dug with methods that are now outdated or 'against the clock' (albeit to modern standards) ahead of road-building, development, quarrying, etc., rather than as pieces of more measured research.

Even if we can reconstruct the original form of archaeological data from our partial sample of their surviving modified traces, there is still the problem of interpretation. Archaeological data do not speak for themselves; they potentially contain evidence that must be decoded in what is, in effect, a forensic manner.[17] It hardly need be said that archaeologists differ greatly in how much evidence they believe can be extracted from data, and the standards of evidence that can be used to support an interpretation. The practical implications of these theoretical and methodological points are wide-ranging.

In this book, therefore, we will give an interpretation of the archaeological data, rather than the only interpretation that any archaeologist might wish to adopt. Yet we will try to indicate some of the alternatives that might be proposed, and set out why we favour the interpretations offered here.

PROBLEMS WITH SURVEY DATA

Archaeological data do not only derive from excavation, and field survey is a key source of evidence about the landscape. This usually employs any of four techniques, and often all are used in conjunction: field walking, aerial photography, geophysical survey and the collation of earlier records of chance finds (such as those recovered during building or farming operations) to produce distribution maps.

Field survey has become one of the archaeologist's most widely used tools for examining the landscape of Roman Britain, yet it has a number of significant problems. These combine with the difficulties already noted to make it impossible to look at a distribution map of concentrations of Romano-British artefacts (the 'sites' of field surveys) and take this as a map of Romano-British settlement patterns, as attractive a prospect as this may be.

First it must be stressed that not all spreads of Romano-British finds necessarily indicate settlements. For example, some may derive from the manuring of fields with domestic rubbish – a point clarified by the important field survey by Gaffney and Tingle at Maddle Farm.[18]

Further problems derive from geomorphological change and later settlement. Geomorphological changes (such as coastal and riverside erosion, hill-wash deposition, the uneven erosion of downland slopes and hilltops, and the effect of wind on sandy deposits) often lead to the destruction, or obscuring, of Romano-British landscape evidence. Not only can settlements be damaged, but artefacts may be moved by the action of water, or in soil shifted by human or natural means, so as to form concentrations of finds at places that were never occupied. Later settlement can have the same effect, either moving objects from place to place – sometimes in large quantities – or obscuring or destroying data. This has been a particular problem in the West Midlands, South Yorkshire and London, where modern cities extend over what were large tracts of the Romano-British countryside.

The use of Romano-British sites for later buildings can also lead to specific patterns of discovery. An example is the use of Roman villa sites for later churches.[19] In such situations the existence of a villa may become apparent through the re-use of Roman stone and tile in medieval church walls, grave-digging, and the archaeological interests of clergy, churchwardens and local parishioners. So, Romano-British evidence at churches has often been more visible, more often discovered, and better recorded than elsewhere.[20]

Differences in the preservation and recovery of evidence and problems of dating limit the utility of extensive surveys of the distribution of Romano-British material as sources for

Romano-British settlement patterns. The recorded sites are only a partial record of what once existed, and some apparent sites may be either illusory or the result of Romano-British agricultural practices rather than settlement. In other cases, seemingly contemporary settlements may be of different dates and of different types, including types that are either unique or rare, as at Stonea, a stone-built tower in the Fens.[21]

These problems are compounded by the general difficulties of interpreting field survey data. A central problem of all archaeological surveys is the tendency for differences in the ease of access to areas of the modern landscape (for instance, the distribution of roads and footpaths) and the specifics of modern landholding (for instance, of farmers favourable or antagonistic to archaeologists) to affect the recovery of data. In upland or pastoral areas, field survey may produce especially clear-cut site plans, but there is even less adequate dating control, because coins and pottery are less easily recovered from pasture than from ploughed fields. So, while such areas may permit more detailed study of the layout of the landscape, including the relationship of field systems to settlements, these settlements can seldom be closely dated and often remain undated.

Survey data are of great significance, but their interpretation depends on excavated sites, and they are probably unable (alone) to answer any important questions about the Romano-British landscape, unless all of the above problems can be overcome. The problems with both excavated and survey data are exacerbated by regional differences in research patterns.

DIFFERENCES IN RESEARCH PATTERNS

Different amounts of research and fieldwork have been undertaken on each site type and in each geographical area. Villas have attracted more attention than 'peasant' (i.e. low-status, non-villa) farms, and the villas of the Cotswolds more than those of Wales. Such disparities are the result of many factors: research priorities and methods, and the distribution of fieldworkers, specialists, archaeological units (professional teams) and universities with research interests in particular areas. Another factor is the distribution and character of rescue threats, such as construction work or quarrying.

The main result of these differences is that there are more data available for towns, villas, temples, and forts than for all other types of site. Geographically, there are more data from the south and east of Britain (modern south-east England and the Midlands, including Humberside) than from most other areas.[22]

Hopefully, more work on the less impressive and artefactually poor sites of the north and west will add sufficient information in the next generation to negate this imbalance, but there are major problems hindering this. Not only are the sites, especially native farmsteads, often visually unimpressive and/or in harsh situations (frequently wet or windy for much of the year), but also there is still a difficulty in dating sites that often produce few intrinsically datable finds. The possibility of radiocarbon dating bone is hampered by the acidity of many of the soils in these regions (reducing the range of suitable material to charcoal), while waterlogging is rare, reducing the possibilities for dendrochronology. Geophysical survey, while of much value in discerning site plans, is of little use as a dating tool on sites where datable features running across unexcavated areas are rare. Thus, most of the settlements known from surveys in the west and north that might be Romano-British lack adequate dating evidence to confirm this. In many cases they could belong to any period from the

Bronze Age to at least the sixth century AD, as recent excavations in north-west Wales have shown.[23]

In contrast, south-east England has a Romano-British archaeology rich in datable artefacts and features: coins, pottery, metalwork, mosaics and sculptured stone.[24] The arable modern landscape is especially suitable for aerial photography and field walking. So it is unlikely that the relative quantity of data from the two areas will change, unless new methods of site-detection and dating are discovered.

Despite the problems and regional imbalances in the archaeological data, the first way they can assist us in discussing the landscape of Roman Britain is by enabling the definition of two distinct regional landscapes. This in turn permits this book to be organized in such a way as to reflect not merely the distribution of archaeological data, but also political, cultural, social and economic differences in Roman Britain.

DEFINING REGIONAL LANDSCAPES

On a site-by-site level of analysis there is a great variety in the settlement evidence from Roman Britain. Detailed discussion of this, even without including other aspects of the countryside (such as temples, roads and natural features), would require several volumes. In relation to a single site, this variation can be understood in terms of the cumulative effect of decisions made by individuals about site layout and use. As no two individuals (however culturally similar) will make identical decisions all of the time, then as more decisions are made, more variability will inevitably occur. Yet beyond this level of analysis, sites can be grouped into regional and sub-regional types, an approach with a long history in Romano-British archaeology.

From this it is only a short logical step to the recognition that regional groups of site types (such as villas, temples, roads and forts) form groups of sites with interconnected functions or similar aspects to their architecture. Each site has a definable relationship with others occurring in the same area at broadly the same time. We will call such groups of sites 'landscape types', comprising recurrently occurring site types with definable functional or architectural linkages.

In Roman Britain the definition of landscape types in this way produces four such groupings of site types (which, when they occur together, we will call 'components' of their landscape type), and two of these have a strongly marked geographical separation into two distinct 'regional landscapes'. The other two lack this regional dimension; that is, not all landscape types are necessarily regional landscapes.

The first of the regional landscapes was centred on south-east England and was dominated by a pattern of romanized farmsteads and country houses (villas) forming the centres of estates, the holding of which was based (at least in part) on written deeds and Roman law. This we will call the 'villa landscape', although, as we shall see, there were many elements other than villas within it. It is this area that scholars of Romano-British archaeology have previously termed 'the Civil Zone'. The latter term is not used here as it relates to a characteristic that is not definable as a landscape feature, unlike the villa, which – despite difficulties discussed in a later chapter – is recognizable in this way.

The second regional landscape is confined to Wales and the west and north of what is today England. This landscape is characterized by a pattern of landholding based on native (i.e. non-romanized, non-villa) homesteads. Although this landscape has aspects other than native sites (such as many Roman military sites), which makes 'native' not an entirely satisfactory term, we will call it the 'native landscape' in preference to 'the Military Zone', which has widely been used as a counterpart to the Civil Zone. While the latter is not misleading, in that the region contains more military sites than are found in the villa landscape, the majority of sites in this region were not Roman forts but native farms.

It must be stressed that using this new terminology is not to discount the potential utility of differentiating between these zones in terms of the means of their administration, or by reference to the relative degree to which their populations were civilian. However, to divide Roman Britain into civil and military zones seems less appropriate to landscape evidence than the division employed here, and may presuppose an interpretation of how it was administered.

Using the classification set out above, it is possible to move beyond the apparent variability resulting from a site-by-site approach, in which every site looks different from every other. By examining sites both as parts of landscapes (components) and in their social and economic context, an intermediate level between the site and the landscape type may be recognized: the 'local group' of components. Such groups represent 'sub-regional' divisions of regional landscapes, as in the case of the 'courtyard house' of west Cornwall. This does not occur elsewhere, but forms a component of a broader landscape type in the areas where it is present.

It is very important to establish a standard terminology of this type to help us to comprehend both differences and similarites between sites, localities, regions and, potentially (but not in this work), between Britain and other parts of the former Roman Empire. This series of levels of analysis can be seen as running from the individual site, through the site type, to the local group, and up to the landscape type, with landscape types potentially making up regional landscapes.

These levels of analysis are the basis of the discussion of the relationship between settlements and other 'artificial' landscape features, and between these and the landscape as a whole, in this book. They also enable us to employ the well-established terminology of Romano-British settlement archaeology, despite some of its problems, so the conventional terminology for site types used by archaeologists of Roman Britain will be employed here.

Before discussing the Romano-British landscape we will, however, begin with a brief examination of the development of the late Iron Age landscape, as this formed both the immediate predecessor of, and the basis for, many aspects of the Romano-British landscape.

THE LANDSCAPE OF BRITAIN IN THE LATE IRON AGE

The natural landscape of Britain on the eve of the Roman invasion of AD 43 was the result of changes operating over thousands of years. Major clearance of Britain's original woodland cover began in the Bronze Age in many areas, and by the Iron Age both arable and pastoral agriculture were widespread in both upland and lowland areas. Late Iron Age society in Britain also represented the outcome of thousands of years of social, political, cultural, economic and religious change.[25]

Prior to the Roman Conquest, Iron Age Britain was divided into a series of tribal territories.[26] In the immediately pre-Conquest period, at least, these were ruled by royal dynasties, although not necessarily with one king ruling each tribe, nor with a direct descent of political authority within a single family.[27] Roman written sources enable us to identify the approximate locations of these groups, and to understand something of their latest pre-Roman political history, at least insofar as this affected the Roman Empire.[28] Late Iron Age kings minted coins, although the exact function of these is uncertain.[29] The coinage of the late Iron Age allows us to recognize tribal boundaries (and perhaps some aspects of their political history) in greater detail, especially if this evidence is combined with attention to natural features, which may have been used as territorial boundaries in Iron Age Britain.[30]

At the end of the late Iron Age, Britain probably had a kin-based, but socially ranked, society.[31] This is demonstrated both by textual evidence and by archaeological indications of a social élite, at least some of whom seem to have been associated with conspicuous display and probably warfare.[32] There were no towns in the Classical sense, and shrines were mainly small timber buildings, as at Hayling Island and South Cadbury,[33] either inside settlements or, perhaps, at natural features and in woods considered to be of religious significance by the local population.[34] The economy was primarily agricultural and the typical rural settlement was an isolated farmstead, often – but by no means universally – enclosed, of curvilinear timber buildings (roundhouses) and frequently either deep grain-storage pits or four-post structures, usually interpreted by archaeologists as granaries.[35] Mortared stone construction was unknown, as was window glass and roofing tile. Flooring was of earth, and perhaps sometimes wooden planks, and buildings were roofed in thatch, turf and possibly hides or wooden shingles.

These farmsteads were densely distributed throughout what is today England and Wales, and were usually associated with field systems.

A reconstruction of the Iron Age landscape. (Painting by John Pearson, reproduced by permission of the Trustees of the British Museum)

Aerial photography has identified many examples of fields that may belong to the Iron Age, but their dating is often uncertain. As will be discussed in chapter 5, convincing examples of Iron Age fields have, however, been found in several areas, in addition to other archaeological evidence for agriculture.

The clearest evidence that arable farming was widespread in the Iron Age comes from pollen analysis, charred plant remains, and a range of archaeological features associated with crop processing and storage, such as quernstones and storage pits, although Iron Age settlements lack some of the more obvious evidence of crop processing found at Romano-British sites, such as so-called 'corn-driers'.[36] Experiments at the reconstructed Iron Age farm at Butser have included an examination of the function of corn-driers and attempts to reproduce the agricultural methods known from the British Iron Age. This work indicates, for example, that Iron Age crop yields were remarkably high, and clearly sufficient to produce a surplus beyond the needs of the farming community.[37] This surplus may have supported both an aristocracy (and their attendants) and craftworking specialists, who produced pottery, metalwork and glass objects, which were widely traded in late Iron Age Britain.[38]

Although some generalizations can be made regarding Iron Age farms, regional variation in site types is also visible, for instance, between the drystone-walled enclosed homesteads of northern England and the timber-built sites of 'Wessex', as at Little Woodbury.[39] The archaeological evidence, therefore, supports the view of a prosperous agricultural economy with accompanying evidence of social ranking and crafts specialization, a view borne out by the few (short) classical written descriptions of late Iron Age Britain.[40]

This flourishing agricultural economy clearly supported a densely populated landscape. Until recently it was thought that Iron Age settlement and cultivation were limited to light, well-drained soils, while heavier clays were avoided. It is now clear, however, that settlement occurred throughout most of Britain and that a range of soils was utilized.[41] Settlements were mostly single farms belonging to families, rather than villages comprising several kin groups, although in all textually attested Iron Age European communities the family unit was probably much larger than it is today,[42] perhaps giving these farms the character of agricultural hamlets. In the north and east of Britain there are, however, larger unenclosed settlements of late Iron Age date, which may be classified as villages by analogy with post-prehistoric sites (see chapter 3).

The settlements may have been connected by a network of paths or trackways but, if so, these are poorly understood at present. There is archaeological evidence for trackways in Iron Age Britain (see chapter 3), but it is not known how common such features were. While paved 'roads' of Iron Age date are represented by strips of cobbling running through many settlement gates, it is unlikely that these extended far into the surrounding countryside.

This brings us to another type of site that was widespread over much of Britain in the Iron Age: the hill-fort. Hill-forts were hill-top settlements enclosed (often defended) by one or more earthen or drystone-built banks, usually with ditches outside them.[43] Hill-forts vary greatly in form, and were built throughout the Iron Age and later. They vary in size from little more than enclosed hill-top farms to very extensive multibanked sites with large-scale earthwork defences and containing many roundhouses and other buildings.

The majority of British hill-forts are Iron Age, but the earliest examples date from at least the Bronze Age (some would say the Neolithic period) and the most recent were built at least as late as AD 600.[44] Both the earliest and the latest British examples are found in western Britain and what is today Scotland, and it is important to remember that in many parts of Britain not all hill-forts can be assumed to be Iron Age without direct dating evidence.[45]

Throughout much of southern England, however, most hill-forts do belong to the Iron Age, although their currently visible earthworks usually represent only a final phase of development, following a sequence of modifications, often over a number of centuries. However, there may have been a move away from hill-forts in the late Iron Age, leaving many sites unoccupied, while a few probably remained important local centres of population.[46]

The exact function of hill-forts is a controversial issue.[47] Excavations, such as that at Danebury, seem to show a close relationship between some hill-forts and local élites, but this does not necessarily mean that all hill-forts were élite domestic settlements.[48] Large sites, such as Maiden Castle, may have incorporated both élite and non-élite populations, and included ritual aspects. However, while not all late Iron Age hill-forts may have been specifically élite sites, archaeological evidence shows that they were directly involved in warfare among Iron Age

Britons.[49] This was probably organized by local élites, as, it seems, was the defence of some of these sites against the Roman army during the invasion of Britain.[50]

The interpretation of some hill-forts as primarily élite sites does not exclude the possibility that others were also religious and population centres. What may be temples occur within several hill-fort sites,[51] so that some may have been ritual centres as well as, or instead of, political centres. The co-existence of élite and non-élite communities may be evidenced by archaeological data from these sites, and can easily be understood in terms of tribalism, and social and economic factors such as 'clientage'. In late Iron Age Gaul, such 'clients' were dependants who voluntarily attached themselves to the élite, providing support and dues in return for protection and patronage.[52]

A pattern of hill-fort dwelling élites and non-élite farms was, however, probably only the basis of a much more complex set of social and economic relationships, and some other site types may be related to these. Specialist production sites, as at Bryn y Castell, manufactured iron and undertook craftworking.[53] Iron-working and other activities could also have taken place in disused hill-forts, as at Brawdy, south-west Wales, where rubbish tips and hearths occupied the interior of a disused single-banked Iron Age enclosure.[54]

There were also some areas without hill-forts, and some with non-hill-fort élite sites, as possibly at Gussage All Saints.[55] There were also (seasonal?) fairs or trading-places, as at Meare,[56] and a series of coastal trading sites, as at Hengistbury Head,[57] which show that long-distance trade was bringing foreign luxuries to Britain during the late Iron Age, some of which ended up in the graves of the élite.[58]

There are other, perhaps less high-status, exceptions to this pattern of agricultural settlement, such as what may be rectilinear timber (fishing?) huts recently discovered below sea level at Goldcliff in south Wales.[59] This raises the question of the seasonal or 'transhumant' exploitation of resources, as Coles has suggested may have occurred at Glastonbury 'lake village'.[60] Glastonbury is an example of a small class of sites that occur on artificial islands or in other lake settings, and that first appeared in Britain in the Iron Age, although Bronze Age examples are known from elsewhere.[61]

Another, especially important, atypical Iron Age settlement type comprises a series of large blocks of land, enclosed but unfortified, as at St Albans and Bagendon.[62] The most northerly example of such sites is at Stanwick in Yorkshire, the subject of detailed examination by Wheeler and, more recently, by Haselgrove and others.[63] At Stanwick there were large but indefensibly long and low-lying earthern banks punctuated by entrances. Inside these were distinct separate foci of activity – settlements, craft zones, etc. – with open space (perhaps for cultivation or stock) in between, and much evidence of wealth and exotic artefacts.

Such sites are usually referred to as *oppida*, a term challenged by Woolf, who sees them as unclassifiable as a single group, although most archaeologists would probably accept that at least some of these can be seen as a related category of sites.[64] Whether or not they are a site type, these large sprawling complexes are certainly one of the most distinctive aspects of British settlement during the late Iron Age. Before leaving the late Iron Age British landscape, however, two places deserve special notice.

The first is the *oppidum* at Colchester (the 'Gosbecks-Sheepen complex'), which may have played a central role in the history of southern Britain at the end of the Iron Age. The site has been mapped by aerial photography and includes a domestic site, a craft-working zone, probably a temple and burials. The late Iron Age witnessed the rise to political dominance of a tribal king, Cunobelinus, and his people (the Catuvellauni), over neighbouring kingdoms.[65] Cunobelinus'

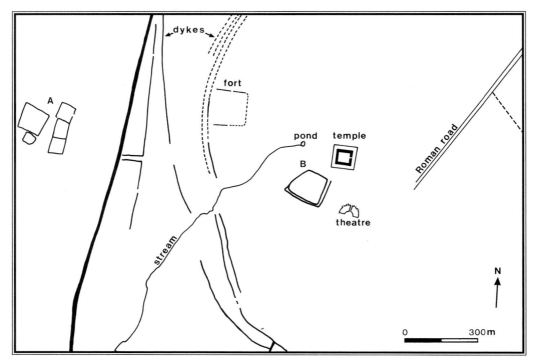

Simplified plan of the Gosbecks area, showing features of the late Iron Age oppidum and superimposed Roman-period fort, road, temple and theatre. Iron Age features shown include: A - enclosures containing high-status burials, B - settlement enclosure, and dykes. (Based on Wacher 1995 after Crummy)

'capital' (the term may not be wholly appropriate to describe a territory that may have had many political centres) was probably at Colchester,[66] and Crummy has suggested that the Gosbecks-Sheepen complex represents this centre.[67] If so, it may indicate the status and function of such settlements elsewhere in Britain.

The complex of sites at White Horse Hill, Uffington, may also have had a special significance in this period. The well-known White Horse (a prehistoric depiction of a horse cut into the chalk) is situated on the hillside below the Iron Age hill-fort of Uffington Castle. The horse has recently been successfully dated for the first time to the late Bronze Age.[68] Interestingly, Uffington is situated at the only point where four late Iron Age tribal territories (convincingly delineated by Sellwood, on the basis of Iron Age coinage[69]) converge. It is possible, therefore, that this figure was used as a landmark to indicate a location in the late Iron Age political geography of southern Britain, or even that the Iron Age tribal divisions of southern Britain also originated in the late Bronze Age. The latter may not be unparalleled. Burgess has argued, on the basis of artefact distributions, that Iron Age territories in Wales also had Bronze Age origins.[70]

It is against this long-established but dynamic background of tribal politics, and in the context of this flourishing agricultural economy, with its social and regional patterning, that we must see the establishment of the Romano-British landscape. This will be discussed in more detail in relation to each of the landscapes examined in this book, but here some preliminary observations may help to set the scene.

THE ROMAN CONQUEST

Some Iron Age British élites put up a sustained struggle in the early decades following the Roman invasion of AD 43,[71] as both archaeological evidence and textual sources attest.[72] The Roman Conquest was, however, surprisingly rapid, and there were areas that did not systematically resist Roman takeover, or only attempted to fight the Romans after having initially tried to cooperate with them.[73]

So, most of what was to become Roman Britain had been conquered by the Roman army by AD 100, and this was followed by an equally rapid establishment of Roman ways of life in south-eastern areas.[74] These regions had already experienced many contacts with the Roman world, and they show traces that suggest the adoption of Roman customs prior to AD 43.[75] Consequently, the adoption of Roman ways of life ('romanization') was already advanced by the time of Britain's one serious native revolt (the Boudiccan Revolt) in the 60s, as remains of destroyed romanized structures at St Albans and London indicate.[76]

It was within the first century of Roman rule, therefore, that new site types and landscapes were being established. The Roman Conquest, together with the process of romanization, did not completely disrupt the native way of life, however, as is evident from the survival of local religious practices and of the Celtic language into the Roman period.[77]

The rich natural resources and the market provided by the new province rapidly attracted businessmen from many parts of the Roman Empire, although it is uncertain how many of these concentrated their activities in the countryside rather than in towns.[78] Even in the countryside there were large non-native populations moving into the province from the first century onwards, in the form of military units.[79] Inscriptions provide us with evidence that these included non-local men who married local women, and whose descendants may have lived in the Romano-British countryside.[80]

This may, in part, be the reason why there is evidence for Latin, and even Latin literacy, in the countryside of Roman Britain from the first century AD onwards.[81] Military groups and the settlement of veterans probably reinforced this pattern of rural romanization, as it would have been difficult to serve in the Roman army without knowing at least some of the language. Latin would also have formed the only common language for western provincials and non-western Roman soldiers. The gradual romanization of rural populations, both as a Roman imperial policy and as an unintended consequence of resettlement and contact, may explain why we see that the names of even unimportant places in Romano-British geography were rendered in Latin by the end of the Roman period. An example is Croydon, south London, where the modern name preserves a local Romano-British Latin version, 'the valley of the saffron flowers', in an Anglo-Saxon form.[82]

Romanization in the countryside, therefore, had a deep-running and pervasive effect during the four hundred years or so of Roman rule, and the population make-up of the countryside was, at least in places, probably significantly changed in such a way as to enhance this process. This is not to say that the British lost their culture or died out, to be replaced by Romans. Most people living in Roman Britain must have been related to the inhabitants of Britain before the Romans came, but many (especially in the towns) probably were not. Some, but not all, of these Britons chose to adopt Roman ways, and romanization did not proceed either consistently or uniformly across the new Roman province. The Iron Age population of Britain had itself not been culturally homogenous.[83] The Roman Conquest, therefore, transformed the countryside, but did not, in every locality, shatter the rural way of life or displace existing farmers.

CHAPTER 2

THE 'NATURAL' ENVIRONMENT

It is debatable to what extent any of the landscape of Roman Britain could have been described as natural, but there were certainly large areas that were neither densely settled nor intensively exploited for agriculture or industry. These areas of woodland, moorland, grassland and heath can be termed 'semi-natural' environments, as they were almost certainly influenced by human activity. It is these areas with which this chapter is concerned.

Human activity has been the most significant factor in causing vegetational change in Britain over the last five thousand years, but this is superimposed on the effects of natural processes acting continually on the environment, on a variety of temporal and spatial scales. Changes in the level of land and sea, which have occurred throughout the period since the last Ice Age, mean that the Roman coastline differed from that of today. Changes of climate affected the ability of Roman farmers to use marginal upland areas, while natural processes of soil change, particularly loss of nutrients due to high rainfall in these upland areas, led to the spread of blanket peat and the loss of potential agricultural land.

Lakes naturally fill with sediment through time, so many of today's lakes would have been substantially larger in the Roman period, and there would have been some that have since filled in completely, as is the case near Hadrian's Wall. River courses also change, a factor that must be taken into account when attempting to understand site location in relation to local topography. Thus, natural processes alone result in a constantly changing landscape. The combination of these changes with human activity means that we can expect to see substantial differences between the present landscape and that of the Roman period.

CLIMATE

Many types of evidence have been used to reconstruct past climates, but they do not usually give the detail required to make them especially useful to the archaeologist or historian.[1] Despite this, by combining a range of sources of evidence for different aspects of the climate, such as temperature and rainfall, it is possible to arrive at an impression of how the Roman climate compared with that of today.

Our knowledge of the climate of Roman Britain must largely be extrapolated from information from various other parts of Europe. A principal source is Roman textual references to unusual weather incidents, such as storms, and particularly cold winters or hot summers. Lamb has collated these, and suggests that cold/wet conditions in the early Iron Age were followed, after about 150 BC, by a shift to a milder climate, which came to resemble that of today by the time of the Roman Conquest.[2] Temperatures continued to rise into the late third and fourth centuries, by which time they may have exceeded those of today by around 1°C. This was accompanied by a period of relatively dry summers, but by about AD 400 there was a return to colder conditions.

The usefulness of textual evidence for climate is limited by a tendency to record only exceptional events such as floods, storms and droughts, leaving the general character of the climate unrecorded. Fortunately, a range of scientific techniques illustrate a broadly similar course of events in the climate of the first millennium AD. These include the study of ice cores from the Greenland ice sheet, the movements of glaciers in the Alps and Scandinavia, tree-rings (dendroclimatology) and variations in peat growth from a range of sites across north-west Europe.

ICE CORES

Snowfall at the Greenland and Antarctic ice caps is deposited in annual layers, which can be identified because of variations in the texture of the snow. Measurement of the proportion of the heavy isotope of oxygen, oxygen-18, to the commoner isotope, oxygen-16, in these layers provides an indication of the temperature at which the snow formed. Where ice has accumulated over thousands of years, isotopic analysis of the annual layers thus provides a means of tracing temperature change over time.

In the record from north-west Greenland, the colder conditions of the AD 400s, suggested by the textual evidence, appear as a minor fluctuation, suggesting that this climatic downturn was of widespread significance.[3] There is some divergence between the textual and ice-core evidence later, however, as the ice-core data indicate a return to relatively warm conditions in the 600s, but written sources suggest that most parts of northern Europe were probably still cold at this time.[4]

GLACIERS

Glaciers respond to climatic fluctuations (changes in temperature and/or snowfall) by changes in size, leading to the advance or retreat of the front of the glacier. Long-term trends in these changes can be reconstructed by study of the deposits left following such movements (moraines) and of sediments from lakes downstream of the glacier. A problem in such studies is that glaciers of different sizes have different response times to climatic change, and obtaining dating evidence for these changes can be difficult. It is perhaps unsurprising, therefore, that not all of the data from different glaciers are in agreement.

While both temperature and snowfall changes can affect glaciers, it has been argued that changes over wide areas are more likely to reflect temperature variations, especially as these correspond to the isotope record from the Greenland ice core.[5] In their study of lake sediments from the Swiss Alps, Leemann and Niessen suggested that the sediment record reflected changes in summer air temperatures in the area. They identified a glacial advance (linked to cooler temperatures) from about 700 BC, and then a retreat (i.e. warmer temperatures) at about AD 100 for around 250 years.[6]

From studies of glacial lake sediments in southern Norway, Matthews and Karlen have constructed a temperature curve (for summer mean temperature) relative to that of today, covering the last 10,000 years.[7] Their curve shows fluctuating temperatures in the Iron Age, reaching a maximum of *c*. 0.5°C greater than today in the middle of the period and then dropping to 0.5°C less than today in the late Iron Age. A recovery followed, leading to a maximum temperature in the middle of the Roman period just *c.* 0.1°C greater than present, followed by a downturn in the late Roman period to *c.* 0.2°C less than today in the mid-sixth century. It cannot be assumed that the magnitude of temperature changes in Britain would have been the same, but the overall trend may have been similar. Further evidence from Scandinavia suggests that several glaciers advanced in the late Iron Age/early Roman period, followed by retreat, and a further advance from the mid-sixth century.[8]

Thus, while there are some discrepancies over the precise dating of glacial retreat in the Roman period, and the advance afterwards, the glacial evidence does again suggest relative warmth during most of the Roman period.

TREE-RING STUDIES

Tree-rings can provide important additional evidence for climate, as the width of the ring of wood deposited each year is related to environmental conditions. The resulting annual variations in ring width are reflected in trees over wide areas and provide the characteristic sequence that forms the basis for dendrochronology. Dated European sequences covering the whole of the last 5,000 years are available for Ireland and Germany, but, unfortunately, their potential for providing a reconstruction of climate has yet to be realized.[9] A shorter sequence of larch tree-rings from Switzerland covering the late Roman period suggests relative warmth from about AD 365, followed by cooling in around AD 400.[10]

There is a further aspect to the tree-ring story that has recently excited much interest, and a fascinating account of this work has been written by Baillie.[11] A link has been found between sequences of exceptionally narrow rings in Irish bog oaks, suggesting unfavourable growing conditions, and peaks of acidity in the Greenland ice cores, linked to volcanic eruptions.[12] Some of these eruptions have been identified, such as that on the Aegean Island of Santorini of 1628 BC, and Hekla 3 on Iceland of 1159 BC, both showing up as periods of narrow tree-rings in Irish bog oaks. Thus, it appears that major eruptions, from such diverse areas as Iceland and the Mediterranean, were affecting climate sufficiently to reduce the growth of trees on Irish bogs. The climatic effects are thought to result from the injection of large amounts of gases, especially sulphur, into the atmosphere. These would have reduced the transmission of the sun's energy to the earth, leading to a fall in temperature. Tree-ring studies suggest that the effects were not long-lived, perhaps lasting for around five years.[13]

From the Irish tree-ring record there are no 'narrow ring events' in the Roman period, but there is one for 207 BC and another for AD 540, apparently corresponding to acidity peaks in the Greenland ice sheet, which again suggests that they were the result of major volcanic eruptions. Both of these dates also tie in with Chinese records of famine and 'dark skies'.[14] A further dust-veil event of 44 BC is recorded in the Greenland ice core, but there are no available Irish trees from this date. This gap in the Irish tree-ring record has, however, been bridged by oak timbers from Carlisle. These show very narrow rings from 40–39 BC, again suggesting a short-lived climatic deterioration.[15] This episode might be connected with records of volcanic glass particles (tephra) found in peat bogs in Scotland and northern England. Estimates of the age of these particles have been obtained by radiocarbon dating the surrounding peat, producing dates that cluster around 2100 BP.[16] Unfortunately, however, when the radiocarbon dates are calibrated, taking into account their error terms, they produce a possible age range for the tephra layer of *c.* 400 cal. BC to cal. AD 100, so it could relate to the 44 BC or the 207 BC eruption.

In view of the apparent frequency of major volcanic eruptions causing widespread climatic deterioration, the Romano-British farmer was unusually fortunate in escaping such events.

PEAT STRATIGRAPHY

Peat stratigraphy is the study of variations in the layers of peat formed in waterlogged environments, particularly blanket and raised bogs. It is one of the earliest methods applied to the reconstruction of climate change in north-west Europe and is one of the few records of climatic change available from Britain. The method uses differences in the degree of decomposition (humification) of plant remains making up the peat as an indication of bog surface wetness and/or temperature at the time of accumulation. Well-preserved plant remains suggest cool/wet conditions while poor preservation suggests warm/dry conditions. Further information can be obtained from the species of plant that make up the peat, since different species require varying degrees of moisture.

The most detailed study of this type, covering deposits of the first millennium, has been provided by Barber's study of Bolton Fell Moss, Cumbria.[17] The results suggested that a relatively wet climate in the Iron Age was followed by a shift to warmer/drier conditions in the mid-second century AD, lasting into the seventh century, followed by a return to wet/cool conditions.

Similar evidence for cool/wet conditions in the Iron Age has been obtained from several peat sites in the north and west of Britain, and is also reflected in many other parts of western Europe.[18] Support for a relatively dry climate in the Roman period is also available from Burnfoothill Moss, south-west Scotland.[19]

The peat bog evidence for climatic deterioration in the post-Roman period is rather variable. Several sites in England, Wales and Ireland suggest increased wetness in the early mid-seventh century,[20] but some, such as Burnfoothill Moss, suggest a drier climate in around AD 400.[21] A problem with this type of evidence is that peat growth in different areas is likely to vary in its response to climatic change, and may also be affected by human activity (see later).

To summarize the evidence for climate, despite the uncertainties attached to the interpretation of the data, it seems clear that the climate of Roman Britain was slightly warmer than it is today, in the latter half of the period at least. This followed relatively cool/wet conditions in the Iron Age. There is also good evidence for a deterioration in climate at the end of the Roman period, although the precise date of this is uncertain.

SEA LEVEL AND COASTLINES

The reconstruction of former sea levels and coastlines faces a number of problems, of which one of the most difficult is that change in the absolute height of the sea surface is not the only factor involved. The height of the land surface also changes, and in different directions in different parts of the country. This is because the north of Britain sank under the weight of the huge ice sheets that covered it during the last Ice Age, while ground further south rose. When the ice sheets melted, around ten thousand years ago, the north began to rise again, and southern Britain started to sink (what is called isostatic recovery). Melting of the polar ice caps has also caused the absolute sea level to rise since the end of the last Ice Age (eustatic changes). Thus, changes in the relative positions of land and sea caused by these factors vary geographically.

Superimposed on these effects are subsidence, plus local factors affecting coastal change, such as the deposition of eroded sediment in estuaries and past attempts at land reclamation. It is, therefore, not possible to generalize about sea level across the whole of Britain from isolated studies at various points along the coast, and data from one area cannot be extrapolated to another. So no general reconstruction of the detailed coastline of Roman Britain can be made, although studies of particular stretches of coast do make local reconstructions possible.

The main sources of evidence for Roman-period sea levels and coastlines come from sediments, and from archaeological sites and finds. Changes in coastal topography since the Roman period are particularly apparent where Roman sites that originally occupied coastal locations now lie inland or have been eroded into the sea. The forts of the 'Saxon Shore' provide an example. These were built on the coast in the third and fourth centuries AD, but several are now stranded from the sea as a result of silting. Burgh Castle fort is currently 6 kilometres inland, while Richborough is 3 kilometres from the sea, overlooking the River Stour.[22]

The most useful sediments are those known to have been formed at a particular point in relation to the boundary between land and sea. These can be mapped and dated, providing an indication of the former coastal topography. Where Roman sites have been submerged and made uninhabitable, dating the base of the deposits formed by inundation provides evidence for the timing of sea-level rise.

Archaeological evidence for sea-level change usually involves the study of artefact scatters and occupation sites in coastal and estuarine areas, assuming that these would have been absent from areas below the maximum reach of contemporary water levels. This assumption may not always be valid, however, since some activities may have specifically required an intertidal location. For example, Romney Marsh and the East Anglian Fens have produced abundant evidence for saltworking in the form of briquetage (a type of coarse pottery probably used to drain salt crystals), but the need for brine makes it likely that such saltern sites were deliberately located between the low- and high-tide marks.[23]

For the Isles of Scilly, Thomas has used the concept of 'minimum occupation level' on archaeological sites now in the intertidal zone to reconstruct the changes in sea level that resulted in conversion of a single land mass to the group of islands present today.[24] This evidence suggests a rise in sea level of 4 metres since Roman times, and Thomas argues that most of the present islands were united until at least the end of the Roman period, becoming separated between the eleventh and fifteenth centuries.[25]

Waddelove and Waddelove have applied a similar approach to Roman sites in various parts of Britain.[26] Their results again suggest a substantial rise in sea level since Roman times, with estimates of 4.2–4.5 metres in Fenland, 4.1 metres (since the first century AD) in London, 2.8–3.9 metres (since the early Roman period) in Dover, and 2.2 metres from Caerleon (since the late third century). They cite some evidence for the extent of sea-level rise within the Roman period. From Roman London, riverbank features in Southwark are argued as suggesting a rise in sea level of 40 centimetres in the second half of the first century, while the position of the Roman quay at Caerleon[27] is taken to indicate a rise in sea level of around 1.4 metres between the late first and late third centuries.

These figures are somewhat greater than the estimated rise of mean sea level of 1.6–2.6 metres since the Roman period produced by Akeroyd from archaeological and sedimentary evidence from a range of sites in southern Britain (the Thames Estuary, Canvey Island, the Thames, the Essex marshes, and the south and east coasts).[28] In relation to the evidence from London,

Akeroyd suggests that figures for a post-Roman sea-level rise in excess of 4 metres are likely to be inaccurate, due to the effects of artificial riverworks and drainage. Other possible explanations of the discrepancies in results between sites include differences in accuracy of recording of levels and dating problems, while in the Fenland there is also the problem of the compaction of peat by overlying alluvial deposits. As mentioned previously, however, some 'real' differences between sites can be expected because of variations in the extent of the vertical movement of different parts of the coast.

Sea-level rise has not occurred as a continuous process, but rather as a series of 'transgressions' separated by retreats of the sea (regressions) during which previously flooded areas could be recolonized. For south-east England, Devoy has recognized five such transgressions since the last Ice Age, one of which ended in the late third or early fourth century AD.[29]

Some of the most detailed recent work on sea-level change in relation to coastal topography has combined archaeological work with sedimentology, notably in the Severn Estuary Levels and the East Anglian Fens.

THE SEVERN ESTUARY LEVELS

The estuary of the River Severn is flanked by several large areas of coastal alluvium and fenland peat deposits termed levels. On the English side the Somerset Levels have been the subject of study for more than fifty years, but attention has recently extended to other parts of the estuary, including, on the Welsh side, the Gwent (Wentlooge and Caldicot) Levels.

At an early stage of the research on the Somerset Levels, observations that Roman material occurred below a considerable depth of alluvium led Godwin to propose a major inundation by the sea – the 'late Roman marine transgression'.[30] Reconsideration of the data by Hawkins and Boon suggested that the Roman material was not, in fact, lying in contemporary deposits but had been redeposited into older layers by erosion from the Roman surface into creeks and inlets.[31] Thus, the principal evidence for a late Roman rise of sea level was removed, and subsequent research on both the Somerset and Gwent Levels has further indicated the need to abandon the concept of this marine transgression.

The peaty nature of much of the Somerset Levels has enabled production of many pollen sequences that illustrate vegetational change from the Neolithic period through to the Roman period and beyond. One such sequence comes from Meare Heath, where shifts in deposition from raised bog to fen peats were argued by Hibbert to reflect an increase in groundwater level, perhaps linked to a higher sea level.[32] Two such shifts are recorded, one beginning at the onset of the Iron Age and lasting into the mid- or late Iron Age, and the second beginning towards the end of the Iron Age and ending in the early Roman period. Similar evidence for an early Iron Age marine incursion has been found elsewhere in the Levels,[33] and radiocarbon dating of deposits from Glastonbury suggests that the estuarine clay once thought to be late Roman in origin belongs to this period.[34] The Gwent Levels also provide evidence of a marine transgression in the early Iron Age, leading to their almost total inundation.[35]

Recent study of the Severn Estuary Levels by Allen, Fulford and Rippon has provided evidence for planned reclamation and settlement at a number of sites in the Roman period, including the Wentlooge Level (at Rumney Great Wharf) and Oldbury Flats.[36] This drainage is discussed in chapter 5, but it is of relevance here that occupation on these reclaimed marshes, which are now below present sea level and protected by a sea wall, suggests a Roman-period sea level that was about 1 metre lower than today.[37]

THE EAST ANGLIAN FENS

The East Anglian Fens consist of a large area of low-lying land around the Wash, encompassing parts of the modern counties of Lincolnshire, Cambridgeshire, Norfolk and Suffolk. Dense settlement during the Roman period is indicated by systems of fields, droveways and drainage ditches, revealed as cropmarks on the alluvial deposits (referred to as the 'silts') bordering the Wash.

The low-lying position of the Fens means that minor changes in the relative position of land and sea can have major impacts on the landscape, and this is reflected in the complex depositional history of the region. The supply of freshwater from the landward side of the basin results in the formation of peat around its edge, while the marine influence causes deposition of clays, silts and sands towards the Wash. A rise in sea level results in a shift of the coastline landwards, increasing the area of mineral deposition and burying areas of peat. Retreat of the coastline increases the area over which peat forms, resulting in layers of interbedded organic and mineral layers reflecting changes in sea level.

The Fens have long been an area of interest in terms of both their sedimentary record and their archaeology, beginning with the work of the Fenland Research Committee in the 1930s and culminating in the recent work of the Fenland Project.[38] Prior to the recent phase of research, the available stratigraphic and archaeological evidence from southern Fenland was interpreted by Godwin as reflecting an extension of marine influence beginning in the Iron Age and continuing into the third and fourth centuries AD.[39] More extensive stratigraphic work by Shennan enabled him to propose a sequence of sea-level fluctuations, including a rise in sea level from the late Bronze Age and thoughout the Iron Age, followed by a fall in the Roman period and a further rise afterwards.[40]

Until recently the sparsity of archaeological evidence for settlement of the Fens in the Iron Age was thought to indicate that they were uninhabitable due to marine flooding,[41] but many

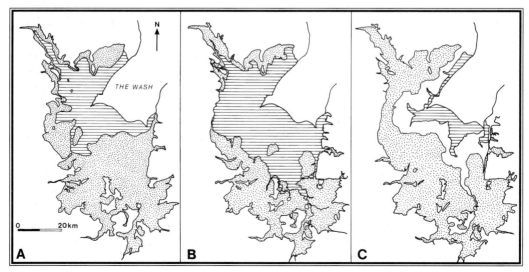

Changes in the area of accumulation of freshwater (stippled) and marine (hatched) deposits in the East Anglian Fenland. A: early Iron Age, B: early Roman, C: post-Roman. (Based on Waller 1994)

settlement sites are now known.[42] The area did get wetter in the Iron Age, with a marine incursion in the central region, but much dry land remained in the southern part of the Fens. The fall in water table in the Roman period enabled an expansion of settlement onto the silts of central Fenland,[43] but some sites appear to have been abandoned in the third or fourth century AD as a result of flooding.[44]

The recent collation of all available data by the Fenland Project has enabled construction of a series of maps showing the development of Fenland palaeogeography and provides the latest data on sea level movements.[45] These data illustrate the extension of marine influence throughout the Iron Age and into the early Roman period, affecting the south and east Fen edges 600–800 years later than the north and west.

To summarize the evidence for sea-level change in Roman Britain, regional variations in the relative changes of level of land and sea, plus the concentration of study on a limited number of areas, mean that it is impossible to produce a general reconstruction of Roman-period coastlines. Furthermore, different approaches to reconstruction often produce conflicting results, so that events are often uncertain, even on a regional scale. Estimates of the extent of post-Roman sea-level rise vary from around 1 to more than 4 metres in different areas. Some of the variability will reflect genuine differences due to the interplay of changes in level of land and sea, and local factors such as inland sediment supply, drainage and reclamation, but others are likely to be the result of errors introduced by the effects of compression of peats by overlying deposits, dating problems, and so on.

In low-lying coastal areas, even minor changes in sea level had a significant effect on the landscape and caused shifts in occupation patterns during the Roman period. Despite the potential for flooding of these areas, evidence from the Severn Estuary Levels and East Anglian Fens for drainage and reclamation indicates that they were considered to be worth the considerable effort involved in their exploitation.

RIVERS

River courses vary through time due to a variety of factors, including climate and sea-level change, plus human activity in the catchment. Increased rainfall causes not only a rise in water level but also increased soil erosion into streams and rivers. These effects may also result from woodland clearance and agricultural activity: removal of tree cover enables more rain to reach the ground and reduces the uptake of water from the soil so that the water table, again, rises. It may, therefore, be difficult to distinguish between human- and climate-induced river-channel changes. Superimposed on these may be deliberate attempts to change river systems, such as drainage.

Archaeological evidence of changes in rivers is provided by excavation of Roman structures that were originally associated with waterways, particularly bridges. An example is provided by the bridges at Chesters, where Hadrian's Wall crossed the River North Tyne.[46] At the point where the river was bridged, the course has subsequently shifted so that the east bank now lies some 15 metres west of its Roman position, with more marked changes upstream and downstream. Hadrian's Wall made a further river crossing, of the Irthing, at Willowford. In this case the divergence of the river from its Roman course is particularly marked – the excavated bridge abutment now lies in a grassy field, with the present course of the Irthing 72 metres to the west.[47]

A further example is provided by changes in the River Thames in London since the Roman settlement of the site in the mid-first century AD. In the first century AD the river flowed up to

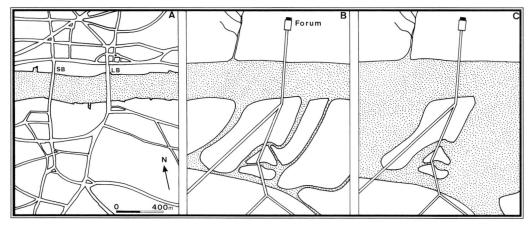

The River Thames in London, comparison of the modern river (A) with the river in the mid-first century at low tide (B) and high tide (C). SB = Southwark Bridge, LB = London Bridge. (After Milne 1985)

700 metres south of the present Southwark waterfront along a network of intersecting channels between islands of higher ground and mudflats.[48] The discovery of first-century waterfronts on the north bank indicates that it lay about 100 metres north of the current channel, and a series of later waterfronts show the gradual advance of the north bank to its present position.[49] The river was tidal in the mid-first century, with a range of at least 1.5 metres, and may have been up to 1 kilometre wide (including areas of marshland) at high tide. At low tide it was about 275 metres wide at its narrowest point, compared with 200 metres today.

ALLUVIATION

Rivers may also cause landscape change by depositing large amounts of sediment (alluvium) on their floodplains due to a combination of climate change and human activity in the catchment. Recent reviews of the alluviation history of rivers throughout Britain reveal a major period of sediment deposition in southern Britain in the late Bronze Age/early Iron Age, and a more significant phase, recorded across the whole of the country, spanning the entire Roman period.[50] The Roman phase corresponds with evidence for a drier/warmer climate, so it is unlikely to reflect climatic deterioration. Pollen evidence, discussed later, indicates increased woodland clearance in many areas in the Roman period, and it seems probable that this resulted in both a rise in water table and increased input of eroded soil into rivers. This brings us to the evidence for the nature of soils in the Roman period.

SOILS

Soils in the Roman period cannot be assumed to have resembled those of today, because fifteen hundred years of agriculture, weathering, and erosion must have resulted in major changes. Some indication of the nature of Roman soils can be found where they have been buried and sealed from subsequent agricultural activity beneath large earthworks or erosion deposits, but such soils have received little study, except where they contain evidence of ancient ploughing.

The vulnerability of soils to change depends to a large extent on their parent material. Upland soils on acid rocks tend to be fairly thin and poor in nutrients. The nutrients are lost as rainwater moves through the soil, and this leaching effect results in major natural changes in the soil and the vegetation it supports. Metal ions (especially iron and aluminium) washed down the soil profile may be deposited as a solid 'iron pan' that does not allow water through and so leads to waterlogging. This, in turn, results in the death of trees growing on the soil, and replacement by bog plants tolerant of waterlogged, nutrient-poor conditions. The main species involved in the accumulation of peat deposits in upland areas is *Sphagnum* moss, which forms raised bogs on flat areas and blanket bogs on sloping sites.

In high-rainfall areas these changes can occur naturally, but at some sites there is evidence that the process was at least accelerated by woodland clearance.[51] This can be explained by the effect of tree removal on the water table, described earlier, triggering the formation of peat in areas where rainfall is already high. Peat formation thus reflects an interplay between local conditions of climate, topography, and degree and nature of human activity, and began at different dates in different areas. By the Roman period, many upland areas were already extensively covered in open peatlands, and the extent of these increased throughout this period and afterwards.

SOIL EROSION

As we have seen, woodland clearance can cause significant soil erosion, and this is particularly severe on arable land. Exposure of the land surface to the rain causes soil to move downhill, where it may be deposited as hill-wash (colluvium) towards the base of slopes or as lynchets where the free movement of the soil is interrupted by field boundaries. Lynchets are associated with the patterns of 'Celtic' fields on the chalk downs, most of which date from between the Bronze Age and Roman period.

The degree to which erosion occurs is influenced by the relationship between periods of high rainfall and the degree of soil exposure. For example, sowing crops in autumn is linked to increased soil erosion, because ploughing is likely to coincide with rainfall.[52] There is evidence from weed assemblages that spelt wheat was often autumn-sown in the Iron Age and Roman period (see chapter 5), so erosion might have increased in these periods.

Loss of soils to erosion was a problem long before the Iron Age, however, particularly in chalk and limestone areas in southern Britain. The original woodland soils of most such areas seem to have been lost by the Bronze Age, presumably due to extensive woodland clearance and preparation of the ground for cultivation. Bell provides an illustration of the problem from a limestone area at Brean Down, Somerset.[53] Here, excavations identified several phases of erosion, beginning in the Neolithic period and becoming so severe in the middle Bronze Age that most of the topsoil from the slope was lost, exposing the underlying limestone. This was attributed to arable activity, and was calculated to have caused the loss of up to 20 centimetres depth of soil. Following a period of abandonment, the site was reoccupied in the late Bronze Age and then again in the Iron Age/Roman period. The erosion associated with the latter phase could be traced to slopes too steep for cultivation, and the trigger for erosion was suggested to have been overgrazing or land clearance for construction of a late Iron Age hill-fort. Eroded soil depth during this phase was estimated at 14–24 centimetres. Subsequently this eroded soil was used for agricultural purposes, indicated by the presence of plough furrows, before being buried by wind-blown sand.

Clearly, then, on many areas of chalk and limestone bedrock, soils may already have been thin by the Roman period. Further thinning is suggested by the fact that colluvium recorded in some Wessex sites had a higher chalk content in the Roman period than previously, presumably because the bedrock surface itself was beginning to be affected.[54]

Eroded soils may be deposited in lakes, where they can result in changes in sediment formation. For example, at Llangorse Lake, south Wales, there was a switch from organic muds to silty clays in the Roman-period deposits, attributed to intensified arable cultivation leading to increased soil erosion.[55]

SOIL NUTRIENT DEPLETION

We have already mentioned changes in the nutrient content of soils in upland areas due to high rainfall and human activity, but lowland soils may also become depleted of nutrients. This is particularly likely if they are not underlain by carbonate-rich chalk and limestone bedrock.

Evidence for soil depletion comes from changes in weed assemblages found accompanying crop remains on archaeological sites. Legumes can grow in soils with a low nitrogen content, and records of weedy legumes may indicate the local presence of soils poor in nutrients. The frequency of such plants tends to increase in abundance in carbonized assemblages from several sites in the late Iron Age and early Roman periods, suggesting progressive soil depletion. For example, at Ashville, Abingdon, legume frequencies increased gradually between the mid-first millennium BC and the third century AD.[56] Lambrick points out that this gradual trend is atypical, however, with major peaks of legumes in the late Iron Age/early Roman period at Mount Farm, Gravelly Guy, and at Claydon Pike, also on the Thames gravels.[57] There is also some evidence of manuring from the Roman period (see chapter 5), suggesting attempts to overcome problems of low soil fertility.

Soil erosion and nutrient loss were clearly problems long before the Roman period in many areas, but they seem to have become more serious as a result of increased intensity of land use at this time. Pressure on the land required not only measures to increase the productivity of depleted areas, but also (as we shall see later) expansion of agriculture onto areas of marginal soils, such as those prone to waterlogging.

VEGETATION

Much of Roman Britain seems likely to have been exploited for agriculture, on the basis of the distribution of settlement evidence alone, but archaeological excavations provide little indication of the extent of semi-natural vegetation types. We saw in chapter 1 that pollen analysis provides the key method of reconstructing the natural vegetation of the Roman period, but its use in the past has been limited due to a sparsity of sequences from many parts of Britain and a concentration of interest in human impact on vegetation in prehistory. The geographical distribution of the evidence is strongly biased because peat deposits and lakes are much more abundant in the west and north of Britain than in the south and east, and even where peat does occur the upper (Roman and later) layers are often missing due to peat cutting.

Furthermore, early attempts at reconstructing vegetational change in relation to human activity were hampered by a lack of radiocarbon dates, and phases of clearance and regeneration in pollen diagrams were assigned to particular periods on the basis of the presence or absence of archaeological evidence for activity nearby. For example, it was often assumed that woodland regeneration phases identified in undated pollen sequences reflected the Roman withdrawal from Britain, as it was assumed that this event would have led to widespread land abandonment.[58]

By the late 1970s sufficient radiocarbon-dated pollen diagrams had been produced from north-east England to enable Turner to attempt a reconstruction of the environment in the Roman period.[59] She argued that much of the area was cleared of woodland in the late Iron Age and farmed throughout the Roman period until at least the sixth century, followed by woodland regeneration (see chapter 7). The applicability or otherwise of this pattern to the rest of Roman Britain remained largely a matter for speculation, as few sequences covering this period were available.[60]

Over the last decade many new radiocarbon-dated pollen sequences have been produced from most parts of Britain, and the rest of this chapter will largely be concerned with using all available 'off-site' pollen data to provide a reconstruction of the distribution of different vegetation types present in Roman Britain, and how this environment compared with that of the Iron Age. Pollen evidence also adds to our picture of agricultural activity, an aspect discussed in chapter 5. Pollen from archaeological sites is not included due to its very local character – it is hardly surprising if on-site assemblages from settlements show open conditions! The aim here is to provide a picture of the landscape as a whole, rather than that immediately associated with individual occupation sites.

Details of how the data have been analysed will be published elsewhere, but it should be mentioned here that an effort has been made to include in the distribution maps only those sites that are well dated so that the Iron Age and Roman parts of the sequences can be identified with confidence.[61] For each site, frequencies of tree and shrub, heather, and herb pollen have been calculated for the Iron Age and Roman periods, reflecting the abundance of woodland, heath/moorland and grassland/other open land respectively.[62] At most sites there is insufficient detail to show changes in the different vegetation types during the course of these periods, so an average figure is shown. More detailed sequences, and areas where concentrations of sites occur, are discussed in the regional case-studies later in this chapter.

An obvious problem is that, despite increasing efforts by pollen analysts to study deposits from southern Britain, there is still a strong bias in the data to the north and parts of the west, but excluding Cornwall. Work on Bodmin Moor and Dartmoor has produced detailed pollen sequences with acceptable radiocarbon dates only for the early prehistoric period.[63] Thus, there is plentiful information from parts of the native landscape, but little relating to the villa landscape.

In attempting to interpret the patterns reflected in the pollen evidence it must be remembered that much vegetational variation between sites will result from differences of local topography, geology, soil and climate, independent of land-use practices. Any vegetational response to changing pressure of land use will also vary accordingly. In most lowland areas, abandonment of land leads to the formation of scrub and ultimately woodland. In upland areas, initial woodland clearance may be followed by severe soil deterioration and changes in the water table, so that trees are unable to colonize abandoned regions. In such areas, cessation or reduction of grazing can result in the spread of heather (*Calluna vulgaris*).

Changes in land management can also produce dramatic and rapid changes in the type of vegetation – burning heather-dominated vegetation on mineral soils at around 3–6 year intervals causes a switch to grassland, whereas less frequent burning at 10–20 year intervals maintains the heather and helps to prevent colonization by trees. A switch from heathland to grassland can also occur (in three years or less) under heavy grazing and trampling.[64] Such rapid changes are beyond the means of conventional pollen analysis to detect, but the possibility of their existence must be borne in mind in the interpretation of the smoothed picture of vegetational change represented by the pollen record.

THE IRON AGE

Of the forty-one sites in the database that span the Iron Age, nineteen indicate more than 50 per cent tree and shrub pollen. Most of the rest have 26–50 per cent tree and shrub pollen, and only four sites have 25 per cent or less, of which two are in the Fens where the pollen assemblages are likely to have been strongly influenced by the local wetland vegetation.

Interpretation of these figures is not straightforward as they cannot be directly converted to a percentage of woodland cover in the landscape around the site. However, studies comparing modern pollen samples with the surrounding vegetation suggest that percentages of tree pollen in excess of 50 per cent may reflect a substantially wooded landscape.[65] So the pollen evidence indicates that in most areas for which there is evidence the landscape contained both woodland

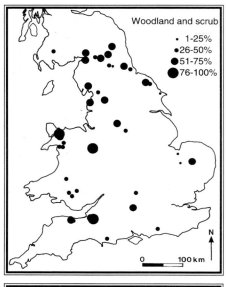

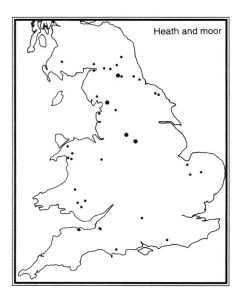

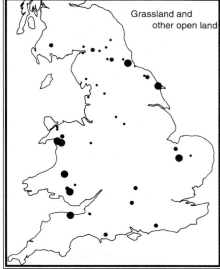

Distribution of pollen sequences spanning the Iron Age, showing the frequencies of tree and shrub pollen (indicating the extent of woodland and scrub), heather pollen (indicating mainly heath and moor), and herb pollen (indicating mainly grassland and other open land)

and open land, although it is uncertain whether the woodland occurred as large tracts or smaller isolated woods in a mosaic of grassland and fields.

The nature of the unwooded areas is illustrated by the non-tree pollen. Pollen of heather occurs in most of the sequences, but tends to be slightly more abundant in the north. This plant grows on heaths, moors and drier bog surfaces, and sometimes in open woodland on acid soils. The pollen data also suggest that cereals were grown near most of the sites, in both the north and south (see chapter 5), while grassland was also widespread. It can, therefore, be seen that the Iron Age landscape was a mosaic of woodland, pasture and arable land in most areas, with heath and moorland in some parts.

THE ROMAN PERIOD

Of the forty-six sequences available for the Roman period, thirty-five have tree and shrub pollen frequencies of 50 per cent or less. Most sites had less woodland in the Roman period than in the Iron Age, and clearance is particularly marked in the north of England, especially close to Hadrian's Wall. Here a cluster of sites shows a major decline in the extent of woodland, and at four sites tree and shrub pollen percentages drop below 25 per cent, suggesting an almost totally cleared landscape.

At least some woodland remained in most areas, however, usually consisting of oak (*Quercus*) and hazel (*Corylus*) on well-drained sites, with alder (*Alnus*) and birch (*Betula*) on damper soils, the latter also occurring on abandoned open sites reverting to woodland. Willow (*Salix*) was locally abundant around some wetlands.

At most sites, frequencies of heather pollen are similar to those of the Iron Age, suggesting that the new areas of open land were not usually given over to heath. There is some evidence for an expansion of the extent of arable land, however, since cereal pollen is recorded at several sites from which it was absent in the Iron Age (chapter 5).

To gain a better impression of the extent to which the landscape was wooded, a comparison has been made between the amount of woodland in the Roman period and that present today. This has been achieved by selecting pollen sequences that cover the whole of the last two millennia up to the present – the number is less than available solely for the Roman period as the upper layers of several sequences are missing. Tree and shrub pollen frequencies from the Roman period have then been compared with those in the surface deposits, the latter being a reflection of the modern extent of woodland.

An interesting pattern emerges. In Wales

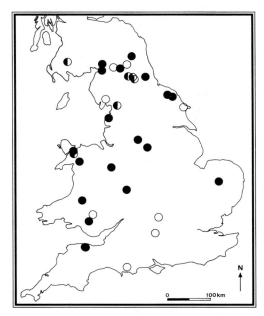

Comparison between the extent of woodland in the Roman period and that present in the late twentieth century. Filled circles: more wooded in the Roman period, open circles: less wooded in the Roman period, half-filled circles: extent of woodland similar

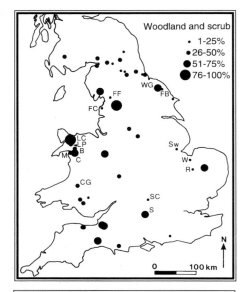

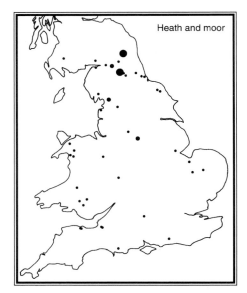

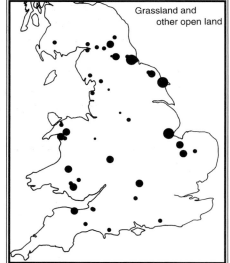

Distribution of pollen sequences spanning the Roman period. Sites discussed in the text are labelled: FF, Fairsnape Fell; FC, Fenton Cottage; WG, Wheeldale Gill; FB, Fen Bogs; Sw, Swineshead; W, Wiggenhall St Germans; R, Redmere; SC, Sidlings Copse; S, Snelsmore; LC, Llyn Cororion; LP, Llyn Padarn; B, Bryn y Castell; M, Moel y Gerddi; C, Crawcwellt; CG, Cefn Gwernffrwd

and western England most sites were more wooded in the Roman period than they are today, but in central southern England all three sites were less wooded in the Roman period. In northern England many sites had more woodland than now, although near Hadrian's Wall there are five sites indicating a Roman-period landscape similar to, or more open than, that of today. This is an intriguing distinction between the different landscape types defined in chapter 1. Most of the native landscape (with the exception of the Hadrian's Wall zone) was relatively well wooded, and seems not to have been exploited to the full extent of its agricultural potential, whereas much of the villa landscape (where, admittedly, the data are sparcer) seems already to have been exploited to the full in the Roman period, at least in terms of the area of land used for farming.

Having established this general picture of the distribution of major vegetation types, we will examine areas where a concentration of pollen data, or availability of particularly detailed sequences, enables trends within the Roman period, and between regions, to be examined.

THE HADRIAN'S WALL ZONE

Hadrian's Wall runs through an area of abundant lakes and peat bogs (mosses), providing the source of the densest concentration of pollen sequences covering the Roman period from any part of the British Isles. The first synthesis of some of this pollen evidence was provided by Turner in 1979, who interpreted the radiocarbon-dated pollen diagrams then available to suggest that much of the area was substantially cleared of woodland in the late Iron Age and Roman periods.[66] Since this initial survey, much new work has been undertaken in this area, supporting the picture of a dramatic increase in clearance during the Roman period.

The pollen sequences most closely associated with Hadrian's Wall are from Fellend Moss, Fozy Moss and Glasson Moss. Fellend Moss lies adjacent to the vallum – a large ditch, flanked by banks, running to the south of the Wall. Here the first significant woodland clearance apparently coincided with the start of the Roman occupation, and it is marked by substantial increases in abundance of grasses, ribwort plantain (*Plantago lanceolata*, a plant commonly associated with pasture), and heather, with cereal pollen recorded from only a single sample.[67] This sequence of events is most easily explained as reflecting clearance of the military zone prior to construction of the vallum and Wall.

Fozy Moss lies immediately to the north of the central sector of the Wall, and its pollen sequence again indicates a major, and apparently rapid, reduction in the extent of woodland in the Roman period, resulting in an almost treeless landscape.[68] This clearance again appears to

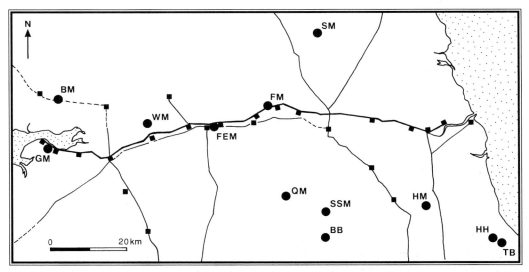

Locations of pollen sequences near Hadrian's Wall. BM, Burnfoothill Moss; GM, Glasson Moss; WM, Walton Moss; FEM, Fellend Moss; FM, Fozy Moss; SM, Steng Moss; QM, Quick Moss; SSM, Stewart Shield Meadow; BB, Bollihope Bog; HM, Hallowell Moss; HH, Hutton Henry; TB, Thorpe Bulmer. Squares indicate forts. (Forts and roads after S. Johnson 1989)

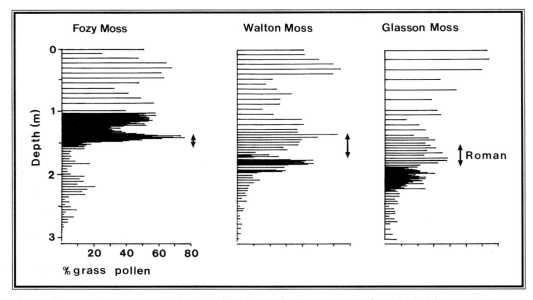

Grass pollen curves from sites near Hadrian's Wall, indicating the changing extent of open land. The approximate location of the Roman-period deposits has been calculated from series of radiocarbon dates on the peat from each site. (Modified from Dumayne et al. 1995)

have been connected with the construction of Hadrian's Wall,[69] but some arable land seems also to have been created, as there is evidence for the local cultivation of rye (*Secale cereale*) and other cereals.

At Glasson Moss, just south of the western end of the Wall, Roman-period clearance was less marked than at Fozy Moss, and it followed a sustained increase in the extent of open land from the middle of the Iron Age.[70] Intriguingly, local cereal cultivation apparently stopped in the early Roman period, perhaps because establishment of the military zone in this area put some arable land out of use.

At Walton Moss, 3 kilometres north of the Wall, significant clearance also began in the Iron Age, but was followed by woodland regeneration and a decline in the extent of open land at the beginning of the Roman period.[71] Dumayne and Barber suggest that this reflects abandonment of land during the resistance of the Brigantes to the Roman occupation.[72] Renewed clearance followed, suggested to have been linked to acquisition of timber for the Wall forts.

Further north of the Wall are Burnfoothill Moss, to the west, and Steng Moss, towards the east. At Burnfoothill Moss, major woodland clearance began in the late Iron Age or early Roman period.[73] Corresponding increases in grass pollen and ribwort plantain suggest the spread of grassland, but cereal pollen is rare. At Steng Moss, sustained major clearance from the early Iron Age was accompanied by cereal cultivation.[74] A further major increase in activity in the late Iron Age/early Roman period included an expansion of cereal cultivation and a massive increase in occurrence of heather pollen, suggesting an extension of moor/heath as well as pasture and arable.

A cluster of pollen sequences has been produced from the Durham area, south of the Wall. At Hallowell Moss and Bollihope Bog major clearance began in the Roman period, while at

Stewart Shield Meadow clearance from the Iron Age resulted in an almost treeless Roman landscape.[75] At Hutton Henry clearance began much earlier, in the Bronze Age, but the Roman period was marked by a further reduction in woodland and extension of heath.[76]

At Thorpe Bulmer significant clearance apparently began in the late Iron Age, but it is possible that a substantial part of the Bronze Age and Iron Age deposits is missing so that earlier clearance is not represented.[77] This sequence apparently indicates local cultivation of hemp (*Cannabis sativa*) in the Roman period (see later). At Quick Moss, 25 kilometres south of the central sector of Hadrian's Wall, major clearance began in the Iron Age and continued into the Roman period, although some local woodland persisted throughout.[78]

The pollen evidence overall suggests that some areas were already extensively cleared long before Hadrian's Wall was built, but at several sites further clearance was connected with Roman military activity. This appears to have been for a variety of reasons, including clearing the military zone prior to construction first of the Stanegate road and its forts, and then the Wall and vallum, provision of timber for building purposes, and creation of new arable land in response to the increased demand for agricultural produce by the army. Activity at the forts would have maintained a need for fuel and agricultural produce, while further fuel and food requirements would have accompanied the growth of settlements outside the forts (*vici*), as at Housesteads.

Supporting evidence that at least parts of the Hadrian's Wall zone were already open before the Wall was built comes from the discovery of plough marks underlying both it, and its forts, in some areas (see chapter 5). The use of turf in the construction of the western sector of the Wall, and in the ramparts of some of the earliest forts, such as Carlisle, Vindolanda and Corbridge, also indicates the presence of grassland.[79]

NORTH-WEST WALES

This area has several pollen sequences, some of which, such as Bryn y Castell, Crawcwellt and Moel y Gerddi, have been produced from wetland areas adjacent to excavated archaeological sites. Bryn y Castell is a small hill-fort, occupied during the late Iron Age and Roman periods, with evidence for major iron-working activity.[80] The three pollen sequences from immediately next to the site might be expected to show a major reduction in woodland associated with this activity, but clearance actually began in the late Bronze Age/early Iron Age, pre-dating occupation of the hill-fort.[81] The clearance affected alder woodland particularly severely, and is evidently attributable to occupants of sites elsewhere. The landscape remained fairly open during the Iron Age and Roman period, with only limited further clearance and evidence for cereal cultivation. Iron-working seems to have had little impact on the extent of the remaining woodland, despite the necessity of a charcoal supply for smelting, perhaps because it relied on managing woodland rather than destroying it.

Similar evidence for intensive iron-working comes from the late prehistoric upland settlement site at Crawcwellt West.[82] The adjacent pollen sequence shows major woodland clearance, associated with evidence for burning, from the late Bronze Age.[83] Once again, alder was significantly affected. Clearance continued throughout the Iron Age, resulting in a predominantly open landscape. Local recovery of birch and hazel woodland apparently followed in the Roman period, after the site was abandoned, although much open land remained.

At Moel y Gerddi a pollen sequence is associated with a late prehistoric enclosure.[84] Major clearance began in the early Bronze Age, before occupation of the settlement, but significant areas of woodland remained throughout the Iron Age and Roman periods.

A contrast to the predominantly local vegetational record provided by these sites comes from Llyn Padarn, a large lake in the heart of Snowdonia.[85] This shows that the extent of woodland began to decline in the late Bronze Age/early Iron Age, followed by a major increase in clearance in the late Iron Age/early Roman period that resulted in an almost totally deforested landscape. A similar sequence is recorded at Llyn Cororion, on the plain between Snowdonia and the Menai Strait. Here, clearance of local woodland began in the early Iron Age and increased dramatically during the Roman period, with a major decline in hazel.[86]

Pollen sequences in north-west Wales, then, suggest that significant woodland clearance usually began in the late Bronze Age or early Iron Age. The Roman period coincided with further major deforestation of the lower-lying sites, producing an almost totally cleared landscape. Some woodland did remain in the Roman period, however, and its extent increased at one upland site at least.

MID WALES

The most detailed pollen sequence in this area is from a peat-covered plateau at Cefn Gwernffrwd, close to the site of a Bronze Age stone circle and ring cairn.[87] Blanket peat began to form in the early Bronze Age, probably as a result of a raised water table following woodland clearance. Pollen analysis of the peat showed that by the beginning of the Iron Age most local woodland had disappeared, but this was followed by a return of some woodland in the Iron Age. Renewed clearance began in the Roman period and resulted in an almost totally treeless landscape. Increases of ribwort plantain, grasses and heather suggest that the woodland was largely replaced by moorland and grassland, although cereal cultivation increased slightly.

Comparison may be made with events at the well-known site of Tregaron Bog, 15 kilometres to the south-east, investigated by Turner.[88] Probably only two samples from the Tregaron sequence belong to the Roman period, and the site is not included in the maps because the published sources show selected pollen types only. The Tregaron sequence does, however, suggest that major clearance occurred much later than at Cefn Gwernffrwd, beginning towards the end of the Iron Age and increasing throughout the Roman period and after.

LANCASHIRE

There are two particularly detailed pollen sequences from Lancashire, one from blanket peat on Fairsnape Fell in the central Pennines, and the other from a peat deposit discovered during archaeological investigations at Fenton Cottage in the lowlands around Over Wyre. At Fairsnape Fell, blanket peat formation began in the Iron Age, by which time considerable woodland clearance had already occurred and cereals were grown locally.[89] Further clearance in the late Iron Age was accompanied by an increase of heather, suggesting an expansion of heathland areas. During the Roman period, woodland remained sparse, but a decline in heather and increase in grasses and plantain, probably in the early mid-third century AD, may reflect the increasing use of heathy areas for grazing by sheep and cattle. Cereal cultivation occurred throughout the Roman period, probably at a similar level to that in the Iron Age. Towards the end of the Roman period the extent of woodland apparently began to expand again, as alder and hazel frequencies increased.

Despite the differences in local topography, a surprisingly similar sequence of events is recorded at Fenton Cottage.[90] The onset of major clearance in the late Iron Age followed a history of lesser woodland interference and cereal cultivation from the Bronze Age. Clearance reached a peak towards the middle of the Roman period, when corresponding increases of grasses and ribwort plantain suggest that much woodland was replaced by grassland. A minor increase in cereal pollen suggests some expansion of arable cultivation also, and local heathland is evidenced by an expansion of heather. Even at the peak of this clearance phase some local woodland remained, however, and the extent of this woodland increased dramatically towards the end of the Roman period.

THE NORTH YORK MOORS

The North York Moors have been a focus of attention for pollen analysts for many years due to the widespread presence of peat, but most research has concentrated on the prehistoric environment.[91] There are two radiocarbon-dated sequences covering the Roman period, however, of which the most detailed is from Fen Bogs.[92] Here, significant clearance began in the middle of the Iron Age, perhaps connected with local evidence for iron-working activity, although cereal cultivation also occurred locally. All tree species were affected, and the continuation of clearance throughout the Roman period resulted in an almost treeless landscape.

At Wheeldale Gill, the Roman period saw a dramatic decline in the extent of the locally abundant alder woodland.[93] Some cereal cultivation seems to have occurred, but the replacement of woodland predominantly by pasture is suggested by the large increase in abundance of ribwort plantain.

CENTRAL SOUTHERN ENGLAND

The most detailed pollen sequence from this area spanning the Roman period is from a valley bog at Snelsmore on the Berkshire Downs, although only a summary diagram has been published.[94] Significant clearance of local woodland began in the late Bronze Age/early Iron Age, followed by a minor episode of regeneration in the early Iron Age. Continuous clearance then occurred through to the Roman period, although significant expanses of local woodland remained. Towards the end of the Roman period, however, major woodland regeneration suggests a reduction in the intensity of agricultural land use.

This can be compared with the situation at Sidlings Copse, Oxfordshire, adjacent to the site of Headington Wick Roman villa.[95] Here, much of the original woodland on dry land was cleared in the Bronze Age. As at Snelsmore, woodland regeneration in the early Iron Age was followed by continued clearance into the Roman period, but at Sidlings Copse there is no evidence for major late Roman woodland regeneration (see chapter 7).

THE FENS

Reconstructing the vegetational history of the Fens is complicated by the fact that variations in intensity and type of human land use are superimposed onto the natural changes in local vegetation caused by the fluctuating sea level and flooding. Rising water levels during the Iron Age resulted in the inundation of much of the Fen area closest to the Wash, but the southern

Fens seem to have escaped marine incursions. Reconstructing the Roman-period vegetation of this area has recently been assisted by the publication of several Fenland pollen sequences by Waller.[96]

Redmere is a former lake in the south-eastern part of the Fens, and was at least 10 kilometres from the probable coastline in the Roman period.[97] Woodland seems to have been sparse from the Iron Age, and close sampling of the Roman-period deposits revealed that trees almost totally disappeared from the area at this time. A significant increase in local cereal cultivation seems to have accompanied this change.

Wiggenhall St Germans, on the eastern edge of the Fen basin, has yielded a peat deposit spanning the Bronze Age to early Roman period sandwiched between layers of marine silts and clay.[98] During the Roman period the landscape was very open, perhaps with some local development of heathy vegetation plus pastoral and arable agriculture, but the site was inundated by brackish water in the early/mid-Roman period.

Another peat deposit between clays has been sampled from Swineshead, near the north-western Fen edge in Lincolnshire.[99] The peat formed between the late Roman and early post-Roman periods, and the Roman deposits contained mainly pollen of grasses and sedges, with virually no trees. This again indicates a very open landscape.

ON-SITE EVIDENCE FOR NATURAL PLANT COMMUNITIES

The pollen data enable the broad distribution of the different types of semi-natural vegetation to be established, and provide some indication of their species composition. Additional information about these various plant communities can be obtained from assemblages of larger plant remains from archaeological sites – on-site evidence. Of particular interest is the question of how, if at all, the different vegetation types were exploited and even managed. The on-site evidence for arable land, the extent of which is almost certainly underestimated by the pollen record, is discussed in chapter 5.

WOODLAND MANAGEMENT

Woodland can be managed to increase its production of useful materials, such as timber of specified sizes, and smaller poles for wattle-work (used to construct walls and fences). Much woodland in Britain was probably managed in the Roman period, in view of the demand for wood for building and fuel, and the apparently limited extent of woodland remaining in many areas. The most likely type of management is coppicing, in which trees, often hazel, are cut down almost to ground level on a cycle of about ten years. In the interim the regrowth consists of long straight poles, which can be used for wattle, fuel, etc. In the medieval period, coppiced woods often contained scattered large trees or 'standards', usually oak, which were cut at longer intervals than the coppice and provided timber.[100]

Suggestions have been made that coppicing can be detected from pollen evidence, usually based on the argument that high hazel pollen percentages reflect this type of management because it encourages hazel to flower more profusely.[101] An abundance of hazel pollen may simply indicate an abundance of hazel woodland, however, coppiced or not. It is not possible to demonstrate the existence of coppicing from conventional pollen sequences, since the sampling interval is too wide to reflect the ten-year, or shorter, cycle.

There is good archaeological evidence for coppicing from long before the Roman period, notably from the wooden trackways of the Somerset Levels, which range in date from the Neolithic to the Roman period.[102] Interestingly, the only Roman trackway on the Somerset Levels (Difford's 1 and 2) was not made of coppiced wood, but consisted of cut brushwood.[103] Most of the identified wood was from alder and birch, with a range of other species that could have grown on the wetland area, and it seems that this wood was collected at random from natural growth of scrub.

Some of the surviving Roman texts on agriculture include references to the management of woodland, and tree planting, summarized by Meiggs.[104] While describing practices in Italy, these methods may have been exported to the more romanized areas of Britain. Cato, writing in the mid-second century BC, provided a list of land uses, in order of profitability, in which woodland features in several forms. These include willow beds, coppice woods and 'mast-wood' (*glandaria silva*). The latter could apparently apply to oak woods or beech, both of which provided nuts that were valued for feeding pigs. He also referred to planting elms and poplars to provide leaf fodder for cattle and sheep, illustrating another valuable resource provided by woodland.

Further information on coppice woods is provided by Columella, writing in the first century AD. He stated that the best woods for coppicing were oak and chestnut, the chestnut being cut on a five-year cycle and the oak at seven-year intervals. He went on to describe the planting of chestnut coppices.

Chestnut (*Castanea sativa*) is not native to Britain but may have been introduced in the Roman period.[105] There is no certain evidence that chestnut coppices were planted in Roman Britain, although there is a possibility that a coppice stool found in a Roman pit at Farmoor, Oxfordshire, identified as most probably of oak, could have been chestnut.[106] Pollen evidence for the tree is lacking, but even if chestnut woods did occur, low pollen production and poor dispersal mean that they would be unlikely to be detected in pollen sequences.

Evidence for the deliberate planting of willow groves is also sparse, and particularly difficult to detect in view of the native status of the tree. A possible instance is provided by the Sidlings Copse pollen sequence (mentioned earlier).[107] Here the frequency of willow pollen increased significantly in the Roman period, at a time when other trees were apparently being cleared. This could represent either planting of willow or encouragement of existing stands. Willow grows remarkably quickly and could have provided a valuable renewable source of fuel for the villa hypocausts and for the pottery kilns that operated locally.

Archaeological evidence of Roman woodland management is becoming increasingly abundant as more waterlogged sites, with good preservation of wood, are excavated. For example, at Barton Court Farm, Oxfordshire, a Roman well was lined with wattles of oak, hazel and willow, and the mosses present were suggested to have come from managed woodland.[108] A pit at Farmoor, also in Oxfordshire, contained further evidence in the form of long, straight poles of oak, accompanied by hazel and ash (*Fraxinus excelsior*), used in its construction.[109] This site also produced the coppice stool mentioned above.

Roman wooden buildings provide further clues to the nature of the woodland used to provide the timber. Oak was by far the preferred structural timber for Roman sites across Britain, and is almost universally recorded at sites where timbers survive, such as at the fort at Vindolanda, Northumberland, and in the Roman towns of York, London and Carlisle. Other species commonly used in Roman building included birch, ash, alder and elm.[110]

Much timber has come from the former waterfronts of Roman London, although in many cases the emphasis of study has been on tree-ring dating rather than on evidence for the way in which the timber grew.[111] A Roman timber building in the City was found to contain re-used oak timbers cut in the first century AD.[112] Tree-ring counts suggested that the wood came from young trees, mostly 26–60 years old. Other buildings in Roman London had wattle-and-daub walls, using rods that probably came from short-rotation coppice. For example, imprints of rods were found in daub from first- and second-century buildings in Newgate Street and Watling Court.[113]

Excavation at New Fresh Wharf, also in the City of London, revealed a wooden quay dated by dendrochronology to AD 225–245.[114] Most of the oaks used had narrow or average-width rings, suggesting that they had grown in woodland, in competition with other trees.[115] This woodland had contained trees of a range of ages and hence sizes, some mature, up to 250 years old when felled, and others much less than 100 years old.

Excavations at Castle Street, Carlisle, have revealed timber buildings dating from the late first to the early second century.[116] These used predominantly oak and alder for stakes, posts and wattle-work, with some wattles also of hazel and birch. Ring counts on a sample of the smaller wood remains suggested that most of the stems were cut at less than 10 years of age, and at least some of the alder, hazel and birch appeared to have come from coppice. Some of the oak wood, however, apparently came from branches rather than coppiced stems.[117] Tree-ring analysis of the oak timbers provided some indication of the age and origin of the larger trees.[118] They had been felled at ages ranging from 25 to more than 400 years, and seemed to have come from a variety of sources. Some grew in dense woodland, as was the case for the New Fresh Wharf timbers, while others may have grown in more open environments.

From Roman York, waterlogging has again preserved timber buildings, this time from the second to early third centuries. These provided further evidence for the use of hazel rods, which had between four and ten annual rings.[119]

The excavated evidence indicates, therefore, that woodland was managed to provide the springy poles needed to produce wattles, but the use of coppice wood probably extended beyond structural purposes. It provided a renewable resource that would have been vital in areas where large quantities of fuel were required. Examples include pottery production centres and sites of large-scale metal smelting (see chapter 6). Domestic use would also have placed a considerable drain on the supply of wood for fuel, especially where villas were common, with their hypocausts and baths.

The tree-ring evidence from Carlisle adds some useful information to the reconstruction of the extent of woodland provided by the pollen data.[120] Pollen sequences suggest that the Hadrian's Wall area had very little woodland left in the Roman period, and it is notable that the tree-ring data point to the use of timber from a variety of sources, both woodland and more open areas. Assuming that the timber was obtained fairly locally, it might be argued that this suggests that woodland was sufficiently scarce that it could not provide enough good timber, forcing the use of less suitable trees from open areas, such as hedges.

GRASSLAND

The pollen data indicate that grassland was widespread in the Roman period, most owing its existence to human activity. In lowland areas of Britain, on soils with adequate drainage, grassland quickly reverts to woodland unless colonization by trees and shrubs is prevented by grazing or mowing. Different combinations of these practices result in different types of grassland, with further variations resulting from different conditions of soil and climate.[121]

Hay meadows, for example, are a type of species-rich grassland that are mown at intervals. A range of species accompany the dominant grasses, including tall herbs such as, on the marshier type of meadow, meadowsweet (*Filipendula ulmaria*), great burnet (*Sanguisorba officinalis*) and meadow rue (*Thalictrum flavum*). On drier soils, characteristic plants include ox-eye daisy (*Leucanthemum vulgare*), red clover (*Trifolim pratense*) and sorrel (*Rumex acetosa*). These plants are intolerant of heavy grazing, and species richness declines if mowing becomes too frequent. Hay meadows can be used for grazing for part of the year, but animals must be excluded for most of the growing season to prevent loss of the hay crop. Grassland that is heavily grazed has a different flora from that of meadows, including plants that are able to survive grazing due to their low-growing form (such as daisies), or are avoided due to prickles (such as thistles) or toxicity (such as buttercups).

The varied species composition of the different grassland types is rarely distinguishable from the pollen record, because many of the key species do not have characteristic pollen, or their pollen is not sufficiently well dispersed to occur often in pollen sequences. The larger plant remains found on archaeological sites have the advantage of enabling closer identification, although grassland plants are less often recorded than arable species.

On the basis of plant remains from archaeological sites in the Upper Thames Valley, it has been suggested that hay meadows first appeared in Britain in the Roman period.[122] Perhaps the best evidence comes from Farmoor, Oxfordshire, where a second-century well contained cut hay, including seeds of ox-eye daisy, yellow rattle (*Rhinanthus* sp.) and knapweed (*Centaurea nigra*). The site also produced a late Roman hay scythe.[123] Roman wells from several other sites provide further evidence for hay, discussed by Greig.[124] These include a well at Lancaster that contained horse droppings with such characteristic hay meadow plants as fairy flax (*Linum catharticum*), clovers (*Trifolium* sp.) and knapweed. Greig suggests that meadows were probably managed by a single mowing late in the summer, followed by grazing in autumn and early winter, then prevention of grazing until after mowing again the next summer.

Further evidence for hay meadows comes from plant remains in a fourth-century latrine pit at the temple site of Uley,[125] and from Roman York, in late second-century deposits inside a timber building.[126] From York the presence of both grassland weevils (such as *Apion* and *Sitona*) and plant remains (such as meadowsweet and perhaps great burnet) suggests that hay had been brought to the building, probably for stable litter. Excavations at York have also revealed evidence for the exploitation of other natural types of vegetation, notably saltmarsh and heathland.

SALTMARSH

Saltmarsh vegetation develops in coastal areas and estuaries subject to tidal flooding by the sea. Surprisingly, remains of various saltmarsh plants have been found in Roman York, despite the fact that it was 30 kilometres from the estuarine stretch of the River Ouse. These plants include sea arrowgrass (*Triglochin maritimum*), and may derive from dung of animals that had grazed on saltmarsh and were then brought to the town for sale.[127]

HEATHLAND AND MOORLAND

The presence of heather pollen in many sequences suggests the widespread existence of heathland and moorland in the Roman period, and it seems that such areas provided a range of useful products. Peat from moorland areas could have provided a valuable source of fuel, particularly where woodland was sparse. Possible evidence for the use of peat for this purpose comes from several sites in Roman York. Here, fragments of raised-bog peat, and peat-bog plants, such as *Sphagnum* moss and cotton-grass (*Eriophorum vaginatum*) have been recorded, some of which were charred.[128]

Heather has also been recovered from York, and may have arrived with the peat or have been brought for its own sake, for bedding or fuel.[129] On the south coast, Iron Age and Roman deposits from Hengistbury Head also included remains of heather, perhaps used for similar purposes.[130]

CONCLUSION

The pollen evidence indicates that much of Britain was already a predominantly agricultural landscape before the Roman Conquest. In southern Britain much woodland was removed in the Bronze Age, while in Wales major clearance occurred in the late Bronze Age and early Iron Age. The late Iron Age seems to have seen the most significant increase in pre-Roman woodland clearance in the north of England, and the arrival of the Roman military at Hadrian's Wall led to further clearance.

In some areas of Roman Britain, notably central southern England and the far north, the landscape was probably not dissimilar to that of today in general character, although specific details, such as the course of rivers and the size of lakes, would have differed. Also, much of the woodland present in these areas today consists of conifer plantations, for which there is no evidence from Roman Britain. In contrast, western Britain seems to have been rather more wooded in the Roman period than today.

This suggests that there was a difference between the native and villa landscapes in terms of the utilization of natural resources. In the villa landscape it appears that pressure on land was greater, so that almost all available agricultural land was used. The extent of agricultural land was increased by large-scale drainage of the Fens and probably smaller-scale drainage in other areas. Only a minimal amount of woodland seems to have remained to supply essential needs, and most of this must have been managed to increase its productivity. It is even possible that some planting of willow coppice occurred on wetland areas that were not worth draining for arable.

Those parts of the native landscape that were most intensively used for agriculture in the Roman period were areas of military occupation, which provided an (apparently temporary) impetus to production. The ability of the native landscape to produce a surplus of agricultural products may have been enhanced by the slightly higher temperatures, and perhaps lower rainfall, prevailing in the Roman period than today.

Formation of the villa landscape clearly did not require major efforts in terms of bringing the land into cultivation – a more significant problem may have been overcoming reduced soil fertility and loss of soil due to erosion to supply an expanding market. The native landscape provided more scope for the extension of the area used for agriculture, but in many places it was never exploited to its full capacity. Having provided an environmental context for Roman settlement in these areas, we will examine the archaeological evidence in the following two chapters.

CHAPTER 3

THE VILLA LANDSCAPE

DEFINING THE VILLA

The key component of the villa landscape was, of course, the villa itself.[1] In Latin, villa means a farm or country residence, and in this sense villas are often referred to in written sources from various parts of the Roman Empire.[2] This evidence mostly relates to the early Roman period, and to long-romanized parts of the Continent. Most Romano-British villas were established in the late Roman period, however, and in much more recently romanized contexts. So it is debatable how relevant these continental sources are to Romano-British villas.[3]

It could be argued that the villa, as it appears in written sources, is essentially the same as the villa we see in the archaeology of Roman Britain, because of shared features of Roman imperial social and agricultural organization.[4] Alternatively, the Mediterranean evidence might be seen as irrelevant to Britain, because the situation in Britain differed fundamentally from that in other parts of the Empire.[5]

This, of course, raises the questions of how can one identify the villa in Roman Britain, and whether it is worth attempting this identification at all? Might it be simpler to abandon the term altogether and opt for some, supposedly 'neutral', archaeological expression, such as 'high status rural settlement', for such sites? To address these questions, perhaps it is first worth examining what we mean by a villa in archaeological terms. Archaeologists of Roman Britain usually define the villa by the presence of both 'prestige' and 'romanized' attributes, including mosaics, Roman baths, tessellated floors, sculptured columns, marble wall veneers, painted plaster and aspects of the ground plan of the buildings.[6] Using a definition of this sort we can examine a site, such as Dalton Parlours or Vineyards Farm, and say whether or not it is a villa in these terms.[7]

In Britain there is no inscription, or other direct link, between this archaeological definition and textual sources, and there has been a long-standing discussion over the degree to which, if at all, the archaeological category of 'villas' is identical to that in written sources. The only Romano-British site described as a villa in a Roman text (the *Villa Faustini* of the *Notitia Dignitatum*) is unlocated, although it is sometimes identified as the very 'un-villa-like' site of Scole, a 'small town' in modern archaeological terminology.[8]

So, we have two definitions of the villa: one based on textual evidence, the other on archaeology. This has led some scholars to differentiate between villas defined on archaeological and textual grounds. Millett has suggested that we adopt a new terminology to separate them[9] so that, in his terms, a villa is archaeologically defined and a Villa textually defined. An alternative, as yet surprisingly neglected in print, is to examine this question on an Empire-wide scale.[10] Using such an approach, it can be argued, it is possible to identify those archaeological characteristics specific to sites directly defined in textual evidence as villas. These characteristics can be used to suggest archaeological correlates of the textually attested villa, so connecting textual and archaeological definitions of the villa. This coincides informatively with work in

Britain, which has demonstrated that a restricted range of ground plans characterizes those Romano-British sites usually considered to be villas on archaeological grounds. This range of plans also occurs at those sites elsewhere in the Roman Empire associated with textual sources identifying them as villas. These sites share other attributes (baths, wall plaster, sculpture, etc.) with their British counterparts. So, the two definitions of the villa may be closer than often supposed, even if they do not exactly correspond.

THE PRINCIPAL TYPES OF VILLA PLANS[11]

There are several distinctive types of architectural plans commonly found at what archaeologists call villas and which also occur at these continental sites. Such plans can be closely related to the usual scheme for classifying British villas first established by Collingwood and Richmond.[12]

The simplest or 'cottage villa' is a simple rectangle with additional rooms provided by subdivisions, without a corridor or wings. This was often achieved by dividing the end into two rooms by a central wall along the long axis. This type cannot be directly related to continental textual evidence in the way suggested above. Its claim to villa status rests on the fact that the known examples of such structures developed into buildings that can be so related. Examples of cottage villas include the earliest structures at Lockleys and Park Street.[13]

Next most complex in plan is the 'aisled house'.[14] This is a simple rectangle, occasionally with subdivisions at one or other end, and small side rooms. The key feature is a pair of parallel walls or rows of posts or pillars along the long axis of the main room, producing aisles. Examples in mortared stone include those at Stroud, Meonstoke and Landwade, and there are also instances built in wood, as at Denton, which was later rebuilt in stone.[15]

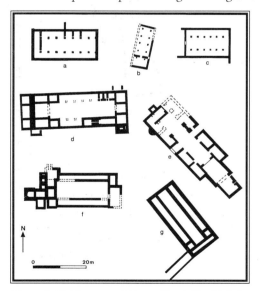

Plans of aisled houses: a, Ickleton (Cambridgeshire); b, Holcombe (Devon); c, Spoonley Wood (Gloucestershire); d, Mansfield Woodhouse (Nottinghamshire); e, Landwade (Suffolk); f, Titsey (Surrey); g, Meonstoke (Hampshire). (a, c, d, e after Collingwood and Richmond 1969, b after Pollard 1974, f after Bird 1987, g after Crummy (in King) 1996)

The most widespread type of building at sites with villa attributes is the 'winged corridor house', a rectangle with two projecting rooms set at each end – the 'wings' of the building. This type of villa is very common, both in Britain and elsewhere in the Roman Empire – where it can be directly related to textual evidence. Examples include Darenth, Ditchley, Farmington (Clear Cupboard) and Shakenoak.[16] Again, there are examples entirely in timber, as at Boxmoor.[17]

The 'courtyard villa' comprises an open area framed on three sides by a single building, with one side either left open or bordered by a wall. Such buildings are the most complex, in terms of plan, among Romano-British villas and can be closely related to continental sites. In Britain, sites of this type include North Leigh, Woodchester and Bignor.[18] So far as is known, there were no entirely timber courtyard villas.

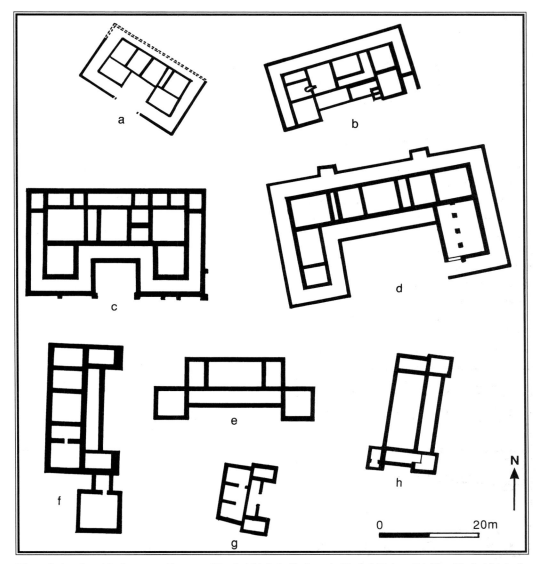

Plans of winged corridor houses: a, Boxmoor (Hertfordshire); b, Shakenoak (Oxfordshire); c, Ditchley (Oxfordshire); d, Gadebridge Park (Hertfordshire); e, Great Staughton (Cambridgeshire); f, Mansfield Woodhouse (Nottinghamshire); g, Hibaldstow (Humberside); h, Plaxtol (Kent). (a after Neal 1970, b after Brodribb, Hands and Walker 1971, c, e, f after Collingwood and Richmond 1969, d after Neal 1974, g after R.F. Smith 1987, h after de la Bédoyère 1991)

The term 'courtyard villa' is often used somewhat more loosely to refer to all villas where the buildings were arranged around a courtyard. Here it is used only to refer to those villas at which a single building itself forms a courtyard, and the term 'villas with courtyards' used for those in which several buildings form a courtyard. Some of the latter were far from palatial, as at Orton Hall Farm, Peterborough.[19]

Subsequently, other scholars have suggested some other consistently occurring types of villa plan. The 'hall-type villa' comprises a large rectangular room (the hall), which forms the

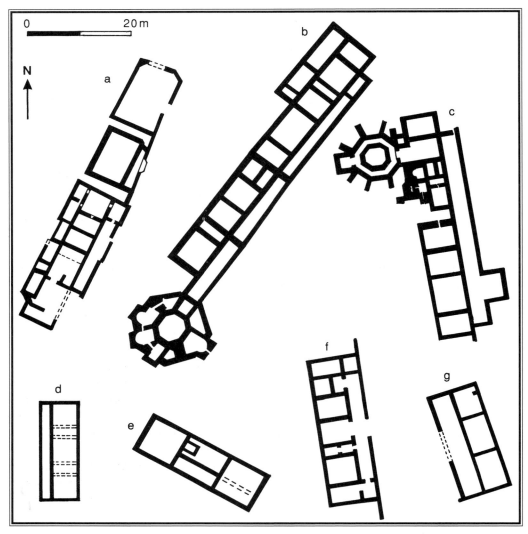

Plans of corridor houses: a, Ham Hill (Somerset); b, Holcombe (Somerset); c, Lufton (Somerset); d, Broad Street Common (Surrey); e, Langton (North Yorkshire); f, Sparsholt (Hampshire); g, Marshfield (Gloucestershire). (a, b, c after Branigan 1976a, d after Bird 1987, e after Corder and Kirk 1932, f after Johnston 1978, g after J.T. Smith 1987)

centrepiece of the plan.[20] A clear example of this is provided by the sites at King's Weston and Wraxhall, while others include associations with winged corridor designs, as at Chew Park.[21]

The 'corridor house' is similar in plan to winged corridor houses but without wings.[22] This is evidenced at a series of sites, mostly in the West Country, as at Downton, Whatley, Ham Hill, Iwerne, Holcombe and Lufton,[23] but also elsewhere, as at Sparsholt and Barton Court Farm.[24]

These types were not mutually exclusive. For example, Brading has both a winged corridor villa and an aisled house in the same compound.[25] Such a combination of distinctive building plans may suggest an association between the different types of plan. Villa plans were also elaborated by the addition of further rooms, while retaining these types as the basis for architectural embellishments, as at Woolaston.[26]

Consequently, there is an inter-related group of structural plans, some of which can be related, by architectural comparison, to continental sites textually identifiable as villas. These often share other features (such as baths) in common both with each other and with those sites. In this way, a close correlation between Roman and modern archaeological definitions of the villa can be achieved. So, the Romano-British villa was probably a socially, culturally and perhaps economically distinctive settlement type, rather than an architectural style alone.

THE CONSTRUCTION OF VILLAS AND THE FORMATION OF THE VILLA LANDSCAPE

Defined in this way, villas are also able to be associated with other characteristics, including glazed windows (sometimes with iron window grilles), marble veneers, sculptured architectural elements and floors that were at least partly tessellated or covered with concrete or mosaic. Although such characteristics are found at other types of site also, for example at temples, the decoration of villas in these ways is one of their most outstanding features. This decoration was plainly intended for those both inside and outside the main house.

Important rooms might be plastered and provided with mosaics and tessellated floors, as well as with elaborate furnishings,[27] and some villas were also plastered and painted on the exterior, as at Piddington.[28] Villas could also be positioned to display picturesque views of the local terrain to those inside them. For example, the fourth-century villa at Great Witcombe has an impressive vista over the local countryside.[29] Sometimes, architectural features were even constructed to enhance the opportunities for viewing the surrounding landscape, as at the fourth-century site at Farningham Manor House, Kent. Here, the winged building plan frames a (probably roofed) open-sided court, provided with a mosaic, at the rear of the main house overlooking the River Darent.[30]

Villas were also often provided with Roman baths, usually in a separate structure from the main house, and frequently the main rooms of the principal house were heated by hypocausts. These aspects, and the rich artefacts often associated with villas, suggest that their occupants, in general, had a higher material standard of living than the majority of those living at non-villa rural sites, where these facilities are absent.

Although the construction of a villa landscape started in the villa itself, it extended far beyond the villa structure and furnishings. The villa building and bath-house were frequently surrounded by an enclosure, or wall, as at Ditchley, Hambleden and Norton Disney.[31] Within this there were usually several buildings in addition to the main villa house, but their layout often focused on the principal house, as at Littlecote and Rockbourne. Entrance to the enclosure might be through an elaborate gateway, as at Littlecote,[32] and sometimes there were formal gardens within this compound. Such gardens were probably much more common than current evidence suggests, but there are two well-attested instances of Romano-British villa gardens: at Frocester and Fishbourne.[33] An ornamental basin seems to have stood in the forecourt at Eccles villa, perhaps implying a formal garden there also.[34]

Such aspects of the villa complex separated its principal buildings from the outside world and controlled access to the surroundings of the main house. Inside the enclosure an element of structural planning and functional unity, in addition perhaps to well-ordered gardens, would give

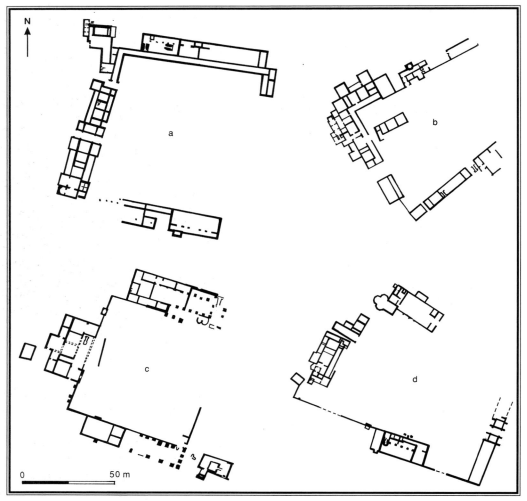

Plans of villas with courtyards: a, Halstock (Dorset); b, Rockbourne (Hampshire); c, Brading (Isle of Wight); d, Littlecote (Oxfordshire) (a after Lucas 1993, b after RCHM (England) 1984, c after Tomalin 1987, d after Walters 1994). Note: these are not 'courtyard villas'

an impression of order and control. This impression, and that of 'sophisticated' romanization, might have been further emphasized by the aspects of symmetry in the architectural style of the main buildings.

THE CHARACTERISTICS OF THE VILLA LANDSCAPE

Other features closely connected with the villa site were often located nearby. Unsurprisingly, perhaps, they often included cemeteries, as at Bletsoe.[35] Mausolea and walled cemeteries, built in mortared stone with classical sculpture and inscriptions, are found close to several villas and seem architecturally related to them, as at Lullingstone, Keston and probably Chedworth.[36] These contained romanized burials: probably those of the villa owners, although not all owners were

Reconstruction of a temple site, showing the temenos *enclosure. (Painting of the temple at Ivy Chimneys, Witham, Essex, by Frank Gardiner, reproduced by permission of Essex County Council)*

buried in mausolea, as evidence from Claydon Pike suggests.[37] There, a cemetery probably associated with the late Roman villa was focused on an especially deep grave containing the body of an adult man, perhaps a member of the villa-owning family.

Another related landscape feature is the romanized temple.[38] Unlike pre-Roman Iron Age temples, these again have shared plans and close architectural affinities both with villas and with continental classical architecture.[39] Like villas, such buildings are stone-built and have tessellated floors, sculptures, stone columns and occasionally even mosaics. The artefacts left at temples were derived from a range of Romano-British contexts, but include many similar items to those found at villas. Villas, temples and mausolea are also connected architecturally, as exemplified by the temple-like mausoleum at Lullingstone villa.

As adult burial was almost certainly prohibited at pagan religious sites in Roman Britain,[40] the connection between temples and mausolea was not through their association with death. It was either based on a common link with paganism or with the rural social élite. This is in contrast to the dissimilarity between the unromanized shrines (such as the remarkable partially waterlogged example from Milton Keynes[41]) and such mausolea.

Villas, mausolea and temples were not the only aspects of the villa landscape. Other features were present, including roads linking these landscape components with each other and with towns. 'Roman roads' (that is, roads built in a romanized fashion) had been established for the most part during, and immediately after, the Roman Conquest and were maintained, or at least in use, in the villa landscape until the end of the Roman period.[42] Although they were almost certainly used for everyday civilian travel and the transport of materials, the formal road network was not primarily designed for rural estates to transport their produce to town, or for travel

A Roman road. Aerial photograph of the Foss Way, North Wraxall, Wiltshire. (Cambridge University Collection of Air Photographs: copyright reserved)

between villas, temples and other sites. It was essentially a military and official communication system, linking forts, towns, wayside staging posts and official centres.

It seems that as more villas were built the occupants of some of these sites, as at Langton, Yorkshire, decided that they required their own stretches of road. Consequently, new romanized approach roads linking villas (and temples, as at Claydon Pike) to the main road system were constructed.[43] Although not always straight, Roman roads, both official and locally commissioned, were distinguished by their linear routes, regardless of local topography, and their paving with cobblestones and gravel (metalling), unlike pre-Roman tracks. In the areas away from these roads, trackways, which seem to have included both ditched and embanked paths and apparently deliberate holloways, formed the network of paths between sites. These non-Roman roads did not adhere to the linear Roman model, nor were they metalled, and they meandered through fields and other landscape features, partly following the contours of the land.

The 'prehistoric' landscape through which these roads passed was also re-used in the Roman period. It is still uncertain whether any hill-fort was constructed in the villa landscape during the Roman period, and secular hill-fort occupation seems to have entirely ceased in most parts of south-east Britain after the Roman Conquest. In the fourth century, however, several previously deserted hill-forts seem to have been re-used, perhaps for military purposes, as at Cissbury (which had been under the plough in the early Roman period) and Highdown in Sussex.[44]

Small villages seem to have been established immediately outside the gates of some hill-forts deserted in the early Roman period, and probably comprised the descendants of the Iron Age hill-fort dwelling communities. Examples include the sites at Wolstonbury in Sussex and Cannington in Somerset.[45] Deserted hill-forts were, however, more often re-used for temple sites (perhaps due to a persisting tradition of their pre-Roman religious functions), as at Maiden Castle and Lydney.[46]

Other prehistoric ritual monuments were apparently used in the Roman period for burials rather than for temples, as at Juliberries Grave.[47] Even at Avebury and Stonehenge, concentrations of pottery and food debris might suggest 'funerary feasts' in connection with Romano-British internments.[48]

A few pre-Iron Age sites were afforded even more Romano-British attention. For example, at Slonk Hill, Sussex, a pre-Roman enclosure was used for a Romano-British settlement, including a fenced-off area surrounding prehistoric barrows, which were re-used for Romano-British burials.[49] At Silbury Hill, what may be Roman-period ritual shafts, and other features, were found at the foot of the prehistoric conical mound.[50]

However, unlike Gaul, in Britain Roman-period temples were seldom located at pre-Iron Age ritual sites. There are only two examples of temples at prehistoric barrows (at Stanwick and

Haddenham), despite many hundreds of excavated burial mounds. Their contexts, one on the Fens where imperial involvement seems to be suggested by the exceptional site at Stonea,[51] the other close to a major villa site with possible official aspects, suggest the possibility that this was due to immigrants from Roman Gaul or elsewhere in the Empire, where such re-use was commonplace.

The Romano-British interest in pre-Iron Age ritual monuments may have been the result of Romano-British folklore about the landscape. Such beliefs might explain both the use of such sites for burial and, if they were not specifically part of pagan religions, the lack of similarly-sited temples. The siting of some Romano-British temples in Iron Age hill-forts may be seen as a different trend, such temples being close to the sites of their Iron Age predecessors.

There were, of course, many other rural Romano-British cemeteries unconnected with villas. These are mostly small in size, often in curvilinear or rectilinear enclosures, and they include cremations and (especially in late Roman Britain) inhumation burials. Together these features were, therefore, the main parts of a common landscape found throughout most of east and south-west England and south-east Wales. The close association between villas and temples, and the probable role of villa estates in reordering the landscape, suggest that this can be said to have come into existence as a result of the establishment of villas – that it is a 'villa landscape'.

For the most part the rural population clearly lived at non-villa sites. The homes of this, mostly lower-status, rural population have been the subject of much less intense archaeological research than have villas. These sites comprise both villages and farms, although there is an unclear division between the larger farms and smaller villages.

VILLAGES IN THE VILLA LANDSCAPE

In the archaeology of Roman Britain the term 'village' is usually used to indicate an unwalled group of many buildings occurring together, as at Chalton Down, Meriden Down and Chisenbury Warren, although some scholars include what are here considered to be small towns under the term village.[52] The latter site, recently partly excavated for the first time in the course of a wide-ranging survey of Salisbury Plain, can be taken as an example of these sites. Chisenbury Warren comprises a series of structures set on terraces along the sides of a trackway (a holloway) and probably occupied from the first to the fifth or sixth centuries AD.[53]

As the defining characteristic of a Romano-British village, such as this, is the combination of several homesteads within a single settlement, there is some scope for debate over how closely spaced these have to be to constitute a village. Partial excavation, or incomplete survey, can also lead to further problems in recognizing whether a site was a village or a farm, and confusion may derive from the existence of temple sites with dependent settlements, as at Nettleton.[54] This is usually classed as a temple or a small town, but has been referred to as a village.

The relationship between villas and villages is also problematical. Elsewhere in the Roman Empire, scholars have noted that villages have strong links with villa estates, but the British evidence is ambiguous. Not all villages seem to be associated with villas, but some are, as at Lockington and Fotheringhay.[55] At other sites, such as Chalton and Grandford,[56] however, there is no reason to connect these villages with any villa. Rather, they seem to relate to local patterns of farms, fields and tracks.

Villages could include buildings analogous in plan to villas, as at Kingscote,[57] although these were at the smaller and less sophisticated end of the villa range. While this may suggest a link

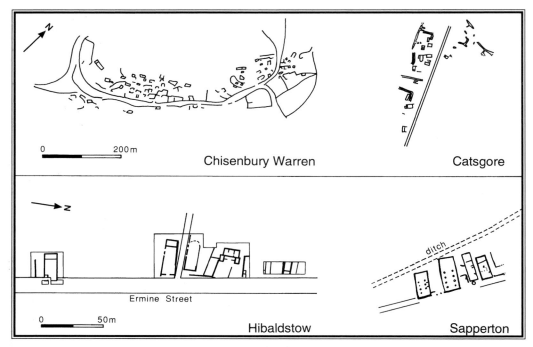

Plans of villages and roadside settlements: Chisenbury Warren, Wiltshire (after C. Taylor 1983); Catsgore, Somerset (after Leech 1982); Hibaldstow, Lincolnshire (based on R.F. Smith 1987); Sapperton, Lincolnshire (based on B.B. Simmons 1985)

with villas, the villa-like buildings in villages are probably too small and simple to be landowner's residences. Other villages, even prosperous sites on the Fens, such as Grandford, had no villa-like buildings. At Grandford the village consisted of timber-framed buildings constructed in the early Roman period and later rebuilt in mortared stone in the third century, when romanized architectural elements such as plastered walls, along with glazed windows, were added.[58]

The evidence, in general, suggests that villages were not at the core of villa estates, with estate workers clustered around the villa owner's house but, if so, these villa-like structures in villages require explanation. They may have been the homes of, for example, village elders, or of estate supervisors (bailiffs) acting for landlords. Bailiffs were part of the continental imperial estate system, in which villas were not always operated directly by their owners. Absentee landowners operated estates using bailiffs, and textual sources tell us of what may be such landowners with property in Britain, so the possibility of bailiffs bears special consideration.

The lack of villas in the Fens and Salisbury Plain, and the supposedly large number of villages in these areas, has led to claims that they were imperial estates owned directly by the Emperor.[59] There is no inscription from Britain that unambiguously enables the identification of such an estate, however, and this interpretation rests on the claim that villages were otherwise rare in Roman Britain.

A convincing case that some villages were founded in the Roman period can be made on several grounds, and is illustrated by the examples of Catsgore in Somerset and Monkton in Kent. Catsgore was apparently established in the late Roman period and contained mortared stone buildings associated with romanized artefacts.[60] While there may have been many sites like

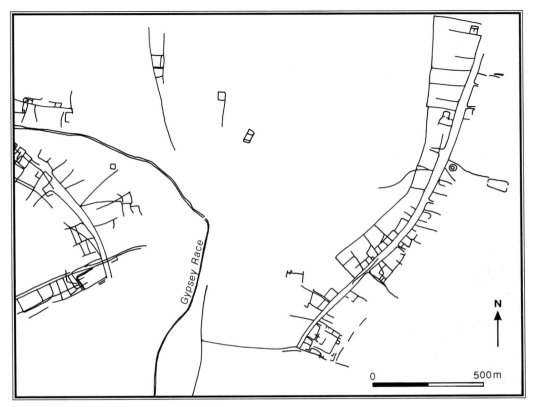

'Droveway settlements' in north-east England, near Burton Fleming. (After Stead 1976b)

Catsgore, Monkton is apparently unique in Roman Britain. It consists of sunken-featured buildings (SFBs), used for a short period, probably less than a century, entirely in the early Roman period.[61]

Not all Romano-British villages lack a pre-Roman background, however, as evidence from Yorkshire shows. There, a series of so-called 'droveway settlements' have been found by both excavation and aerial photography, at sites such as Burton Fleming, Kirmington and probably at both Wharram Percy and Sherburn.[62] These seem to have developed from local Iron Age sites, and contained clusters of buildings (constructed in timber or drystone) concentrated around a holloway, the 'droveway' of their title. Regional differences of modern archaeological terminology should not be allowed to obscure the fact that these settlements share all of the defining features of Romano-British villages such as Chisenbury Warren and Chalton Down.[63] These sites were apparently entirely unconnected with both villas and official establishments and were, in origin, pre-Roman. Some villas, as at Rudston, were later built on droveway settlements, but the evidence for continuous occupation is at least ambiguous, and this might equally be seen as reminiscent of the eighteenth-century clearance of villages for the estates of the wealthy.

So, villages were found in areas other than the Fens and Wessex, and could have both pre-Roman and Roman-period non-official origins. They were not usually founded to accommodate villa estate workers, even if some such employees lived in them. It is also worth stressing how widespread villages were in other parts of the villa landscape.

Between the villages of the Fens and the droveway settlements of Yorkshire there were many other villages, also apparently with non-official origins, as at South Ferriby, where an extensive domestic site was probably occupied from the Iron Age through to the fifth century AD.[64] At Winteringham, a (28 hectare) settlement close to a Roman road contained second- or third-century stone buildings on a site with both Iron Age and fourth-century finds.[65] At Dragonby there is evidence of another contemporary form of village.[66] This was occupied from the Iron Age through to the late fourth century. In its Romano-British form it consisted of rectilinear buildings and corn-driers within rectilinear ditched plots, set along a metalled road.

To the south of the Fens there are other sites that might be termed villages, although their pre-Roman origins are less clear-cut, as at Maxey, where a Romano-British non-villa secular settlement (of 8 hectares) included ditches, pits and occupation evidence.[67] At Thundersbarrow Hill, Sussex, there was a sizable Romano-British settlement of roundhouses associated with fields on either side of a trackway, a well and several corn-driers, immediately outside a disused hill-fort.[68] In the West Country yet more villages apparently await discovery, as the recent evidence from Butterfield Down near Amesbury suggests.[69]

Evidence for villages – many with Iron Age origins – is, therefore, widespread in the villa landscape from North Yorkshire to Sussex, and from the West Country as far east as the Fens and Kent. So it is doubtful if there were any large areas of this landscape completely without villages, and many less well-known large rural settlements may be sites of this type, for example Ducklington and Appleford in Oxfordshire, and Lansdown Hill near Bath.[70] To these must be added 'roadside settlements' – villages along Roman roads – as at Wilcote and Hibaldstow, which may also be classified as villages.[71] At the latter site, for example, occupation extended for more than 800 metres along the road and separate plots (defined by ditches) were used for different purposes. In contrast with other, simpler buildings, one plot contained an aisled house, eventually replaced by a very small winged corridor house. This is noticeably smaller than the other structures at the site, so is unlikely to represent the home of a landowner rather than a bailiff or village official.

Another example of roadside development was at Portway, where timber buildings were set in defined plots on one side of the road, while on the other there were both similar buildings and shrines.[72] Interestingly, most such settlements, and the sub-class of 'river-ford settlements' (roadside settlements at river crossings), as at the aptly named site of Oldford, were probably unofficial in origin.[73]

Far from being without villages, the villa landscape was, therefore, also a landscape of villages, large and small. The frequency of villages in Roman Britain, and the Iron Age origin of many of these sites, undermines both a consistent association between villages and official policy, and the argument that any area was an imperial estate because it contained many villages. It must be stressed, however, that villages and villas merely comprise definable categories in a divisible (into farms, villas, villages, small towns, etc.), but still continuous, scale of settlement size and nucleation.

NON-VILLA FARMS IN THE VILLA LANDSCAPE: A REGIONAL REVIEW

By far the most common type of Romano-British secular settlement was neither the village nor the villa, but the isolated farmstead. As they are relatively unknown, a brief regional review of these sites may provide a general impression of their character and regional variation. Dividing

Roman Britain into broad areas (moving roughly north–south) we may begin with the north-east of the villa landscape: the area between Catterick and the Humber, although there are a few villas north of this zone.

THE NORTH EAST[74]

In this area there are many enclosed farmsteads known from aerial photographs and field survey that can be attributed to the Roman period on the basis of associated finds or excavated evidence, such as three sites identified by the Wharram Percy Project: Birdsall High Barn, Burdale Tunnel Top and Wharram Grange Crossroad.[75] These are all rectilinear univallate (i.e. with a single barrier) enclosures occupied from the Iron Age to the fourth century AD.

Excavated examples of such sites can be found in many parts of the north east, for example in North Yorkshire at Middle House,[76] or at Salthouse Road, Hull, where a double-ditched enclosure of the first century AD associated with three roundhouses was sited on an island of higher ground close to the Humber.[77] Enclosed farms are known from the very north of this area, as at the early Roman site of Potto in the Tees valley,[78] a ditched enclosure containing two timber roundhouses with adjoining ditches linking these to its surrounding fields. In North Yorkshire a series of 'square enclosures' (up to 70 metres square), with both domestic artefacts (such as querns) and first- to fourth-century AD pottery, are apparently sites of this type, as at Nunthorpe, Whorlton, Lounsdale, Egton Church and Ingleby.[79] Most of these remained 'native' in character throughout the Roman period, but a few became villas, as at Beadlam.[80]

Although many sites originated in the Iron Age,[81] not all northern sites show long-term

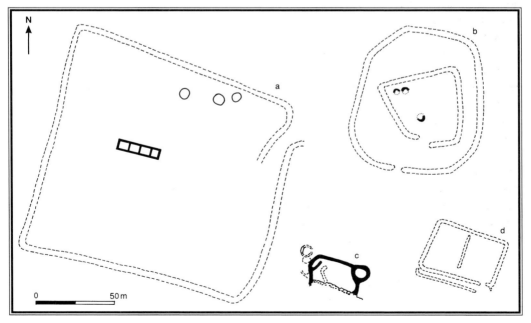

'Square enclosures' and an enclosed hut-group in north-east England: a, Brough Hill, Settrington; b, Staxton; c, Trougate; d, Langton (a and b based on Ramm 1978; c based on Raistrick and Holmes 1962; d based on Corder and Kirk 1932). Stone walls shown in black, ditches in outline

continuities from the pre-Roman landscape: at Wetwang Slack, three farms were founded in the first century AD on the periphery of a ditched land unit with a pre-Roman and earlier Romano-British farm in its centre, apparently abandoned when the farms were established.[82] This pattern then survived until the fourth century.

An interesting, and much more diffuse, pattern of occupation was found at Welton.[83] This had been a villa site until the second century, but the villa was then disused and occupation continued in the form of corn-driers and small domestic structures (including SFBs) built amid the ditched enclosures of the Roman-period field system. Burials were placed in some of the ditches and in the flues of disused corn-driers.

THE MIDLANDS[84]

In the Midlands (the area of England south of the Humber and north of the Thames) there were also large numbers of small, ditched, rectilinear and curvilinear enclosures containing curvilinear and rectilinear timber buildings, of probable Romano-British date. Excavated examples in the

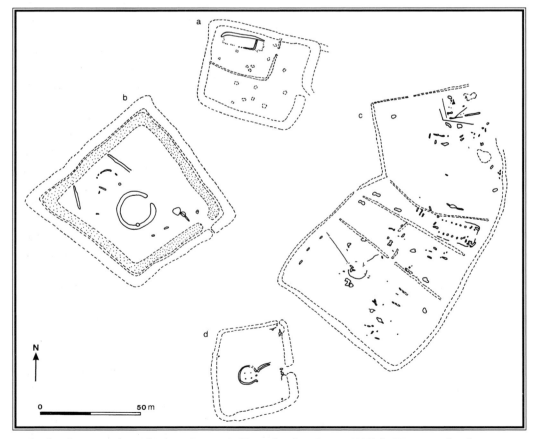

Enclosed settlements in the Midlands: a, Dunston's Clump (based on Garton 1988); b, Werrington (based on Mackreth 1988); c, Wakerley (based on Jackson and Tylecote 1978); d, Sharpstones Hill (based on Jenks in G. Webster 1991). Earthworks stippled, ditches in outline

East Midlands include the sites at Tallington, Rampton, Colsterworth, Breaston and Dunston's Clump. As these examples show, such sites were in use from the Iron Age long into the Roman period.

At Colsterworth[85] a curvilinear enclosure containing a farm comprising five or six roundhouses built in timber was used from the Iron Age up to, and probably after the start of, the Roman period. At Tallington a similar Iron Age settlement was succeeded by a small early Roman farm set within a rectilinear enclosure.[86] The associated features included both a granary and working-hollows, although the main house had probably been destroyed by quarrying before the excavation began.

The site at Rampton shows that not all sites were short-lived: a single roundhouse of the first century AD was found in a low-lying location amid a complex of enclosures, the finds from which seem to attest occupation until the fourth century.[87] Breaston provides another example of such a site,[88] comprising roundhouses within a sub-rectilinear enclosure but, in this case, occupation more certainly seems to have commenced in the Roman period rather than before, showing that the presence of roundhouses alone cannot preclude a Roman-period foundation.

At Dunston's Clump the rectilinear ditched enclosure contained rectilinear timber structures, occupied from the first to the third centuries AD.[89] Consequently, we can see strong excavated evidence for the occupation of these sites (as a group rather than at any individual enclosure) between the Iron Age and mid-Roman period.

Some such sites were developed by their occupants in ways that adopted more romanized features. A clear example is the site at Odell,[90] where a ditched enclosure containing timber roundhouses, with a small adjacent cremation cemetery of the first century AD, was occupied in the Iron Age. Occupation shifted in the early Roman period to a nearby location, where an open settlement was established. At first this also comprised timber roundhouses, but then in the late Roman period it was replaced by a rectilinear building of conjoined rooms – which might be viewed as a more romanized plan – probably also of timber but with broad gravel foundations. Adjacent were a small curvilinear timber building and two stone-lined wells, while a probably (at least partly) contemporary corn-drier stood within a rectilinear enclosure nearby.

There were less romanized enclosed settlements in the East Midlands, as at Werrington and Cat's Water in Cambridgeshire.[91] Similar sites existed as far south as Essex, where the Romano-British settlement at Stansted, close to and perhaps associated with the rich early Roman cremations at Bury Lodge Lane, was a rectilinear ditched enclosure of this type established on an Iron Age farmstead.[92] Interestingly, although this settlement probably contained no stone buildings (only a few areas of cobbling and shallow gullies survived ploughing), finds from fieldwalking included hypocaust tile.

In the West Midlands there were also large numbers of ditched early Romano-British settlement enclosures, to judge from aerial photographs and other survey data. Excavated examples include the sites at Sharpstones Hill and Weeping Cross.[93] At Sharpstones Hill a rectilinear enclosure surrounded a farm originating from the Iron Age, but in the Roman period comprising first curvilinear and then rectilinear buildings. A similar but larger enclosed site occupied both in the Iron Age and early Roman period has been excavated at Weeping Cross.

There were also dispersed Romano-British unenclosed settlements in the Midlands, analogous to Welton. Excavated examples include North Shoebury and Bulpham in Essex.[94] The settlement at North Shoebury comprised a trackway with associated roundhouses, pits and other minor features, apparently occupied from the Iron Age throughout the Roman period.[95]

Evidence from Bulpham suggests curvilinear hut sites, and many pits were found over an area of 6 hectares associated with Roman-period finds.

There were also smaller, and more concentrated, unenclosed settlements in this area. Examples include the small cluster of roundhouses at Staunton, dating from the first to the fourth centuries, and the four timber curvilinear huts found on the foreshore at East Tilbury, associated with early Roman pottery and roof tiles.[96]

CENTRAL SOUTHERN ENGLAND[97]

In central southern England, as further north, there are Roman-period enclosed farmsteads that were established on the sites of, and similar to, those of the late Iron Age. These include the curvilinear enclosures at Rotherley and Woodcuts, which were occupied throughout the Roman period.[98]

Not all Romano-British settlements in this area were located at pre-Roman sites. An interesting case of a site showing the complexities of the range of relationships represented is at Winterbourne Down.[99] There, building platforms associated with Romano-British pottery were connected by a trackway to a curvilinear enclosure containing Romano-British burials, which overlay an Iron Age settlement. This may show discontinuity, the abandoned settlement being designated useless waste ground, or perhaps evidence of continuity – the signalling of descent and legitimacy by relating the burial of more recent ancestors to more ancient ones who, it was claimed, had lived in the then deserted settlement.

Similarly the Romano-British site at Farmoor, Oxfordshire, was established on a new site adjacent to an Iron Age settlement, possibly evidence of discontinuity due to disuse, possibly of continuity – merely the shifting of the location of the settlement, not its desertion.[100] Whichever was the case, in the early Roman period Farmoor was probably the site of an enclosed farm, set within a rectilinear ditched enclosure with a well, linked to another area of small fields or paddocks by a linear ditched trackway. This may have been associated with a small settlement, although the excavated data are ambiguous.

Another Oxfordshire site, at Ashville, also had Iron Age origins, and in the Roman period consisted of wells, pits and an associated field system.[101] There was more evidence of domestic activity at this site, although the associated structures were not located. Building debris suggests an undiscovered tiled construction nearby. Of special interest, however, is a small fourth-century inhumation cemetery, apparently belonging to this settlement. This comprised both rows of east–west graves without grave-goods and north–south burials with grave-goods. Some of the latter were beheaded, a practice probably indicative of pagan funerary practices. The excavator suggested that this was a burial ground with separate zones for Christians and pagans, analogous to the dual cemeteries found (with more supporting evidence) at the small town at Shepton Mallet, Somerset. Similar small cemeteries (both enclosed and, as at these sites, unenclosed) are widespread in the villa landscape of central southern England, as at Lynch Farm[102] and Barrow Hills, Radley,[103] although the religious affinities of those buried in them are frequently unclear.

The clearest excavated example of an unenclosed farm with a trackway in this region is perhaps Overton Down, where a pair of rectilinear drystone buildings were associated with a trackway and field enclosure and Roman-period pottery.[104] Unenclosed settlements also occur widely in this region, as at Thornhill Farm.[105] There, the early Roman settlement comprised

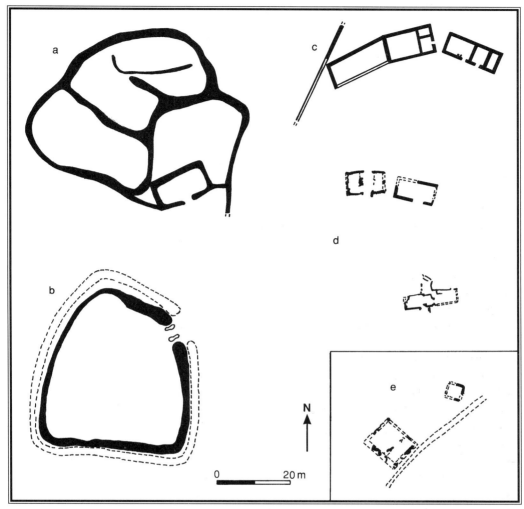

Non-villa settlements in central southern (inset e) and south-west England: a, Row of Ashes Farm, Butcombe (based on Fowler 1976); b, Kingsdown (based on Gray 1930); c, Bradley Hill (after Leech 1981); d, Studland (based on Field 1965); e, Overton Down (based on Fowler 1967). Stone walls shown in black (with conjectured continuations in out-line), ditches in outline.

small timber roundhouses, animal pens and other minor agricultural features, set amid rectilinear fields covering approximately 15 hectares.

SOUTH-WEST ENGLAND AND SOUTH-EAST WALES[106]

In the south-west of the villa landscape, in the West Country and south-east Wales, there were also both enclosed and unenclosed settlements. In this area hill-forts were sometimes occupied during the Roman period, as at Balksbury, Castle Ditches and Llancarfan.[107] Evidence from an extensive survey of the relevant evidence in Somerset suggests that such Romano-British secular domestic occupation at hill-forts, while it occurred at some sites, was not a common aspect of the villa landscape.[108] Several apparent examples, such as Kingsdown – probably built in the Roman period as a secular domestic settlement in a curvilinear enclosure – may be more correctly termed enclosed farms than hill-forts, and others, as at Cadbury Tickenham, may have been temple sites.[109]

Consequently, the Romano-British domestic occupation of hill-forts in the West Country and south-east Wales may have involved relatively few of the many known hill-forts. The construction and reoccupation of hill-forts in this area during the immediately post-Roman period[110] complicates this issue. Post-Roman hill-forts are frequently associated with Roman-period artefacts, even when (as at High Peak) Romano-British occupation probably did not precede the post-Roman phase.[111] So, it is insufficient evidence for Romano-British domestic occupation simply to find unassociated Roman-period objects in a hill-fort.

Otherwise the settlement-types from this region are closely comparable to those from other parts of the villa landscape. The site at Studland near Poole Harbour gives a clear example of such an unenclosed settlement, in which timber roundhouses were replaced by rectilinear structures on drystone foundations.[112] There are many less well-known sites of unenclosed Romano-British non-villa rural secular settlements in this area. An example is Poxwell, south of Dorchester, where a third- or fourth-century rectilinear building with stone foundations, containing corn-driers and an iron-working furnace, lay in the lee of a field terrace.[113]

There were also unenclosed settlements more closely analogous to Overton Down in the south west. These varied both in size and exact form. To compare two late Roman examples: at Maddington Farm, Shrewton,[114] a small timber roundhouse was set amid fields, near a similarly small inhumation cemetery, while at Bradley Hill in Somerset[115] the unenclosed settlement consisted of rectilinear mortared stone buildings. The Bradley Hill example included domestic structures (each used for a single pre-occupation burial) and a barn. The latter building was later employed as a cemetery for infants, while another, probably Christian, cemetery, including adults, was established outside the settlement. Perhaps a similar site, albeit previously not compared with Bradley Hill, may be the pre-cemetery farm at Poundbury (buildings R12, R13, R14), which was associated with the earliest east–west inhumations on the site. This included some burials that may have been pagan, but others that could easily have been Christian (see the case of Farmoor, mentioned above). Perhaps the origin of the late Roman Christian cemetery at Poundbury lies in a pre-existing Christian burial focus, at first serving some or all of the inhabitants of this farm, but later attracting more graves as the Christian population of Dorchester grew in the fourth century.[116]

The discovery of Christian (or possibly Christian) burials at several of these sites raises the important point that there is an increasing amount of evidence for Christianity in the Romano-British countryside in general. Most of this evidence is located in the villa landscape, and although it was once claimed that Christianity was more often found in the towns, in Britain (unlike many other parts of the Roman Empire) recent evidence suggests that there may have been many rural Christian communities by the end of the Roman period.[117]

This view is supported by new data from small towns, closely connected with rural society despite their 'urban' designation, notably at Shepton Mallet.[118] There, apparently juxtaposed Christian and pagan late Roman cemeteries co-existed in the same settlement. There is also evidence of rural churches, as at Icklingham,[119] and of Christian burials, as at Bagshot and Wells, not associated with urban communities.[120] This evidence seems often more closely related to the inhabitants of non-villa rural settlements than to villa dwellers, although a few villas (especially in the West Country) have produced evidence of Christianity, as at Lullingstone and Hinton St Mary.[121] Such sites suggest that, in some areas, both low- and high-status groups were being converted to Christianity during the Roman period.

Enclosed sites are also known from the south west, although these may have been rarer in this area than in the north or the Midlands. A well-known example is at Row of Ashes Farm, Butcombe.[122] This site began in the Iron Age, when the settlement comprised at least one timber roundhouse. In the first century, rectilinear timber buildings were constructed, and these were replaced in the second century by stone-footed structures associated with stone-flagging. In the later third century the settlement was rebuilt as a series of small enclosures, each containing a small stone- and timber-built rectilinear house, possibly aisled. The site may have been associated with neighbouring fields and other features, and is perhaps most usefully seen as a group of small farms rather than a village site.

Clear evidence for enclosed settlements also comes from south Wales, as at the pre-villa

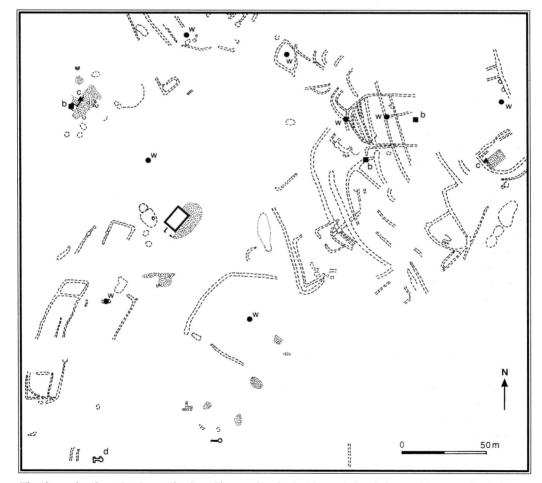

The 'dispersed settlement' at Lower Slaughter, Gloucestershire: b - burial, c - coin hoard, d - corn-drier, w - well, stipple - paved area (after RCHM (England) 1976)

farmstead at Whitton, a rectilinear earthwork enclosing curvilinear and rectilinear buildings.[123] A similar site, but without the subsequent villa, is known at Cae Summerhouse, while the small, approximately oval, enclosure at Mynydd Bychan was occupied in the Iron Age and Roman periods as a settlement containing curvilinear buildings, with a single rectilinear Roman-period structure.[124] The site at Brockworth, close to Gloucester, may also be classifiable as an 'enclosed' settlement.[125] This comprised two early Roman timber roundhouses within conjoined rectilinear ditched compounds, replaced in the second century by more rectilinear timber structures both in the same, and in adjacent, ditched compounds.

As in the Midlands and the north east, there were also dispersed settlements in the West Country, where occupation spread over many hectares, as at Lower Slaughter.[126] This site was apparently in use from the Iron Age until the late fourth century. It extends over more than 10 hectares and consists of ditched enclosures, other ditches, wells, pits, burials, a corn-drier, and various other structures. Two excavated rectilinear buildings were set adjacent to paved surfaces.

SOUTH-EAST ENGLAND[127]

Finally, there is the south east (represented here by Kent and Sussex), comprising England south of the Thames. Although rectilinear enclosed settlements did occur in this area, for example the early Roman farm at Bishopstone,[128] the commonest form of non-villa secular rural settlement in the south east seems to have comprised small unenclosed groups of timber or turf/cob-walled rectilinear structures. Partial excavations at sites throughout the area hint at the widespread distribution of settlements of this form, for instance in west Kent, as at Fox Hill and North Pole Lane in West Wickham, Leafy Grove in Keston, and Calfstock Lane in Farningham, all of which show evidence of ditches or gullies associated with domestic finds, including early Romano-British local and mass-produced pottery.[129] At Park Brow,[130] five structures were associated with Roman-period pottery, window glass, roofing tile, wall plaster and a door key, showing that apparently 'simple' timber structures need not have been architecturally primitive. At Bullock Down there were nine buildings, probably turf or cob-walled, also associated with Roman-period finds.[131]

SUMMARY OF NON-VILLA SECULAR CIVILIAN SETTLEMENT TYPES

On the basis of this review it will be clear that four broad types of non-villa, non-industrial, secular civilian rural settlements can be observed: enclosed farms, unenclosed farms, dispersed settlements and villages.

Enclosed farms are single farms, each comprising a group of rectilinear or, more usually, curvilinear timber buildings in rectilinear or curvilinear ditched, sometimes embanked, usually univallate enclosures. These can be recognized in all areas, but are most common in the north east and the Midlands. They often, but not always, have pre-Roman origins, and may have been especially common in the early Roman period, although such sites were plainly still used in both the north and the Midlands until the end of the Roman period.

Unenclosed farms are single farms comprising isolated, or small groups of, curvilinear or rectilinear timber, drystone or mortared structures without enclosures, but set among fields. These may have been especially common in the south and in south central England, and in the late Roman period, but early Roman examples are known. Frequently, such sites seem to be associated with small, possibly family, cemeteries.

Dispersed settlements comprise isolated rectilinear and curvilinear timber, or perhaps also drystone, structures and kilns set amid ditched enclosures over several hectares, sometimes with associated, but also dispersed, burials. These can be recognized in most areas, but are perhaps especially common in the Midlands. At some sites they seem to originate in the Iron Age, but they were also founded and in use throughout the Roman period.

Villages are large unenclosed rural nucleated settlements, without villa or small town characteristics, but also without evidence of a major ritual or industrial focus. These seem to derive more commonly from Iron Age origins in the north east and some, especially in the south and the East Midlands, may be associated with official or tenurial control. Villages are found in all areas, but especially perhaps in the north east, the Midlands and central England.

The range of these settlement forms shows scant evidence of regional variation, with most or all types occurring in all areas. Even such gaps as currently exist in the distribution of these sites might be explained by a lack of archaeological data rather than Roman-period absences. All types of site often had their origins in local pre-Roman settlements, but all include settlements founded in the post-Conquest period on sites without pre-Roman occupation.

This lack of regionalism is borne out by the remarkably similar range of artefacts found at such settlements, yet, as we shall see, regionalism is apparent in other categories of sites, and textual sources make it clear that tribal (later *civitas*) divisions were maintained in the east of Britain throughout the Roman period. Interestingly, however, both *civitates* and these settlement-types represent patterns continuing from the Iron Age, although modified by Roman-period changes.

THE RELATIONSHIP BETWEEN VILLAS AND NON-VILLA SETTLEMENTS

Many non-villa sites were situated in a landscape dominated by the villa-estate system, and these may have provided villas with labour, as the close physical relationship between them suggests, as at Stanwick and Lockington.[132] Likewise, at least some temples also probably had dependent farming populations, as the settlements around sites at Nettleton and Frilford suggest,[133] and the close relationship between temples and villas has already been noted. Temples were apparently frequented by both the landowning élite and members of the lower-status farming population, but it must not be assumed that such social divisions are necessarily those of villa/non-villa populations.

The early Roman site at Claydon Pike, with a large complex of romanized timber buildings and rich finds but no villa, suggests that there were non-villa-owning élite groups in the villa landscape.[134] Likewise, the existence of field systems attached to, and focused on, non-villa sites, as at Thornhill Farm,[135] hints at independent farming units based on sites of lesser status, rather than the inclusion of all such sites in unitary managed estates. Although it is unclear to what extent the inhabitants of non-villa farms owned, rather than farmed, land, it is likely that there is no simple equation to describe the relationship between landowning farmers and villa owners. In areas without villas – which in the early Roman period may have been extensive, as most Romano-British villas date from the late Roman period – many landowners presumably lived in non-villa settlements. As more villas were built the villa-dwelling portion of the landowning class presumably increased, probably resulting in a decrease in non-villa-owning landowners.

Villas and non-villa sites were also physically linked by routeways. Tracks, rather than formal Roman roads, seem to have run between several, perhaps most, villa and non-villa settlements, as at Roughground Farm villa, and similarly to have linked these farms and their field systems.[136] There is less evidence for tracks providing access to temple sites, except where these were also sizable settlements. Temples, such as Pagans Hill[137] and Brean Down,[138] may have been isolated in the contemporary landscape, possibly deliberately to emphasize the sense of 'separation' evoked by travelling to them, and related patterns of movement may have had a seasonal or periodic character, as Isserlin has recently suggested.[139] As these may have involved movement across estate boundaries, it is interesting to ask whether this would have been legally possible for all but the élite in the late Roman period, when such movement was officially restricted,[140] and when such temples seem to have been most common in Britain.[141]

We have seen that the background to all other rural settlement forms in the Romano-British landscape lay in the Iron Age. It is also clear that the Roman Conquest did not fundamentally transform the agricultural economy, so why was the villa adopted so widely by native Britons as a settlement form? The answer may lie in the social and political circumstances in which the villa system was established in Britain.

The villa landscape was a product of cultural change (romanization) affecting a landscape already partly established before the Roman Conquest. This change was itself a product of political change (the Roman Conquest and occupation), and its origins are to be sought in the political and cultural aspects of Iron Age and early Roman Britain. The inclusion of Britain in the Empire enabled the rapid romanization of existing social groups and established new aspects of society and politics.

THE ORIGINS AND DEVELOPMENT
OF THE VILLA LANDSCAPE

Although most Romano-British villas date from the late Roman period, the earliest in Britain belong to the first century, and it is with these sites that we must begin in order to understand the origins of the Romano-British villa. First-century villas, such as Boxmoor,[142] are characteristically simple, both in plan and decoration.[143] Most of them are either 'cottage houses', as at Lockleys,[144] or winged villas, as at Titsey, with aisled buildings apparently only introduced (perhaps from Germany, where the form is common) in the second century.[145]

In Sussex an exceptional group of first-century sites, comprising very elaborate courtyard villas, has been discovered.[146] This includes the villas at Southwick and Eccles, possibly emulating the 'palace' at Fishbourne.[147] The latter was a very large courtyard villa established in the first century on a Mediterranean-style plan with elaborate furnishings and formal gardens. This was used until the third century, when it was destroyed by fire, although occupation may have shifted to a villa-like aisled building at an adjacent site, built at about this time and occupied into the fourth century.

The existence of this unusual group of first-century courtyard villas in Sussex, displaying very high levels of romanization and wealth, is perhaps easily explained. The Regni of Sussex were a 'client kingdom' of the Romans in the late Iron Age. It is unsurprising, therefore, that their élite, perhaps even no more than their royal family, retained high rank after the Conquest, nor that they chose to express this in a romanized idiom.[148]

Other than this small group of unusually elaborate courtyard sites in Sussex, most of the

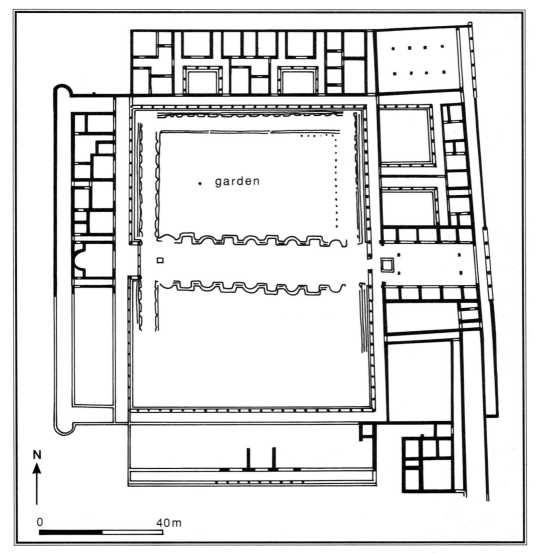

Plan of the villa at Fishbourne (West Sussex), c. AD 75, showing formal garden (after Cunliffe 1994b)

certainly first-century villas are found in a geographical zone that also shares two archaeological characteristics belonging to the late Iron Age.[149] The first is elaborate élite burials,[150] and the second is the use of coins of the Catuvellaunian/Trinovantian rulers.[151]

This evidence of a distinctive zone in the late Iron Age archaeology of south-east England is made more significant by the clear links between these two types of Iron Age evidence. The burial evidence is closely connected with the local élite. Elaborate élite burials continued in this part of Britain through the early Roman period, and this is the area in which all known early Romano-British barrow burials, including the barrow cemetery at Bartlow Hills, are found.[152]

The late Iron Age coins were minted on behalf of, and probably for use by, the same sort of people being buried elaborately and in local political control. The distinctiveness of these

Comparison of the distribution of villas constructed before AD 100 (western/northern boundary of counties containing pre-AD 100 villas shown as dashed line) with that of coins of the Catuvellaunian/Trinovantian rulers of the late Iron Age. Stipple indicates counties with more than two coins. (Coin distribution after B. Jones and Mattingly 1990)

characteristics from those of surrounding areas also merits stressing: élites in neighbouring areas of Iron Age Britain disposed of their dead in ways that archaeologists have found undetectable (in rivers?), and they used other coins. As these coins may have signalled political identity, it may be significant that the whole area was probably dominated by Cunobelinus' late Iron Age kingdom, as attested by textual sources.

The elaborate late Iron Age burials found in this area contain artefacts that may attest both a degree of pre-Roman romanization and an élite interest in conspicuous display.[153] Further, artefactual evidence may support this view, such as the distribution of Dressel 1 amphorae – bringing wine from the Roman world – which have a similar and limited distribution in Britain.[154]

The distribution of first-century villas also seems to bear a general correlation with this area. Some villas in this zone may also be more specifically associated with elaborate burials, as at

A Roman-period barrow burial at Bartlow Hills, Essex. (Photograph: P. Dark)

Ashdon villa close to the Bartlow Hills barrows.[155] This may enable us to employ the scant textual evidence for the way in which romanization proceeded after the Conquest to explain how this pattern was produced.

Most important among the textual sources is Tacitus' *Agricola*.[156] This is a biographical account of the first-century governor of Roman Britain who gives his name to the work. It describes, among much else, how a deliberate policy of romanization was promoted by the imperial authorities in the area under Roman control, resulting in the widespread aristocratic adoption of aspects of Roman culture. As it was this zone which was most firmly under imperial control in the first century AD, and as the British aristocracy of this area was apparently susceptible to romanization prior to the Conquest, if there is any truth in Tacitus' claim, then it is here, rather than elsewhere, that one would expect rapid élite adoption of Roman ways to have occurred.[157]

This brings us back to the first-century villas. As these are élite romanized structures, designed for displaying status, then it seems reasonable to link the adoption of villas, at least in part, with the romanization of this élite. The small scale and simple architecture of the majority of these sites contrasts with those in Sussex, suggesting perhaps that less grand members of the élite were responsible for their construction.[158] Direct archaeological evidence also suggests that the majority of first-century villas resulted from the romanization of local inhabitants. This is provided by the discovery of Iron Age roundhouses beneath some of these sites, as at Park Street and Latimer.[159]

Given that everyone wishing to construct a romanized house need not have built it on top of their old home, there is no reason why all sites have to show this pattern for it to be convincing.[160] That is, as Branigan and others have argued, there seem to be strong archaeological grounds for the claim that the villa-owning élite of Roman Britain were partly

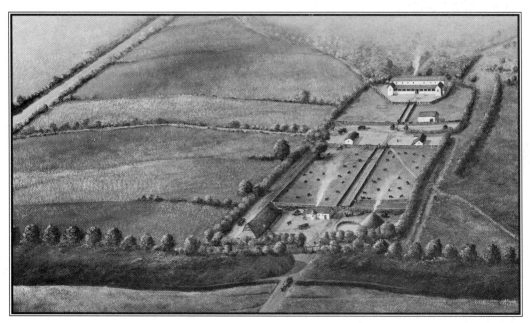

Reconstruction of the villa at Gorhambury c. AD 180. Much of the enclosure within which the villa was built dates from the Iron Age. (Painting by Frank Gardiner, reproduced by permission of English Heritage)

derived from the élite of the late Iron Age. A particularly instructive case-study is provided by the villa at Gorhambury, close to a late Iron Age tribal centre at St Albans.[161] Here, a bipartite late Iron Age enclosure, dating from the first century AD, contained an Iron Age-style settlement with a timber aisled building, replaced in around AD 100 by a masonry villa, also with an aisled building.

Throughout the south east, romanization, and the display opportunities and tenurial security offered by the villa estate system, may have appealed to local élites no longer able to express status in traditional modes. This had wide-ranging and long-lasting effects in relation to the British landscape, because it led to the establishment not only of a new type of site but also to a new kind of landscape. The characteristic features of the villa landscape are first found in Britain dating from approximately the same time, and in the same areas, as the earliest Romano-British villas, as at the temple sites at Hayling Island and Harlow.[162] The rebuilding of such sites as Romano-Celtic temples may, therefore, show the same pattern of romanized élite continuity, through the romanization and patronage of local cults.[163]

The spread of élite romanization, and consequently of this villa landscape, to the rest of what was eventually Roman Britain began to accelerate after the first century. Even at the start of the second century, villas were built in the very north of the villa landscape at Holme House, near Piercebridge.[164] The rapid establishment of romanized sites at such remote locations may suggest that the immigration of provincials from elsewhere in the Empire, and the resettlement of retired servicemen and government officials, may be responsible for some of these sites. Likewise, the investment by overseas proprietors in British estates may have, in part, promoted this transformation.[165]

The vast majority of villas, however, probably represent the romanization of the local British élite rather than these factors, as is suggested by a replication of the pattern of rebuilding Iron Age-style native homesteads as villas in these 'new' villa areas in the second and even later centuries. This may explain the location of villas in what could have been late Iron Age political centres, as at Tidbury Rings and at Ditches, and may suggest that the majority of late Roman Britain's villa owners were themselves British in origin.[166]

The reasons prompting the romanization of local British élites (and the adoption of villas and associated site types over a wide area of Roman Britain) in the second century and later may have been varied. These could have included both the emulation of already romanized, villa-dwelling, south-eastern élites and acculturation into romanized culture by participation in town life. The potential settlement of non-local groups in Britain as a result of military service, trade and official duties has already been mentioned. Through service in the army or bureaucracy, at least some of these non-local elements had adopted a

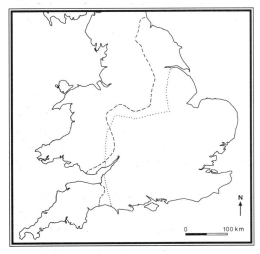

Comparison of distribution of villas (dashed line shows western boundary of main area containing villas) and Romano-Celtic temples (dotted line shows western boundary of main area containing Romano-Celtic temples). A few outlying villas and temples are also known. (Distributions based on Millett 1995)

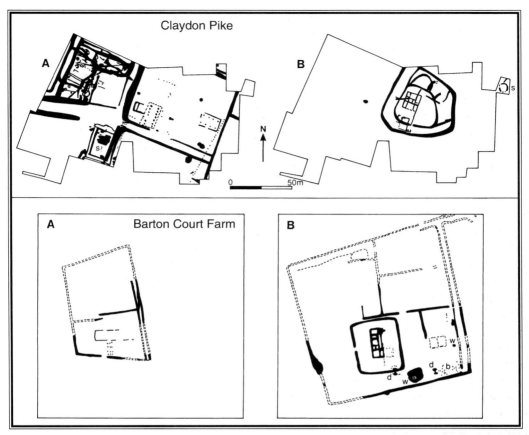

Two examples of the transition from non-villa to villa sites: Claydon Pike, Gloucestershire (after D. Miles 1984), and Barton Court Farm, Oxfordshire (after D. Miles 1986). A: early Roman non-villa settlements, B: late Roman villas, b - infant burials, d - corn-drier, s - shrine, w - well

high degree of romanization prior to their immigration to Britain, and others came from already thoroughly romanized parts of the Empire and became rich through trading activities. In this context the settlement of veterans inside the province may have been the key factor in this second stage in the development of the villa landscape. Finds of military equipment and links between villa and military architecture have suggested to Black that retired soldiers were among the groups responsible for the spread of rural élite romanization.[167]

The biggest expansion in the number and grandeur of Romano-British villas was, however, in the fourth century. The most elaborate villas of this period had more architectural sophistication, a greater complexity of plans, a larger scale at many of the biggest establishments, and lavish decoration. Such sites, as at Bignor,[168] North Leigh,[169] and Woodchester,[170] were plainly the centres of the estates of magnates, even if these were not always resident. The scale of opulence was sometimes 'imperial': Woodchester, for example, has the largest mosaic floor in the north-west provinces.[171]

Although there were large and complex villas, such as Gadebridge Park, the majority of late Roman villas in Britain were much simpler structures, as at Crofton and Chilgrove 2.[172] These

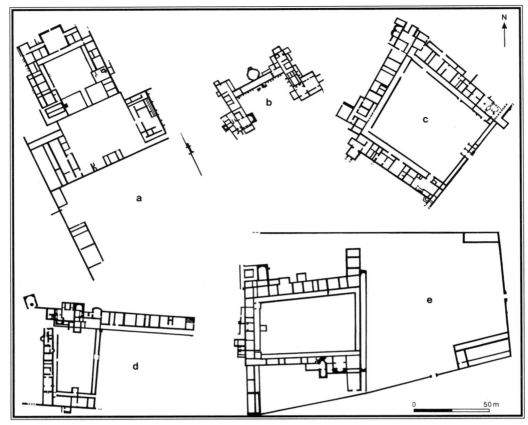

Elaborate fourth-century villas: a, Woodchester, Gloucestershire (after G. Clarke 1982); b, Great Witcombe, Gloucestershire (after RCHM (England) 1976); c, North Leigh, Oxfordshire (after Collingwood and Richmond 1969); d, Chedworth, Gloucestershire (after R. Goodburn 1981); e, Bignor, Sussex (after Aldsworth and Rudling 1996)

were still, however, buildings that seem to have been intended to impress. They often had hypocausts and baths, and conformed to the villa plan types so far described.

The cause of this late Roman expansion in the number of villas is uncertain, although the fact that Britain was relatively unaffected by the 'third-century crisis' of Roman imperialism, had a thriving economy and, apparently, a considerable agricultural surplus, may suggest a period of unusual prosperity.[173] That economic changes were producing other effects on the landscape is suggested by the establishment of new rural industries, and presumably new wealth derived from them.[174] Several scholars have suggested that both romanization and the monetary economy were making significant inroads into rural society at this time.[175] Likewise, the movement of élites from the towns to the countryside might explain some of these new villas, but this is uncertain as a general observation.[176]

That a wider distribution of rural wealth, and perhaps increased rural romanization, may have led to a new demand for villa building is probably hinted at by the large number of fourth-century villas that were built on a relatively small scale, notwithstanding the palatial courtyard villas referred to above.[177] The former may suggest a newly wealthy group of landowners who wanted to express their status in a romanized idiom and could afford a villa, but not a very big villa.

Although clarifying the chronological development of the villa landscape, its origins, and its social and political operation, none of this, however, answers the question of how villa landscapes functioned in economic and legal terms. To understand this we may again begin with the villa itself.

THE VILLA ECONOMY

The economic operation of the villa landscape was clearly based on tenurial control, land-ownership, and the ability to extract wealth from the land.[178] In more extensively documented parts of the Roman Empire these questions might be discussed on the basis of written evidence, but this is not available for Roman Britain. Land tenure, even in Britain, had to be founded in legal concepts of ownership, so discussion of the operation of the villa economy must start with an examination of its legal basis.

The extent to which Roman law operated in Britain is a matter of controversy,[179] but there is a small amount of textual evidence. At Chew Park villa a wooden tablet from the well is part of a legal transaction, under 'Roman vulgar law', that details the transfer of land.[180] In a Roman legal text an example is cited showing that in the fourth century the Theodosian Code, a late Roman legal framework, was in operation in a rural context somewhere in Britain.[181] There is also textual evidence that continental Romans owned estates in Britain, presumably held under Roman imperial law.[182] This and other evidence hints that the villa landscape functioned at least partly within a Roman legal framework, including the buying and selling of property under contract.

Assessing the extent to which Roman law operated in the villa landscape has important implications for how we interpret villa sites. J.T. Smith and Stevens argued that 'Celtic' law (which they reconstructed by 'retro-projecting' medieval Welsh law onto Roman Britain) was of more use in understanding Romano-British villas than Roman law.[183] In their interpretations, such 'Celtic' law was based on landholding by the kin-group or extended family, and was widespread among the villa owners of Roman Britain.

In an interesting series of detailed studies, Smith applied this interpretation to Romano-British sites. Identifying recurring patterns of rooms, he argued that when similar groups of room plans could be seen recurring at the same villa, or the plan could be seen as divisible into two or more 'houses', this meant that more than one family group occupied the villa. So, he argued, at least some villas were joint property, and he explained this by reference to the patterns of kinship that he claimed were characteristic of native society in the Roman period.

Similar arguments have been proposed by Applebaum[184] and, more recently, by Hingley.[185] Hingley's interpretation built on Smith's, and placed much importance on David Clarke's interpretation of Glastonbury Lake village,[186] in terms of Iron Age social structure. While there is still much of value in these studies, especially those by Smith and Hingley, recent work on the records of the Glastonbury excavations has made Clarke's interpretation of the site untenable.[187] This inevitably affects Hingley's interpretation. Simon Clarke's recent reinterpretation of the patterns identified by Smith strongly argues that they are more easily accommodated within wider fashions in western Roman architecture than previously seemed possible.[188] As such, it is doubtful whether these patterns reflect joint ownership or 'Celtic' Romano-British society. One

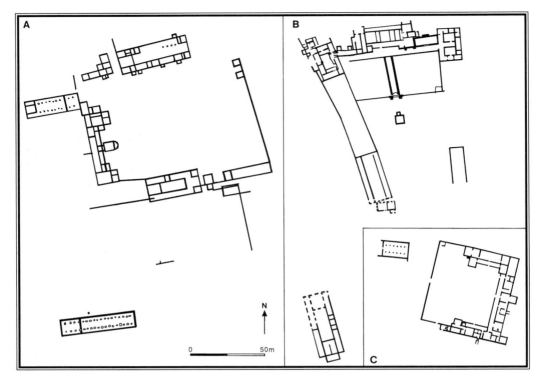

Plans of villas with large buildings outside their courtyard enclosures. A, Winterton, Lincolnshire (after R. Goodburn 1978); B, Darenth, Kent (after Philp 1973); C, Spoonley Wood, Gloucestershire (after RCHM (England) 1976)

might also doubt whether the latter are reconstructable from laws compiled nearly a thousand years after Roman Britain, and geographically distant from the villa landscape.

This raises the question of what we can reliably say about the villa economy. The majority of both villas and non-villa farms were almost certainly agriculturally based, and many villas probably formed the centre of an estate. At some extensively excavated villas, such as Winterton, Rockbourne and Gorhambury,[189] it is possible to see all of the constituent elements of an estate centre. At a smaller group of sites, notably Roughground Farm and Stanwick,[190] and also arguably at Bancroft, the inner parts of the villa estate can be seen in relation to the main house. At Winterton,[191] for example, the walled villa compound seems to have included a winged corridor villa building (including baths), several barns, aisled buildings with domestic occupation (one of which was probably also used as a barn), corn-driers and other ancillary buildings.

The occurrence of large rectangular buildings, often aisled, is widely evidenced both in courtyard villa complexes and at other villa sites, as at Spoonley Wood, Rapsley, Beddington, Beadlam and North Wraxall.[192] The association of some of these buildings with corn-driers and other agricultural features, as at Rockbourne,[193] has suggested to most archaeologists that they are barns,[194] but some examples were used for domestic occupation, as at Keston.[195]

If some of these buildings were barns, the volume of expected produce that they appear to have catered for suggests large estates. This may imply that some of the (apparently lower-status) non-villa settlements were occupied by tenants of villa owners. However, we have already seen that there were probably non-villa landowners, who might also have had their own tenants. So we cannot assume that every non-villa settlement in the villa landscape was socially inferior (or economically subordinate) to a villa, especially perhaps in the early Roman period.

The existence of possible barns at villas may also imply the collection of rents (paid in grain) from such tenants.[196] If so, it is reasonable to ask what (and where) was the market enabling villa owners to profit from this. The urban and military communities both required food, but probably could not fulfil their own food requirements with the resources of time, labour and land available to them. So, these may have formed a ready market for this produce.

This view is supported by data from Kent. A series of large buildings, likely to have been barns, has been recognized at late Roman villas in the Darent Valley of west Kent (including Lullingstone and Darenth), which may be related to the proximity of these villas to urban markets. Such markets probably existed in Canterbury, Rochester and, depending on one's interpretation of the late Roman sequence there, possibly also London.[197]

If rents were collected and villa populations engaged in large-scale commerce, it is reasonable to seek evidence of estate administration. Many writing styli have been found at some villa sites, as at Hambleden (where there were seventy),[198] suggesting that literacy played a role in estate management. This may also imply professional estate administrators attached to villas or living nearby. Other sites, such as Barnsley Park, have such large numbers of coins as to suggest rent collection or the storage of wealth in the form of coinage.[199] These data tend to support the view that villas were the centres of organized estates, from which their owners gained revenue by the payment of dues.

In arguing for joint ownership, Smith and others have noted the existence of two apparently contemporary villa houses at some sites (as at Newton St Looe, Rivenhall and Gayton Thorpe). Although not all claimed examples of such 'double villas' seem credible, and their numbers have probably been overstated in the past, the provision of an additional villa house within villa enclosures requires explanation. We have seen that, when found in association with villages, such buildings may be interpreted as bailiffs' houses. Could this also be the case at villas? Some absentee landowners controlling estates in Britain may have retained houses at estates which they only occasionally, if ever, visited. The everyday operation of such estates would have been run by administrators, who might be expected to have emulated the fashions and customs of their 'superiors'. Perhaps this explains at least some double villas and the widespread occurrence of aisled buildings with domestic occupation both inside, and immediately outside, villa compounds, as at Keston, Norton Disney and Mansfield Woodhouse.[200]

The interpretation of these buildings as bailiffs' houses could be extended to at least some of the other sites where aisled houses stand alone, as at Exning, where an isolated aisled house is close to a contemporary village.[201] It is also interesting in this context that isolated aisled buildings occur most frequently in the Fens and in Hampshire,[202] where villas are rare. Perhaps this is because such rich agricultural areas were especially prone to outside investment, and so to absentee landowners. This seems a more convincing interpretation for the absence of villas than imperial estates, but it must be stressed that all aisled houses need not have been occupied by bailiffs, and landowners may have dwelt in sites other than villas.

Although formal estates seem to have been a common feature of the villa landscape, no Romano-British estate boundaries are definitely known. There have been many attempts to identify these, at sites including Barton Court Farm and Gorhambury.[203] While natural features may have been used as estate boundaries, without evidence of boundary markers it is unlikely that these could be archaeologically identified. An alternative approach is retro-projecting the

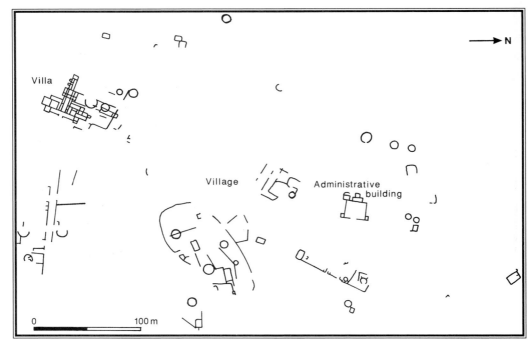

Stanwick, Northamptonshire: villa, associated structures in surrounding landscape, and village (based on Salway 1993 after Neal)

earliest textually attested post-Roman estate boundaries – those of seventh-century Anglo-Saxon England – onto Roman Britain. This assumes, perhaps implausibly, high levels of continuity in landscape divisions between the Roman and Anglo-Saxon periods, and even the most well-known possible example, at Withington villa, is not usually seen as credible.[204]

It is also feasible that several villas could be within a single estate. This may be illustrated by the juxtaposition of the large villa at Stanwick (which has a village with a possible bailiff's house adjacent to it) and the smaller winged corridor villa at Redlands.[205] At Redlands the villa house was preceded by, and incorporated, a water-mill, possibly one belonging to the Stanwick estate. Patterns of ownership may also have led to ranked estates. For instance, a major landowner may have resided in a courtyard villa at the core of the estate, with tenants or officials in less elaborate villas, either at subsidiary estates or on the same estate. Such patterns need not have involved contiguous land units, nor in every case similar types of villa houses.

Complex patterns of land tenure may, therefore, render Romano-British estates unreconstructable on current evidence. Progress in defining field systems belonging to specific villas, as at Barnsley Park and Brading, may enable the recognition of blocks of organized landscape centred on them, and so the inner parts of their estates.[206] However, problems of association and partial preservation hamper this approach.

While most villas may have been the social and economic centres of farming estates, with outlying dependent settlements within their estates, Branigan has recently shown that some villas had non-agricultural functions probably linked to industry, or were specialist producers of a specific foodstuff or other commodity for the urban market.[207] So, the simple equation of villas and farming may not always hold true.

CONCLUSION

We can, therefore, see the villa landscape as a distinct and clearly related series of components. Most villas were agricultural estate centres, but some were related to 'industry', and a few may have been the palaces of magnates, without direct economic functions. The villa landscape comprised not only villas, however, but also rural, non-villa, agricultural communities, often based on pre-Roman sites and settlement types. This landscape was a product of the romanization of that of the Iron Age, not its complete replacement, both in the form of its settlements and its economy. The origin and development of the villa landscape can, therefore, be explained only by understanding the promotion, and reception, of romanization in Britain.

Through the Roman period both the villa landscape and its extent changed and acquired new attributes. Likewise, the social and cultural system that produced it, and was enacted through it, changed. However, the villa landscape never came to cover the whole of Britain, despite its centrality to the society and economy in those areas in which it was established. In other parts of Britain other landscapes continued to co-exist with it, whether the 'barbarian' native region to the north of Hadrian's Wall (and for a while north of the Antonine Wall) or the 'native' landscape of the north and west.

CHAPTER 4

THE NATIVE LANDSCAPE

CHARACTERIZING THE NATIVE LANDSCAPE

Towns, both large and small, and villas were very rare in the native landscape. Romanized temples, walled cemeteries and mausolea were also rare, especially away from military sites, while the latter were far more common than in the villa landscape. Cemeteries are rarely found, as in Iron Age Britain, and were much less romanized than those of the villa landscape, perhaps suggesting that Iron Age burial practices often continued to be employed.[1]

So, much of the archaeology of the native landscape shows affinities with Iron Age Britain rather than with the continental Roman Empire. There were also a few differences from the villa landscape perhaps derived from topographical factors, notably the prevalence of cave use.

ROMANO–BRITISH CAVE USE[2]

Although there were utilized caves in parts of the villa landscape, cave use was principally a native landscape feature. It closely, perhaps unsurprisingly, correlates with the availability of suitable caves on geological and topographical grounds. Although there is a single example of ritual cave use in Roman Britain (at Culver Hole), most caves seem to have been used either as domestic sites, as at Minchin Hole, or as burial places, as at Dog Holes. Domestic use of caves was much the most common of these, although both forms of use could occur together, as at Ogof-yr-Esgyrn. Apart from the Mendips (also in the villa landscape), where cave occupation seems to have been essentially a late Roman characteristic, cave use was predominantly early Roman, although seldom, if ever, representing a continuation of pre-Roman activity.

This may seem a surprising landscape feature with which to begin a discussion of the native landscape, but it is not chosen by chance: no other features of the native landscape zone have distributions arguably explicable by environment or topography alone. Differences must, therefore, be explained in terms other than by reference to environmental factors or topography. In seeking such factors, many scholars have placed special importance on the role of the Roman army in shaping this landscape.

THE ROMAN ARMY IN THE NATIVE LANDSCAPE

Both the villa and native landscapes contained part of the Roman military and official communications network with its roads and milestones, but the militarization of the native landscape forms one of its defining features. Military sites were rare in the villa landscape after the first century, and even in the fourth century military personnel were mostly stationed near the coast and in towns.[3] In the native landscape, however, military sites (mostly forts but also some naval sites and watchtowers) were the principal aspects of Roman imperialism. They are very common in Wales and northern England, and, of course, along the Hadrianic and Antonine Walls.[4]

Reconstruction of a Roman fort, showing the vicus *and its hinterland. (Painting of the fort at Chesters on Hadrian's Wall by Ronald Embleton, reproduced by permission of Frank Graham)*

Military sites fall into four main groups away from the Walls. There were a few 'legionary' fortresses (as at York), containing units of Roman citizens; forts containing 'auxiliary' units of non-citizens (as at Brecon Gaer and Ribchester); 'fortlets' (as at Nanstallon) with detachments of such units operating locally; and 'signal stations' (as at Martinhoe) – towers for observation and signalling.[5]

Many major forts and some smaller military outposts had *vici* (civilian settlements) attached to them.[6] Recent work has shown that these seem to have been a deliberate part of these forts: rather than simply 'growing up', they were deliberately established outside the fort gates.[7] *Vici* served the non-military needs of the soldiers, providing shops, taverns, temples and so on. Local people seem to have had access to these settlements, but probably not to the forts themselves, making them a meeting point between the military and native populations where subtle romanization could occur.[8] The demand for agricultural produce to support forts also linked them to the local economy.[9]

In the late Roman period the organization of the army in Britain changed considerably,[10] with more troops being stationed in the villa landscape. A series of signal stations was established along the Yorkshire coast, as at Filey and Scarborough, connected with the fort at Malton. Further signal stations may have been established on the west coast (as at Holyhead Mountain), perhaps related to the fort at Segontium (Caernarvon).[11] Although military occupation continued at many sites in the native landscape, the number of forts was reduced, especially in Wales, and military occupation of the south-west peninsula seems to have ceased after the early Roman period.[12] A few military sites, notably Segontium, also seem to have taken on a more important administrative role,[13] and the gradual relaxation of Roman official attitudes to intermarriage, and to military service in one's home province, may have assisted in the integration of soldiers and civilians.[14]

The degree to which such military units could be fully integrated into the surrounding communities in the early Roman period may have been restricted by their functions. Given the low level of threat from Ireland and from the north in the early second to early fourth centuries, these may have been to police the surrounding areas, enforce imperial instructions, collect taxes and serve as a deterrent to aggression.

Of these functions, policing and tax collecting are unlikely to have endeared the military to those locals who perceived themselves as unfairly treated or victims of harsh taxation. These functions would easily have been acquitted by auxiliary troops, assisted by the network of Roman roads that, in the native landscape, primarily linked forts into a framework of imperial control. As military pay and subsistence depended on taxation, there was also an incentive for soldiers to insist that taxes were paid in full. So, while integration commonly occurred, this may have been a far from universal process.

HADRIAN'S WALL

These characteristics are seen most clearly on Hadrian's Wall, the frontier line established across northern Britain in the 120s–30s.[15] This frontier was the consequence of earlier developments in the north of Britain, especially the establishment of forts along the east–west road today called the Stanegate, a system that seems to have reached its most complex form in around 120. The 'Stanegate frontier' was not a walled barrier, however, although minor frontier works – ditches, etc. – may have been employed in places, especially at its western end. The building of Hadrian's Wall fixed this approximate line by the construction of a permanent boundary work, also provided with forts and other installations.

Changes in military strategy, and in the design of the Wall, meant that its exact form was altered during construction. The original plan was to build a 'broad' masonry wall from Newcastle to the Irthing, and then a 'turf wall' (i.e. earthwork) from the Irthing to Bowness in the west. During construction, however, the width of the wall was narrowed, and then (in stages) the 'narrow wall' was extended to take in the east of the turf wall. These changes were undertaken in Hadrian's reign, but later the Wall was extended in masonry, in an 'intermediate' width, to include the entire line of the turf wall – probably in the later second or third centuries. The landscape history of the Wall and its hinterland is extremely complex, with military sites frequently being built, modified, used, disused and then re-used.

Along the Wall there were large forts, fortlets and turrets. The fortlets (today called milecastles) are spaced at intervals of approximately one Roman mile between forts, as at Castle Nick and Poltross Burn,[16] with turrets between milecastles at intervals of one-third of a Roman mile.[17] Turrets seem not to have been intended for more than very temporary (perhaps overnight) occupation, but probably served as watchtowers.[18] Milecastles, which held small units (probably those patrolling the areas between the forts), show evidence of short-term occupation, as at Sewingshields (Milecastle 35),[19] but the Wall garrison primarily lived in the forts, and it was at these that *vici* were located.[20]

Several of the forts have been the subject of important modern programmes of excavation, such as those at Vindolanda (Chesterholm), South Shields, Birdoswald and Housesteads.[21] This work has both greatly clarified the character of the military occupation on the Wall, and served to demonstrate the ways in which Wall garrisons led to more romanization in the environs of their forts than elsewhere in the landscape.

Small towns were founded at Carlisle and Corbridge, and stone-built bridges spanned major rivers.[22] Around these towns and forts there were other romanized structures, such as mausolea, as at Shorden Brae, and temples, as at Carrawburgh.[23]

The shores of the Solway Firth were defended by a series of forts, such as Beckfoot and Maryport, and watchtowers, such as that at Easton (in part associated with a free-standing palisade), along the Cumbrian coast.[24] So, the Wall effectively prevented sudden attack on the north of Roman Britain, and the landward movement of large forces and cavalry into the area to its south. If an enemy force did pass it, the combined forces of the forts in northern Britain would have been able to attack, aided perhaps by legionaries from York and Chester.

Together these defences rendered northern England safe from major attacks throughout most of the Roman period, but this relative success appears to have led to a relaxation of military discipline and an emphasis on non-military activities among the garrisons of the Wall. Several pieces of evidence – changes in the form of barracks, the construction of kilns in the towers and gates of forts, for instance – suggest that a civilian character was predominating in the forts in the fourth century.[25] This relaxation in military standards may explain why, when 'barbarians' attacked in the 360s and after, the Wall proved such an ineffective barrier and was over-run.

The construction of Hadrian's Wall also created a major new landscape feature (in addition to the associated changes in land use discussed in chapter 2). The impact of (in Romano-British terms) a 'permanent' mortared stone barrier across northern Britain, manned by a substantial non-local population, on surrounding communities and economies may have been wide-ranging. More specifically, the rear of the Wall was delineated as a military area by a unique series of features. A road (the 'military road') was constructed to serve the needs of the army, and beyond was a ditch between two banks, today called the 'vallum'.

The vallum is hard to interpret, but is probably most easily understood as demarcating the military area. This might have served both a practical and legal function: livestock and civilians would have been unlikely to cross the ditch and so stray onto the road. If a civilian crossed the barrier it had to be a deliberate act and, therefore, unlawful, so it would have clarified the immediate scope of military regulations and command.

There is, however, evidence of civilian occupation north of the vallum. A typical native enclosed settlement at Milking Gap, for instance, located between the Wall and the vallum, was probably occupied during the period of use of the Wall, if one takes its finds at face value.[26] Unless the Milking Gap settlement is much later in date than usually supposed, civilian sites were apparently permitted within the area defined by the vallum. This does not invalidate the view that the vallum defined the Wall area in legal terms, but may suggest that such regulations did not exclude all civilians from the area.

THE ANTONINE WALL

Understood as a defensible perimeter, Hadrian's Wall forms a discrete line across the landscape of Roman Britain, bounding the northern edge of the native landscape for much of the Roman period. Even if ultimately a military failure, the Wall was one of the most significant and enduring additions to the British landscape made by the Roman army.

For a brief period the Antonine Wall, a similar but less sophisticated boundary defence (of turf and timber), enclosed the Scottish lowlands within the Roman province.[27] The decision to move the provincial boundary north seems to have been taken at the very end of the 130s or in the early 140s, and the Antonine Wall was constructed in the following decade. This wall was also provided with milecastles and forts, as at Seabegs Wood and Croy Hill,[28] although plans for the number and spacing of forts seem to have been altered during its construction, adding many more smaller forts or fortlets.[29] Fortlets were provided to cover the coastal flanks of the scheme, and they were established beyond its line to the north.

The Antonine frontier is usually argued to have been systematically abandoned in the mid-150s, perhaps for no more than a year, and then briefly reoccupied until the early 160s, when it finally fell into disuse.[30] This was also conducted in an orderly way, suggesting that both periods of abandonment resulted from strategic or political decisions, not military necessities. However, Roman forts remained (as at Risingham and High Rochester) beyond the Hadrianic line for generations following the abandonment of the Antonine frontier.[31] These produced a similar effect on the landscape of their environs to that of sites further south, as the small cemetery of mausolea near the fort at High Rochester illustrates.[32]

During the use of the Antonine Wall the inter-wall zone must, of course, have been included within the native landscape of the Roman province.[33] The settlements of this area were, in general, similar to those immediately south of Hadrian's Wall, and there is some evidence of romanization both during and after the use of the Antonine Wall. This zone can, therefore, be seen as an extension of the native landscape to the north of the Wall, albeit encompassing a few specific local variants of enclosed and unenclosed settlement forms.[34]

REGIONAL GROUPS OF CIVILIAN SETTLEMENTS IN THE NATIVE LANDSCAPE

THE NORTH[35]

In northern Britain, north of Catterick and from the Pennines westward, the usual form of settlement was an enclosed group of curvilinear drystone or timber huts, as at Waitby.[36] Many of these enclosures were curvilinear, as at Milking Gap and Ewe Close, although they could also be rectilinear, even if the huts inside were curvilinear.[37] For example, at the early Roman-period settlement at Riding Wood, a rectilinear drystone enclosure contained three drystone roundhouses (to which another was later added) set in a cobbled yard with separate causeways leading from the entranceway to each.[38] Although not the only settlement plan in use, similar plans are known from many sites in northern Britain, for example at West Longlee.[39]

Such settlements were frequently on Iron Age sites, as at Esp Green, Gubeon Cottage and Woolaw, where single-phase enclosures contained sequences of buildings, first in timber and then in stone.[40] A similar sequence is evidenced from many Tyneside sites. For example, at Kennel Hall Knowe, second-century AD drystone houses occupied an earthwork enclosure following a long sequence of timber buildings within a timber-built palisade.[41]

At other sites the enclosures were also of more than one phase, as at Burradon and Hartburn.[42] At both of these sites there were concentric enclosures, the outer of which contained only Iron Age occupation, the inner a Romano-British settlement: a single timber roundhouse at Burradon, and at Hartburn two stone roundhouses in a cobbled yard (following a long sequence of timber roundhouses) reminiscent of the site at Riding Wood.[43]

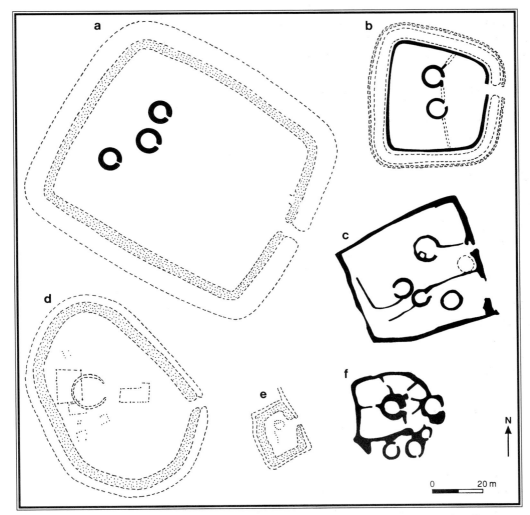

Enclosed settlements in the north of Roman Britain: a, Kennel Hall Knowe (based on Jobey 1978b); b, Belling Law (based on Jobey 1977); c, Middle Gunnar Peak (based on Jobey 1981); d, Penrith (based on Higham and Jones 1983); e, Silloth (based on Higham and Jones 1983); f, Milking Gap (based on Kilbride-Jones 1938). Stone walls shown in black, earthworks stippled, ditches in outline

There is a tendency for drystone buildings to replace those of timber during the early Roman period at many of the excavated sites. We have already seen examples of this, but many others are known, including Forcegarth Pasture South where this development occurred in the second century AD,[44] and Huckhoe, where two buildings with small compounds were built in the early Roman period following occupation as a palisaded enclosure containing timber buildings stretching back into the early Iron Age.[45]

The trend for sub-rectilinear and rectilinear building plans to replace curvilinear plans during the mid- or late Roman period is found at sites throughout this region. For example, at Penrith in Cumbria a single timber roundhouse of the second century AD was replaced, within the same enclosed cobbled yard, by rectangular timber buildings with paved floors.[46] At Roystone Grange

Reconstruction of a Roman-period enclosed settlement in north Britain. (Painting by Ronald Embleton, reproduced by permission of Frank Graham)

in Derbyshire a timber aisled building, albeit one with bowing walls, replaced earlier curvilinear structures.[47] Yet there are also inter-site and local variations within these overall patterns. Some are almost village-like in scale, as at Roystone, with several adjacent houses with their own enclosures. In other cases, as at Silloth, they consisted of a single roundhouse inside an enclosure.[48]

Whatever their scale or exact plan, the enclosed settlements of northern Britain seem to have been small farms, and the existence of a single hut within some such sites may suggest that at least some were inhabited by a single family group. The different scale of settlements of this type need not preclude the extension of this interpretation to the majority of them – even the largest sites of this type may have been occupied by no more than a single extended kin-unit.

NORTH-WEST WALES[49]

Settlements in north-west Wales share many similarities with the northern British group, but there are also differences between these two groups. North-west Welsh enclosed settlements, as at Cefn Graeanog II, Caerau, Din Lligwy, Graenog and Hafoty Wern-Las, more frequently had rectilinear enclosures containing rectilinear buildings than in the north, although both curvilinear structures and enclosures also occur.[50] The buildings within these enclosures were also more often attached to the enclosure wall, and entrance into the enclosure was more often through one of its buildings, than at similar sites in the north. Some north-west Welsh enclosed settlements had rectilinear earthwork enclosures, analogous to the 'square enclosures' of the north-east. In north-west Wales, these comprised settlement within rectilinear earthen banks, as at Bryn Eryr.[51] There (in its final, late Roman, phase), a cobbled yard, provided with drainage

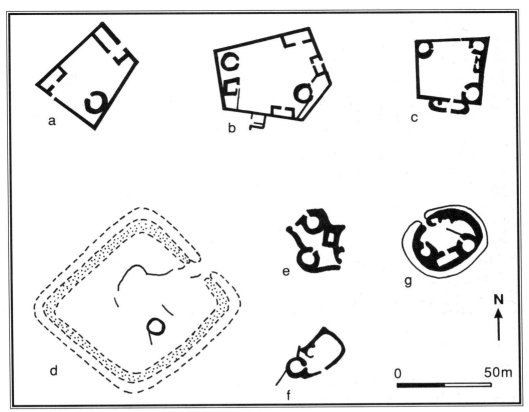

Settlements in north-west Wales: a, Hafoty Wern-Las; b, Din Lligwy; c, Cefn Graeanog II; d, Bryn Eryr (note enclosure out of use); e, Cors-y-gedol; f, Ty Mawr; g, Cae'r Mynydd. (a, b, g after Hogg 1966; c, d, f after Kelly 1991; e after C.A. Smith 1977)

gullies, contained at least one stone-built roundhouse, but the enclosure itself, built in the Iron Age, was already disused.

An especially interesting contrast between the north-west Welsh and northern British enclosures is that iron-working took place in the former. The reason for this is unclear: it may indicate variations in the supply and processing of basic raw materials, the spread of iron-working technology in the local community, or differences in value assigned to iron products. Corn-driers, and possibly barns, at north-west Welsh sites may indicate that the on-site processing of raw materials in general, was more common than at similar sites in northern Britain.

The north-west Welsh sites also have larger numbers of romanized artefacts than their northern British counterparts. This, alongside the use of rectilinear plans, has led some to see them as a local equivalent of villas. However, they are unlikely to have been the homes of major landowners, simply because they were so closely spaced in the landscape, and there are so many enclosed sites of this type in north-west Wales, even compared, for example, with the dense distribution of villas in the Cotswolds. Consequently, the north-west Welsh sites seem most convincingly interpreted as native farmsteads, analogous to those of northern Britain. If this is so, they may attest to a much higher material standard of living in this area in the Roman period and

Reconstruction of an enclosed settlement in north-west Wales. (Painting of Cefn Graeanog by Ivan Lapper, reproduced by permission of The Reader's Digest Association Limited, Roman Britain © 1980)

a greater degree of romanization than in northern Britain. That such a high standard of living and level of romanization was not shared by all of the population of the region is shown by a further group of sites: unenclosed curvilinear drystone huts with simple (mostly undivided) ground plans, as at Ty Mawr.[52]

These unenclosed hut-groups also show much evidence of having been farms, but lack the artefactual richness and architectural sophistication of many of the enclosed sites. As both types of site occur in the same areas, sometimes even juxtaposed, these differences may be explicable in social rather than locational or economic terms. For example, unenclosed hut-groups may have been the residences of the socially inferior 'clients', or even slaves, of those resident in enclosed hut-groups.

There was also contemporary hill-fort occupation at sites in north-west Wales, as at Bwrdd Arthur and Dinas Emrys.[53] While not necessarily true of all such sites, evidence from Dinas Emrys suggests a more wealthy domestic settlement than that of the enclosed settlements. It is, therefore, possible that at least some hill-forts belonged to the social superiors of the inhabitants of the enclosed farms. The relative rarity of Romano-British hill-fort occupation in this area, compared with the enclosed farms, might suggest that the hill-fort sites include the residences of the local élite.

NORTH-EAST WALES[54]

Much less is known of the Romano-British settlements of mid- and north-east Wales (east of the River Conway, the approximate boundary for the north-western group) than those of north-west Wales. There is some evidence of enclosed settlements in this area also, and wealthy hill-fort occupation is demonstrated by the large inland site of Dinorben.[55] Excavation of this site has produced a large assemblage of Romano-British pottery, metalwork, glass and other artefacts, and structural evidence, together suggestive of élite domestic use as an agricultural centre.

The enclosed settlements of this area were apparently distinct in plan from those of north-west Wales. Characteristically, these were enclosures defined by at least one (and often two or more) earthen bank with an external ditch. Excavated examples include the sites at Arddleen, New Pieces, and Collfryn – where the entranceway of the Iron Age enclosed settlement was remodelled in the early Roman period and occupation in the interior continued into the fourth century.[56]

SOUTH-WEST WALES[57]

Moving south once again, the next regional group of sites is in south-west Wales. These 'small enclosures', sites such as Woodside, Dan-y-Coed, Walesend Rath and Pen y Coed, are different in form from those of north-west Wales: they are curvilinear earthworks, usually having single banks with external ditches.[58]

Within these enclosures, early Roman buildings included both four-post granaries and roundhouses, in contrast with the rectilinear buildings often found on the north Welsh sites, although – apparently insubstantial – rectilinear timber structures have been found in the early Roman site at Llangynog II in Dyfed.[59] These sites seldom show much evidence of on-site iron-working or of corn-driers, and they lack the barns and entranceway buildings found in north Wales. Characteristically, these early Roman roundhouses were often replaced by a single rectilinear late Roman building. The latter was usually partly built of drystone and was associated with romanized artefacts, which at Dan-y-Coed included imported amphorae and high-quality glass.[60]

The modern archaeological interpretation of these sites has followed a similar pattern of development to that of the enclosed settlements of north Wales. It used to be claimed that these were no more than local 'peasant' farms, but recently archaeologists have suggested that they were high-status residences. However, their numbers, the agricultural basis of their economies and their siting once more suggest prosperous farms, perhaps analogous to the enclosed settlements of north Wales.

As in north Wales, other settlement types also occur in this area. There are unenclosed groups of rectilinear drystone and timber buildings, as at Stackpole Warren, which might be seen as analogous to the unenclosed huts of north Wales.[61] Another similarity to the north Welsh pattern is Romano-British activity associated with rich finds and relatively large quantities of coinage at hill-forts, notably Coygan Camp.[62] There, late Roman occupation was associated with coin forging, but the explanation of this is unclear: it could, for example, represent a local magnate openly emulating the imperial authorities for reasons of status rather than illicit forgery for profit. Other hill-forts seem to have been occupied only during the early Roman period, or disused at the Conquest, as apparently at Castell Cogan.[63]

THE SOUTH-WEST PENINSULA[64]

Another area where a similar threefold division of settlement types is visible is in the south-west peninsula, today divided into Cornwall and Devon, but a single *civitas* (the Dumnonii) in the

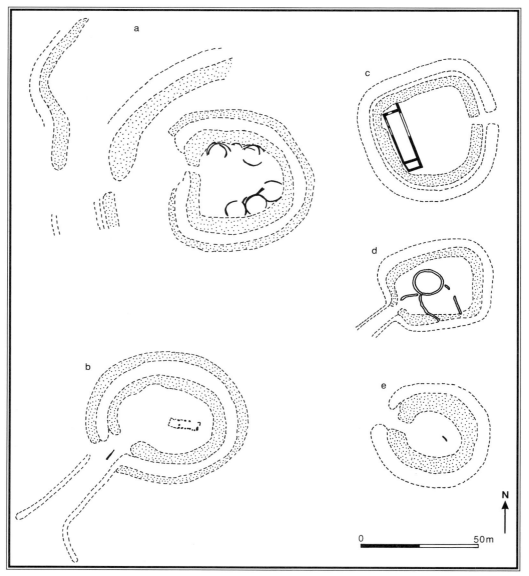

Enclosed settlements in south-west Wales: a, Woodside; b, Dan-y-Coed (a and b shown in their correct spatial relationship); c, Cwmbrwyn; d, Pen y Coed; e, Drim (a, b based on G. Williams 1985; c, based on Ward 1907; d, based on Murphy 1985; e, based on Williams 1988 after Mytum)

Roman period. In both of the modern counties there are enclosed farms analogous to the small enclosures of Dyfed.

In Cornwall these settlements are called 'rounds' by modern archaeologists and have been the focus of intensive archaeological attention during the twentieth century.[65] Aerial photography and surface fieldwork have identified similar, although somewhat more frequently rectilinear, enclosures, in Devon, as at Hayes Farm and Stoke Gabriel.[66] Here these enclosures will be

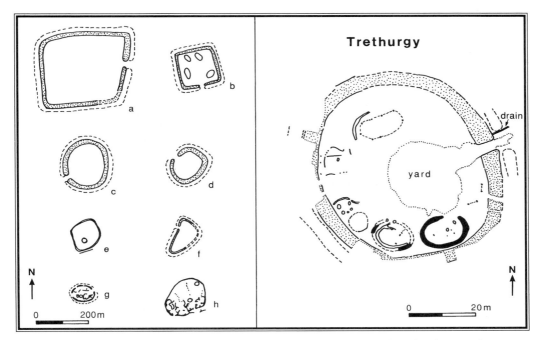

Cornish 'rounds' (a–f) and 'courtyard houses' (g–h): a, Carvossa; b, Grambla; c, Castle Gotha; d, Carwarthen; e,
Shortlanesend; f, Crane Godrevy; g, Goldherring; h, Porthmeor (all after N. Johnson and Rose 1982). The
extensively excavated 'round' at Trethurgy is shown on the right (based on Quinnell 1986).

referred to by their Cornish name (rounds) regardless of modern county divisions, as these have no demonstrable relevance to the Roman period. In west Cornwall there was another distinctive type of enclosed farm – the courtyard house. Such sites comprise conjoined drystone curvilinear buildings, probably forming small villages.[67]

Both rounds, such as at Crane Godrevy, Castle Gotha, Shortlanesend, Carloggas and Carvossa, and courtyard houses, such as at Chysauster, Goldherring, Porthmeor and Carn Euny, characteristically contained curvilinear structures (often oval).[68] Structural romanization seems, in general, rare at rounds, although boat-shaped houses were found in a rectilinear late Roman round at Grambla, which might suggest knowledge of rectilinear building plans.[69]

At rounds, the buildings were enclosed by earthen banks, outside which occupation (similar to that found in the enclosure) sometimes continued, as geophysical surveys have confirmed. Although rounds are probably too widespread in the south-western landscape to be élite sites, associated finds sometimes include imported amphora and high-quality glassware, suggesting that they were wealthy farms. This is supported by the evidence from the almost totally excavated round at Trethurgy, where mass-produced Roman artefacts were associated with curvilinear drystone buildings occupied throughout the late Roman period and beyond.[70] There are other hints that the pattern found in Wales is also present in the south-west peninsula. There are hill-forts probably occupied in the Roman period, as at Trevelgue Head in Cornwall and Milber Down in Devon,[71] and probably also unenclosed hut-groups, as at Trebarveth.[72]

Reconstruction of a village of courtyard houses. (Painting of Chysauster, Cornwall, by Judith Dobie, reproduced by permission of English Heritage)

SUMMARY OF CIVILIAN SETTLEMENT TYPES IN THE NATIVE LANDSCAPE

The range of settlement types in south-west Britain appears so similar to that of Wales, and to that of northern Britain, as to suggest that they represent local transformations of a similar social system, with regional variations being the product of local cultural and economic factors. Four main types of site can be discerned: enclosed settlements, unenclosed settlements, inland hill-forts and coastal promontory forts. Villages were relatively rare, although some (as at Chysauster) were to be found.

Enclosed settlements encompass regional variants such as rounds, small enclosures and enclosed hut-groups. These frequently originated in the Iron Age, although sites of this type were established *de novo* in the Roman period. Unenclosed settlements were small groups of curvilinear or rectilinear timber or drystone buildings. They seem both to have been established in the Roman period and, more often perhaps, to have been on Iron Age settlement sites. Inland hill-forts and coastal promontory forts fall into two groups: sites with early Roman occupation apparently continuous from that of the Iron Age, and sites with late Roman domestic occupation.

CONTRASTING SETTLEMENT TYPES IN THE NATIVE AND VILLA LANDSCAPES

It is immediately clear that the range of non-military settlement types in the native landscape is different from that in the villa landscape. For instance, there were relatively few villas in the native landscape, and relatively few hill-forts were used for Romano-British secular domestic occupation in the villa landscape. Villages and dispersed settlements also seem to have been rare in the native landscape, but they occur widely in the villa landscape.

There were also differences in the form of shared settlement types. Unenclosed settlement in the villa landscape included buildings more often rectilinear in plan and more frequently employing romanized constructional elements, such as roofing tile, wall plaster, window glass and mortared stone walls, than those of the native landscape. These buildings more often comprised structures with two or more rooms than those of the native landscape. Enclosed settlements of the native and villa landscapes also show differences in form not wholly attributable to the availability of raw materials or to environmental differences. Most early Roman enclosed settlements in the native landscape were curvilinear, and they seldom contained rectilinear buildings, unlike those in the villa landscape. This difference became less acute during the late Roman period, however, when rectilinear buildings seem to have been more widely constructed in the native landscape. Consequently, the two zones can be said to represent distinct landscapes, even if romanization in the native landscape eroded some of these differences over time.

THE SOCIAL AND ECONOMIC OPERATION OF THE NATIVE LANDSCAPE

The existence of high-status civilian settlements implies that society in the native landscape was ranked, and suggests that it remained dominated by local élites. These élites were presumably responsible for day-to-day local administration, as purpose-built official administrative facilities seem largely absent. Official administration was probably the responsibility of the army, in view of the lack of other official sites, although local society may have been governed in everyday affairs by native rather than Roman law, unlike that of the villa landscape. If so, the native landscape may truly have been the 'military zone' of Roman Britain. The Roman military constituted an élite in this zone, however, whatever their administrative role, so raising the question of the relationship between the military and the local population.[73]

There are several indications that the effects of the military occupation were less deep-seated than might initially be supposed. For example, away from the immediate hinterland of the forts, most religious activity seems to have been centred on small unromanized shrines, or perhaps on sites without structures at all.[74] These may be recognizable due to their artefactual richness, but can be difficult to distinguish from native domestic settlements, as at Nornour in the Scilly Isles.[75] There are few structures that demonstrate romanization at native secular sites, and there is much evidence for the continued production of local artefacts for use at such sites, alongside more romanized items.

This picture is further supported both by the scarcity of evidence for the regular usage of Latin place-names among what was, almost certainly, a Celtic-speaking rural population, and by the lack of romanized small towns as 'local centres' in this zone.[76] The lack of large towns, except at Carmarthen, is obvious.[77] An involvement in town life may have been important in romanizing the rural élites of the villa landscape, and the lack of such settlements may have had wide-ranging consequences for society and economy in much of this zone.

It seems likely that, given the romanization inherent in Roman military service, there was a clear contrast between the life of imperial military sites and those of the surrounding civilian landscape. Although in cultural, social and economic terms this contrast probably decreased over time as military discipline became more lax and surrounding populations became more romanized, it is probable that the forts remained the most romanized settlements in much of this area.

The intermediary role of *vici* in the acquisition of local supplies has already been mentioned. This produced an economic link between the army and the surrounding civilian population, established through the acquisition of supplies for the military, and by the collection of taxes due to the state. It may also imply the local production of an agricultural surplus. The effect that taxation had on the landscape is uncertain. It may either have acted as a stimulant to production, so as to alleviate the risk of retribution against defaulters, or have had a restrictive effect by reducing motivation because of the reduction of economic incentive.

The overall flow of produce was probably to the forts from the native settlements, although the army was also able to draw on alternative or supplementary modes of supply, such as the long-distance supply of pottery to northern garrisons and the state-controlled manufacture of military equipment. As a local native élite seems to have existed, at least in Wales and the south west (although interestingly perhaps not in the Wall zone), this presumably could also extract its own dues from those of lower status. So, there was apparently a disposable residue remaining to local people after official taxation. As the occupants of most native settlements still managed to obtain traded goods, after both official taxation and any such local renders, this may indicate the size of the surplus produced.

The existence of a native élite may suggest the survival of native social organization in at least parts of the native landscape. In this context, the relationship between the regional groups of settlement forms, discerned above, and the textually attested political structure of Roman Britain may be of interest. The Romano-British *civitates* were derived from the romanization and partial reorganization of the tribal system of Iron Age Britain. So, Romano-British *civitates* (and the textually attested tribal area of the Ordovices of north Wales, who may or may not have been a *civitas*), may be assumed to have had a political meaning for local British populations in these areas.

Turning to the settlement evidence with this tribal framework in mind, there is a surprising correlation. The 'south-western group' of settlements might be equated with the Dumnonii, the 'south-west Welsh group' with the Demetae, the 'north-west Welsh group' with the Ordovices, the 'north-east Welsh group' with the Deceangli and the 'northern group' with the Brigantes.[78] Although the Carvetii seem not to be represented in these groupings, it is unclear whether they were entirely distinct from the Brigantes or a sub-group of that large tribe.[79]

The maintenance of tribal identities might correlate with that of distinctive cultural features or customs, and so could explain the pattern seen here, which cannot be explained in economic or environmental terms. This contrasts with the villa landscape, where tribal groups of settlements are not so obvious.[80]

The existence of a native élite and the production of a substantial surplus raise the question of the role of those villas that are found in this landscape. These are not concentrated in any specific tribal area, but are mostly in south-west Wales and north-east of the Pennines north of Catterick, although at least one site has been found in Cornwall.

Where villas were built in the native landscape zone, a combination of elements found in the two landscape types can be observed. This is evidenced by the combination of characteristics specific to villas with those specific to enclosed native settlements at villa sites. For example, villa houses were built inside enclosures like those of other local settlements. Examples include

Cwmbrwyn, Trellissey, and Llys Brychan, where villas were built inside 'small enclosures'.[81] Such sites were not confined to Wales. Two of the most northerly villas in Britain, Holme House and Old Durham, lay within 'native'-style enclosures.[82] Magor, Cornwall's only certain villa site, is within a round, detected by geophysical survey.[83] These combinations show that elements of both landscapes were not incompatible to all inhabitants of Roman Britain.

THE ORIGIN AND DEVELOPMENT OF THE NATIVE LANDSCAPE

The native landscape of Roman Britain probably developed directly from that of the late Iron Age. Landscape changes were not completely absent, of course, and the formation of a network of Roman military establishments, with their interconnecting roads, constitutes the major innovation in this landscape. Unlike native settlements, these forts were frequently disused, producing a relict pattern of deserted forts as earthworks and ruins throughout the native landscape.

Other military activities gave rise to yet more transient sites and eventually relict aspects of the native landscape. Military manoeuvres involving construction of practice works and the enactment of sieges on pre-Roman hilltop settlements produced another rapidly developing facet of the surroundings of military sites, as probably at Burnswark and High Rochester.[84] Palimpsests of practice works were also the result of such manoeuvres, as on Llandrindod Common, Haltwhistle Common, and Tomen-y-Mur.[85]

The 'throwaway' character of such earthworks, used only for periods of days or weeks, highlights a key contrast between the rate of landscape change produced by military and civilian activities, and may suggest that there were two different 'paces of life' in the native landscape. These can be explained in terms of the different purposes and activities of the civilian and military communities. The army was stationed to take part in military missions, administration, information gathering, policing, and perhaps to act as a deterrent force against attack from beyond the Roman frontier. Secondary activities, such as training and occupying bored troops with 'outside activities', such as building practice works, resulted from the same basis. The relatively fast-moving rate of such military activities was in marked contrast with the slow cyclical character of the agricultural year, which human action could not precipitate, and the everyday life of farming families coping with their environment and their neighbours.

MINOR FEATURES OF THE NATIVE LANDSCAPE

This cultural conservatism and local continuity of the native landscape make it probable that the folkloristic perception of natural features and antiquities led to a mythological view of topography, as in the villa landscape. This may have included a religious dimension, such as the veneration of mountains or lakes.[86]

The archaeological evidence for such veneration in Roman Britain is ambiguous. There may, however, be an unusual piece of evidence that can be brought to bear on this question. Lindow Man, the body of a murdered man preserved as a result of its submersion in a bog (a 'bog body') in Cheshire, and evidence of a concentration of all known Romano-British bog bodies in the north of England, may suggest that human sacrifice was practised in this area in the Roman period.[87] Evidence of unusual dress – many of these bodies were equipped only with shoes –

their unusual locations, and sometimes proof of deliberate killing, may demonstrate that these were Roman-period sacrifices. If so, then the deposition of these bodies in bogs and lakes is perhaps strong evidence of the importance attached to such natural features in local paganism. This evidence spans both landscape zones, so if the practice took place, it was specific to inhabitants of neither the native nor the villa landscapes.

Information about non-settlement features of the native landscape, other than field systems (discussed in chapter 5), is generally lacking. The roads and milestones erected by the Roman army were primarily connected with military activities in this zone, but there may have been an as yet undiscovered pattern of native pathways between settlements and other activity areas.

CONCLUSION

The contrast between the villa and native landscapes represents differences in Romano-British society, economy, culture and politics, as well as in landscape organization. Both landscapes were, however, based on the differential romanization of Britain, and on changes resulting from the introduction of Roman imperial administration. Both these, and the urban and industrial landscapes, as we shall see later, share a common basis in aspects of the Iron Age background of Roman Britain. The economy of much of both the villa and native landscapes was based on agriculture, and this will be the subject of the next chapter.

CHAPTER 5

AGRICULTURE AND THE LANDSCAPE

INTRODUCTION

Agriculture formed the basis of the economy throughout most of Roman Britain and had played a key role in shaping the landscape from as early as the Bronze Age. It has often been supposed that there was a division between predominantly pastoral farming in upland areas and arable in the lowlands, but there is increasing evidence that arable agriculture was widespread in the native, as well as the villa, landscape. This is indicated both by the pollen evidence and by the larger (macroscopic) remains of crops preserved on archaeological sites.

Other evidence for arable land-use comes from cultivation marks left by ploughs and other tools, and the boundaries of fields. Artefacts associated with crop production and processing can provide clues as to the role of sites in the general agricultural economy, but their interpretation is not straightforward.[1] Some such artefacts may have had a range of uses, not all necessarily connected with farming, and even if their function is certain, as with iron ploughshares, their presence at a site need not necessarily indicate local use. For example, finds of iron implements could represent blacksmiths' scrap. The presence of quernstones on a site need not indicate a local arable economy, since the site may have been involved in processing crops brought in from elsewhere. Similarly, structures involved in crop storage, such as pits and granaries, need not imply local production.

Evidence for animal husbandry comes from the bones of livestock and from structures used to house animals, such as byres. It is rarely possible, however, to be certain that a structure has been used for such a purpose.

Because of the problems associated with the interpretation of artefactual and structural evidence for agriculture, these sources are not discussed in detail here. We will begin with the evidence for the most obvious landscape feature of agriculture – field systems – and then consider the biological evidence for the crops and animals that occupied these fields.

FIELDS

IDENTIFICATION AND DATING

Much evidence for early fields has been lost due to continual cultivation, but in areas that came to be considered marginal for arable after the Roman period, early field systems are often preserved and can be seen from the air.[2] Unfortunately, however, the fact that the distribution of surviving field systems is biased to land that was not later ploughed means that they may not be a representative sample of what was once present.

Aerial photography can discover the subtle remains of field earthworks that are not obvious from the ground, especially if enhanced by shadow or light snow cover. Traces of field systems for which no surface remains survive can also be observed, as cropmarks or parchmarks in grass. On sloping sites, the outlines of ancient arable fields may be preserved by lynchets formed by the downslope movement of soil due to long periods of ploughing. Banks of soil build up at the lower end of the field (positive lynchets), with depressions at the upper edge of the field where soil loss is greatest (negative lynchets).

While aerial photography provides evidence for an increasing number of such field systems, their date is often uncertain. A major problem is that fields often remain in use for centuries, so that evidence for the date of their establishment and early cultivation may be obscured.

There are two main approaches to dating fields: from their contents and from their boundaries. Fields tend to contain little artefactual evidence relating to their use, and any that is present is likely to be poorly stratified due to disturbance by cultivation or trampling by animals. Even if a ploughshare is lost, later ploughing may destroy its stratigraphic context and its relationship to any surviving field boundary will probably be uncertain. Scatters of eroded pottery found in fields are sometimes assumed to represent the spread of settlement refuse, mixed with manure, on the fields to increase their fertility.[3] Such material could also, however, reflect later ploughing of a Roman rubbish deposit, or even a settlement.

More credible evidence for a Roman date can be obtained by excavation at a point where a field boundary can be related to a settlement, but examples where this is the case are few. Most field systems have not been excavated, and their dates are usually estimated from their apparent relationship to other landscape features, such as Roman roads, and whether or not these features are 'respected' or cut across by the field system. This approach has been used by Williamson in the analysis of the fields around Scole in Norfolk, where a Roman road appears to overlie a pattern of earlier land divisions.[4]

DISTRIBUTION AND TYPES OF ROMAN FIELDS

Pollen evidence indicates that much of what was to become Roman Britain was already being exploited for agricultural purposes by the end of the Iron Age, so that the scope for the creation of new areas of fields from previously untouched land was small. Thus, in many areas, the Roman agricultural system was superimposed onto a landscape that may already have been under the plough, or grazed, for centuries.

The widespread existence of prehistoric field systems throughout Britain also attests to the extent of pre-Roman agriculture. For example, Dartmoor was divided up by an extensive system of boundaries (reaves) in the Bronze Age, a system apparently connected with stock rearing.[5] Similarly, early systems of major land enclosure can be found on the chalk downs of Sussex and Wessex, indicating a highly organized agricultural landscape long before the Roman period. These prehistoric downland field systems often consist of blocks of fields, apparently laid out *en masse* rather than in piecemeal fashion, suggesting planned enclosure of a landscape already cleared of its woodland. Such fields tend to be square or rectangular in shape, presumably because this was the most logical form to use when cross-ploughing with the light ard (see later), and they are often defined by lynchets. As well as these 'Celtic' fields[6] there are long linear boundaries, sometimes called 'ranch boundaries'. This term implies stock control, but they may have been connected with land tenure.[7] It has been argued that linear boundaries post-date the

Celtic fields, but it has been shown that, on the Berkshire Downs at least, they are probably often contemporary.[8]

Some prehistoric downland field systems seem to have been used in the Roman period and owe their final form to Roman developments. An example is Chalton in Hampshire, where excavation of one of several settlements surrounded by fields and trackways suggested activity from the late Iron Age through to the fourth century, by which time the site had reached sufficient size to be termed a village.[9] A cluster of similar sites occurs in Sussex, including Bullock Down on Beachy Head, where early Iron Age and Roman settlements were associated with trackways and systems of rectangular fields.[10] Excavation suggested that the lynchets associated with these fields were developing during the late Bronze Age/early Iron Age and Roman period, implying re-use of the prehistoric fields. Similar evidence comes from Rookery Hill, Bishopstone, but the Romano-British settlement on Thundersbarrow Hill was surrounded by a large series of rectangular fields with lynchets that apparently first formed in the Roman period.[11]

Field systems and settlements in the Chalton region, Hampshire. Stippling - 'villages', triangles - masonry buildings, circles - other Romano-British settlements, square - cemetery (based on Cunliffe 1977)

On Fyfield Down in Wiltshire there is evidence of a reorganization of field layout in the Roman period: a system of irregular 'Celtic' fields of probable Iron Age date is overlain by a series of rectangular fields laid out from a double-lynchetted trackway.[12] Excavation demonstrated that there was early Roman pottery in the ploughsoil of these fields, presumed to reflect manuring. On the Berkshire Downs a series of excavations across field boundaries suggested that most of the long, narrow fields, and some square or irregular fields, had a Roman origin, with little evidence for the re-use of prehistoric boundaries.[13]

A series of lynchet excavations has also recently been undertaken in the Salisbury Plain area, notably in connection with field systems at Coombe Down and Chisenbury Warren.[14] At Chisenbury the field system in its fullest form was found to date to the Roman period. There were possible indications of a late Iron Age origin for part of the system, but the area under cultivation seems to have been reorganized in the first to second centuries AD.

Evidence of large-scale planned field systems is not limited to the chalklands of the south. For example, 'brickwork' patterns of fields covering up to 200 hectares have been revealed by aerial photography in South Yorkshire and north Nottinghamshire, as at Edenthorpe and between Torworth and Barnby Moor.[15] These consist of ditched strips of land 50–100 metres wide, divided into fields of up to 3 hectares by short cross-boundaries. Limited excavation suggests that these fields were farmed in the Roman period, although their date of origin is uncertain. On a smaller scale, 'ladder' systems of fields have been found linking farmsteads

Fields around Knighton Bushes on the Berkshire Downs. Circle indicates site of a Romano-British settlement. (After Bowden, Ford and Mees 1993)

around Wharram on the Yorkshire wolds.[16] These consist of a series of rectangular enclosures, usually aligned along a trackway. Although probably in use in the Roman period, at least some have an Iron Age origin.

Despite the large number of villas that have been excavated, few have been placed in the context of the fields that must have surrounded them. A notable exception is Roughground Farm, Lechlade, on the second gravel terrace of the Thames.[17] Here the villa was underlain by a system of early Iron Age ditches, assumed to represent land boundaries. The site seems not to have been occupied in the later part of the Iron Age, but in the early Roman period a non–villa farm was established, and this was replaced by a villa in the early second century. The villa was surrounded by a regular system of enclosures, interpreted as paddocks, and larger open fields covering at least 15 hectares, separated by ditched tracks and droveways. Some of the fields, apparently dating to the later second century, appeared to have been laid out to a standard unit of length. The smallest of these enclosures, assumed to be paddocks or gardens, were 17 by 27 metres in size, while others were two to four times as large.

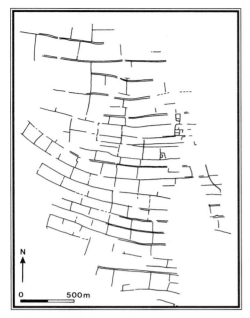

'Brickwork' fields between Torworth and Barnby Moor, Nottinghamshire (based on Riley 1980)

At Barnsley Park villa near Cirencester, walled enclosures of similar size to the Roughground example, clustered around the villa buildings, were interpreted as paddocks.[18] Here, a major system of fields was linked to, and followed the same alignment as, these paddocks.

The gravels of the Upper Thames Valley provide an impressive array of cropmarks revealed by aerial survey, many of which date to the later Iron Age and Roman periods.[19] Settlements with ditched enclosures and fields, associated with droveways, were common, as at Ashville, Abingdon, and Farmoor.[20] The enclosures tend to be close to the focus of settlement and seem to represent paddocks rather than arable fields, but excavations at Drayton have revealed large Roman arable fields, some more than 4 hectares in size, on a gravel island on the Thames floodplain.[21] These fields contained plough marks (see later), were bounded by banks and ditches, and contained scatters of pottery that mainly date to the first to second century, which the excavator interpreted as reflecting manuring.

From the native landscape there are few well-dated field systems known. Enclosed homesteads of the type that is common in north Wales and northern England were occupied both in later prehistory and in the Roman period, and often seem to be associated with stone-walled enclosures and unenclosed fields defined by lynchets. Few such sites have been excavated, and even where they have been, the relationship of a site to the surrounding traces of fields often remains uncertain. It has been suggested that there may be some difference in date between the use of stone-walled enclosures and terraced/lynchetted fields in north Wales, the former belonging predominantly to the Bronze Age and the latter to the Iron Age and Roman period.[22]

At Silloth Farm on the coast of the Solway Firth in Cumbria, a link could be made between a ditch forming part of a field system, visible from the air under drought conditions, and the outer ditch of the enclosure.[23] Another lowland Cumbrian site, Yanwath Wood, was

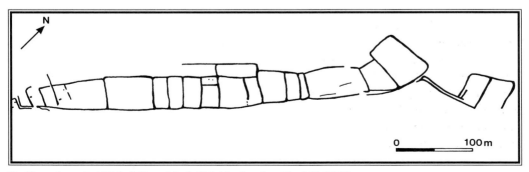

'Ladder enclosures' at Birdsall Brow, North Yorkshire (based on Hayfield 1988)

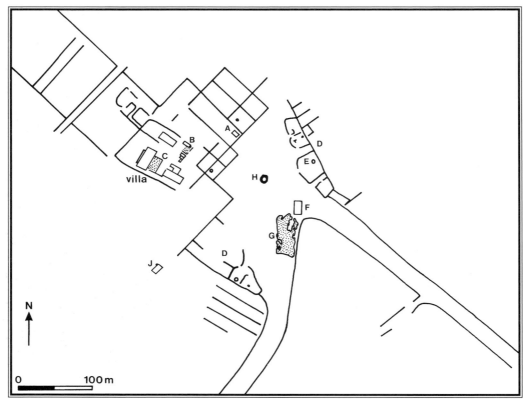

Interpretative plan of the villa complex and fields at Roughground Farm, Lechlade, Gloucestershire: A - ancillary building, B - ?bath-house, C - paved yard, D - domestic and farmyard enclosures, E - well, F - timber building, G - gravel pit, H - mound, J - ?detached bath-house. (After Allen et al. 1993)

also associated with a field system, consisting of small rectilinear enclosures bounded by walls and ditches.[24]

More extensive field systems are known from higher altitude sites, as at Crosby Ravensworth, although few are dated.[25] Perhaps the best known settlement associated with a field system is Ewe Close, where a stone-built Romano-British settlement seems to have undergone several phases of expansion with the addition of enclosures.[26] A further example, which probably dates at least partially to the Roman period, comes from Eller Beck, where fields cover an area of at least 60 hectares and seem to be associated with several settlements and trackways.[27] On the lower slopes of the valley the fields are predominantly rectilinear and defined by banks and stone walls, while further up the slopes they are less regular. Higham has suggested that this system bears some similarities to the well-known site at Grassington, North Yorkshire, where more than 100 hectares of mostly rectangular fields occur, defined by banks and lynchets.[28] A Roman date has been suggested for these fields on the basis of scatters of pottery of second to fourth century date, again assumed to reflect manuring.

Further evidence for fields in the native landscape comes from Northumberland, where there are indications of cultivation prior to the Roman military occupation in the form of plough marks sealed below Hadrian's Wall (see later). As for the fields themselves, clear examples can be

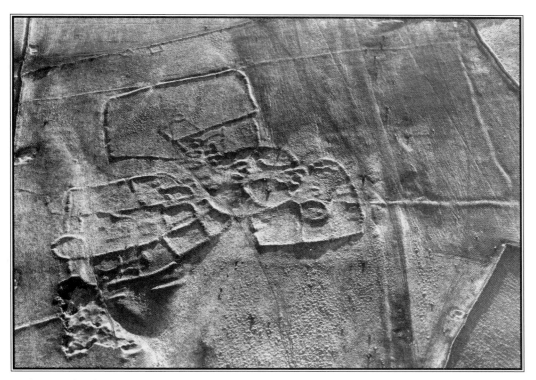

Settlement and enclosures at Ewe Close, Cumbria. (Cambridge University Collection of Air Photographs: copyright reserved)

seen around the fort and *vicus* at Housesteads, where a variety of terraces, lynchets and earth banks occur. Fowler suggests that at least five phases of arable cultivation can be recognized here, the earliest of which are likely to be pre-Roman or contemporary with Roman occupation.[29] Excavation of one of the terraces revealed a series of features below the terrace wall, including a palisade of stakes, a gully and two phases of timber fence, and it links construction of the terrace for arable agriculture with establishment of the *vicus* in the third century.[30] A further example of terracing, possibly of late Roman date, has been excavated between Hadrian's Wall and the vallum at Sewingshields.[31]

Moving to the south of the native landscape, in Cornwall there are again few field systems that can be assigned to the Roman period with confidence. The courtyard house at Goldherring, for example, was surrounded by small rectangular terraced fields.[32] Other undated examples may, as at Maen Castle, also represent field systems used in the Roman period.[33]

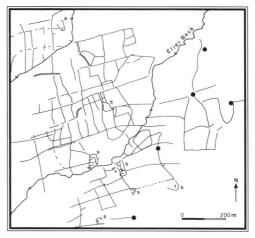

Field systems and settlements (s) at Eller Beck, circles indicate mounds (based on Higham and Jones 1985)

Aerial photograph of the fort at Housesteads, on Hadrian's Wall, showing the vicus *and surrounding terraces and enclosures. Note that some of the terraces are of post-Roman date. (Cambridge University Collection of Air Photographs: copyright reserved)*

FIELD BOUNDARIES

Field boundaries seem to have taken a variety of forms, such as banks, ditches, stone walls, fences and hedges. The lynchets, which often define the edges of fields as seen from aerial photographs, result from soil creep due to ploughing rather than a deliberate form of field demarcation. The form of the boundary often reflects its purpose, which may have included simple marking of ownership, a need to exclude or impound stock, or a combination of these.

Stone field boundaries were most commonly employed, of course, where stone was abundant locally, but their use was not universal in such areas. At Barnsley Park villa, for example, in an area with an abundant supply of limestone, only the paddocks close to the villa had stone walls. The outlines of the fields are preserved as earthen banks and lynchets, and may originally have been bounded by fences or hedges.[34] Indirect evidence for the use of hedging in the Upper Thames Valley comes from Farmoor, where remains of several species of thorny shrub, including rose (*Rosa*) and blackthorn or hawthorn (*Prunus spinosa/Crataegus*), were abundant in Roman but not Iron Age contexts.[35]

Several Roman sites have also revealed the presence of leaves and twigs of box (*Buxus sempervirens*), a shrub well suited to ornamental hedging. Clippings of box were apparently found in a pit in the town of Silchester, while leaves occurred in a well in Skeldergate, York, and in Roman deposits in London.[36] It seems likely that these finds represent use in gardens rather than field boundaries, and planting trenches that may have been used for such a purpose have been excavated at the 'palace' of Fishbourne.[37] The finds of box on poorer sites, such as Farmoor,[38] may indicate that ornamental gardens were not confined to the wealthy, although the plant may have been grown for other than aesthetic reasons.[39]

PLOUGH MARKS AND PLOUGHSHARES

The typical plough of the Iron Age was a light wooden ard with an iron share-tip, pulled by a pair of oxen. This type of implement continued in use into the Roman period, as suggested by the find of a wooden ploughshare in a second-century context at Usk in Gwent, and iron shares from several sites, including in a late third-century context at Coygan Camp, south-west Wales.[40] The continued use of Iron Age plough technology was not limited to the west, however, as witnessed by the find of the wooden share from such an ard in a third-century well at Abingdon,[41] and the criss-cross ard marks in a Roman ploughsoil at the nearby site of Drayton, perhaps dating to the first or second century.[42]

This type of cross-cultivation, with the creation of plough marks in two directions at approximate right angles, seems to have been necessary with this light type of plough to break up the soil adequately, although one-way marks thought to have been made by an ard have also been found. At Slonk Hill, Sussex, grooves running in one direction cut into the chalk were found close to an Iron Age and Roman settlement, and were sealed by a lynchet containing early second-century pottery.[43] An iron ard tip of a type that could have made the marks was found in a pit on the site.

Later Romano-British ploughs were heavier, enabling deeper soil penetration, and from the late third and fourth centuries AD they included a coulter, which ran through the soil in front of the share.[44] This meant that the soil could be broken up more easily by ploughing just one way. Cultivation marks that could have been produced by such a plough are known from several sites, including the villas at Latimer, Gadebridge Park, and Newhaven, and below Rudchester fort on Hadrian's Wall.[45]

A variety of plough marks have been found underlying Hadrian's Wall and its associated structures, in addition to those at Rudchester. These include examples at Denton Burn, turret 10A at Throckley, and below the headquarters building at Carrawburgh.[46] The date of these marks is uncertain, and they need not necessarily relate to ploughing immediately before construction of the Roman frontier. The Carrawburgh marks were predominantly one-way, while those at Throckley were in a criss-cross pattern, which may reflect a difference in the type of plough used, and perhaps a difference in date. Fowler has suggested that the Carrawburgh marks could belong to the second millennium BC,[47] but it is difficult to assign a date purely on the grounds of their form. It should also be remembered that such marks are not necessarily typical of 'normal' ploughing – their survival cut into the subsoil suggests that they penetrated to a greater depth than usual, and they may reflect the initial attempt to break up the soil after clearance or use as grassland, as has been suggested for the Throckley example. It is also possible that some of the marks do not reflect ploughing for agriculture at all, but rather an attempt to level the ground prior to building works.

The marks from Rudchester were cut into the clay subsoil and seem to reflect predominantly unidirectional ploughing, as mentioned above. They lay beneath a ploughsoil with a ridged surface resembling a type of ploughing called 'cord rig'. The plough marks were suggested to have been responsible for the creation of the 'rig', but, as Fowler has pointed out, the location of

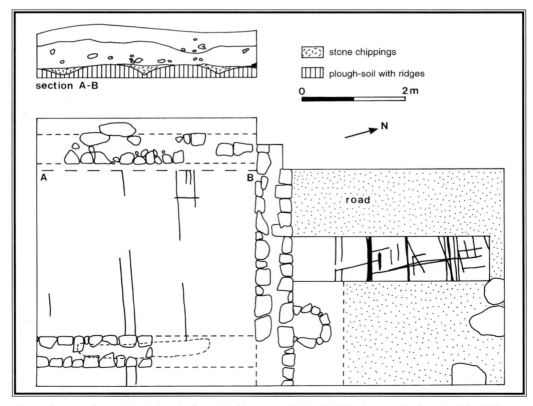

Plan and section of excavations below the fort at Rudchester, on Hadrian's Wall, showing plough marks (after Gillam, Harrison and Newman 1973)

the marks under the ridges rather than the furrows of the rig seems to argue against this.[48] It is possible that they again relate to a much earlier phase of cultivation than the rig, which may have been in use immediately before construction of the fort.

Cord rig typically consists of narrow ridges separated by furrows, the distance between the centre of furrows being about 1.5 metres. It occurs widely in the Hadrian's Wall area, often apparently associated with prehistoric settlements, to altitudes well beyond the current limit of arable cultivation.[49] An excavated example is provided by Greenlee Lough, just north of Hadrian's Wall at Housesteads. Here, cord rig underlay a Roman camp and was arranged in fields aligned on a trackway leading to a curvilinear settlement (which is unfortunately not closely datable).[50] Cord rig cultivation appears to be confined to areas of the native landscape, and its use apparently ended during the early Roman period. The ridging may have been designed to improve the drainage of the soil in areas of high rainfall, perhaps going some way to explain its distribution.

Perhaps the final late Roman development in plough technology was the asymmetric share. Such shares could have been attached to a mouldboard plough, which is characterized by both cutting and turning the soil, although the date of introduction of this type of plough is uncertain. Examples of asymmetric shares have been found at the villas at Folkestone and Brading, from the hill-fort at Dinorben, and in a hoard from the fort at Chester, but there are no datable plough marks known from Roman Britain that could have been made by such a share.[51] Mouldboard ploughing would have affected the types of weed that grew in the fields, with an increase of annuals able to grow quickly from seed on freshly overturned soil.

LAND RECLAMATION AND DRAINAGE

In some areas, pressure on the land in the Roman period was apparently sufficient to prompt major land drainage, as in the Severn Estuary Levels and the East Anglian Fens. As mentioned in chapter 2, there is evidence for planned reclamation and settlement of the Levels at several sites, including the Wentlooge Level at Rumney Great Wharf, and Oldbury Flats.[52] At the former site, a series of drainage ditches cut into the alluvium was probably completed between the late second and mid-third century, and was presumably associated with some form of sea defence. The primary purpose of the drainage is likely to have been the provision of agricultural land, and finds of lamb, calf, and horse bones in excavations at Rumney Great Wharf may suggest the use of the lush grassland on the reclaimed area for pasture.[53] Large quantities of slag found at several sites suggest that metalworking was also an important aspect of activity on the Levels, using ore from the Forest of Dean.[54]

Turning to the Fens, it has been suggested that their reclamation was so huge a task that it must have been carried out at the instigation of the Roman authorities, at a time when the Fenland formed an imperial estate.[55] Some of the more regular areas of fields on the Fens, as on Spalding Common, Lincolnshire, resemble official Roman land division (used especially in southern parts of the Empire) called 'centuriation'.[56] In this system, large areas of the landscape were divided into a grid pattern of fields of specific dimensions. There is no convincing evidence that centuriation was used in Britain, however, despite arguments to the contrary.[57] The resemblance of some Fenland fields to such a layout is probably coincidental, and at least partly due to the relationship of the fields to straight Roman roads. The pattern of fields and tracks across most of Fenland suggests a piecemeal approach to land enclosure rather than a large-scale

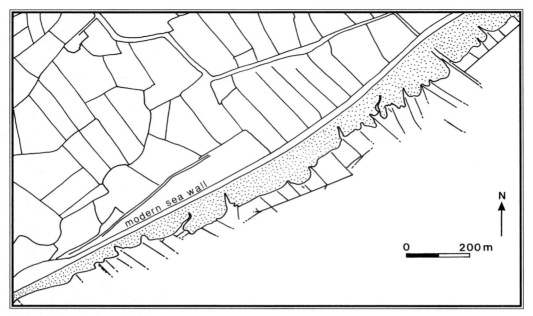

Intertidal ditches and modern field boundaries at Rumney Great Wharf: stippling indicates current extent of saltmarsh. Note that the boundaries of the long narrow fields follow the alignment of the intertidal ditches, suggesting that they are part of the same planned landscape. (After Fulford, Allen and Rippon 1994)

planned layout. The area is criss-crossed by ditched trackways between often irregular ditched fields, an example of which has been revealed by aerial photography and limited excavation at Holbeach in Lincolnshire.[58]

There are some features of the Fenland that do suggest action on a grand scale, notably the Car Dyke, the function of which is a matter for some debate.[59] It has been suggested that it was a canal, used to transport grain to northern Britain, including Hadrian's Wall. However, the necessity for such long-distance transport of grain is diminished in the light of evidence for extensive arable agriculture in northern Britain. In any case the dyke seems unlikely to have been navigable along its entire length, and was crossed by causeways in places, although these seem to be secondary features. It is perhaps most likely that the dyke was primarily designed to drain away floodwaters, while also being of use for local transport.

In addition to large-scale land reclamation, drainage was also employed at individual settlement sites and in fields to enable maximum use of local soils. The ditched enclosures on the Thames gravels have already been mentioned, as at Ashville, Abingdon, where construction of late Iron Age/Roman ditches was accompanied by a decline in the frequency of the spike-rush (*Eleocharis palustris*), a wetland plant, suggesting that the ditches may have lowered the local water table.[60]

THE MAINTENANCE OF SOIL QUALITY

There is some evidence that deliberate attempts were made in the Roman period, and indeed before, to maintain and improve the quality of agricultural land. This includes the widespread pottery scatters, mentioned above, perhaps indicative of the spread of household rubbish and

Fields, settlements and trackways at Holbeach, Lincolnshire. The Roman features are crossed by a modern drainage canal and smaller straight ditches. (Cambridge University Collection of Air Photographs: copyright reserved)

manure on the fields. It is also likely that animals were released onto the fields during fallow periods to provide a direct application of manure. Chalk may deliberately have been applied to clay fields to improve the soil texture: a first- or second-century pit from Bullock Down, East Sussex, may have been a marling pit used for this purpose.[61]

Crop rotation may have been used to reduce soil exhaustion and prevent the build-up of pests. If one of the crops was a legume (such as beans) it would have enhanced soil fertility by returning nitrogen to the soil. Hints of crop rotation are provided by seeds of non-cereal crops mixed with cereal assemblages from some archaeological sites, suggesting that they are survivals from a previous year's crop. For example, flax (*Linum usitatissimum*) and Celtic bean (*Vicia faba*) have been found with cereal remains from a corn-drier at Barton Court Farm, Oxfordshire, and it is highly unlikely that these plants would have been grown together deliberately.[62]

GRAZING LAND

The pollen and other evidence discussed in chapter 2 indicates the widespread existence of grassland, including hay meadows, although the character of much of it is uncertain. Botanical evidence that hay production is a Roman introduction is supported by artefactual evidence. There have been no finds of pre-Roman tools suitable to cut hay, but scythes have been found at military sites in first-century deposits, as at the fort at Newstead.[63] These may have been used to cut hay for horse fodder. Scythes appear later at non-military sites, as at Farmoor in Oxfordshire, and Great Chesterford in Essex.[64] These were much longer than the earlier type of implement and could have been used to cut hay or cereal crops.[65]

Many of the field systems mentioned above probably included at least some pasture. The villa sites, for example, seem to have been surrounded by paddocks with arable fields further away, while the Thames gravel and floodplain settlements appear to have been predominantly involved in stock rearing.

Grassland does not provide the only possible source of grazing. The large expanses of heather moor in upland areas would have provided another source, and there is evidence that heather was brought to some sites, such as York and Carlisle, possibly as a source of winter feed for stalled animals.[66]

CROPS

Evidence for Roman crops comes predominantly from their remains preserved on sites where they were produced, stored, processed or consumed, and from their pollen grains in the type of lake and peat deposits discussed in chapter 2. It is, therefore, possible to distinguish between the on-site record of macroscopic crop remains, mainly cereal grains and fruits/seeds of other food plants, and the off-site record of pollen. Macroscopic remains have the advantage over pollen grains of enabling closer identification of the species of plants concerned, although there is a bias in preservation towards those plant parts likely to be exposed to charring, the commonest means of plant preservation on most archaeological sites. Leafy and root vegetables are rarely preserved, perhaps because they tended to be cooked by boiling, so our knowledge of the cultivation of such plants is limited.

Plant remains from archaeological sites have provided the main evidence for crop production in Roman Britain, but there are few sites where a systematic attempt has been made to study such remains, and there is a strong bias of evidence in favour of the south, that is the villa landscape. This contrasts with the evidence from pollen analysis, which is biased to the north and west: the native landscape. A combination of both sources of evidence provides a broader view of agriculture than is possible from the limited number of sites where macroscopic remains have been studied, but caution must be exercised in comparing them.

EVIDENCE OF CROPS FROM THE POLLEN RECORD

One advantage of the use of the off-site pollen record in reconstructing the distribution of crop cultivation is that most such records reflect the local cultivation of the plant, whereas larger plant remains on archaeological sites may have been brought in from a long distance away. However, there are problems of identification. While cereal grains can generally be identified to a specific type, most of their pollen grains, with the exception of rye (*Secale cereale*), cannot, and attempts to separate rye pollen are not always made. Thus, it is usual for a pollen sequence simply to record the presence of cereal pollen rather than attempting further identification. An additional problem relates to the low pollen production of most cereals. Even in areas of intensive cereal

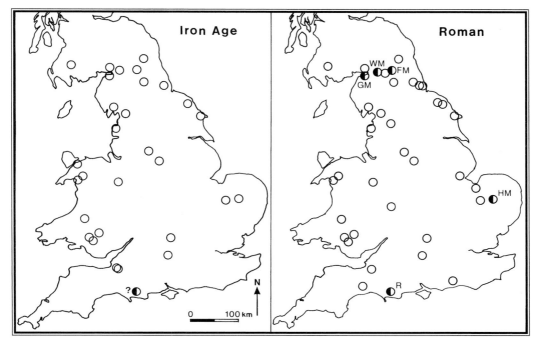

Distribution of sites with pollen evidence for the cultivation of cereal in the Iron Age and Roman periods. Sites where rye pollen has been identified are shown as half-filled circles. GM - Glasson Moss, WM - Walton Moss, FM - Fozy Moss, HM - Hockham Mere, R - Rimsmoor

production, little cereal pollen may occur in local lake or peat deposits because most cereals are self-fertilizing, releasing little or no pollen into the air (but rye is again an exception). Cereals are strongly under-represented in the pollen record as a result.

A survey of the evidence for cereal cultivation from the pollen sequences discussed in chapter 2 reveals rye at five sites in the Roman period: Rimsmoor in Dorset, Hockham Mere in East Anglia, and three of the Hadrian's Wall sequences (Glasson Moss, Walton Moss and Fozy Moss).[67] There is no evidence for an Iron Age presence of rye near any of these, with the possible exception of Rimsmoor. Macroscopic plant remains from archaeological sites do, however, indicate an Iron Age presence of rye in southern England, and pollen evidence from other sites suggests that the plant may have been present in Britain in the Bronze Age, although probably not deliberately cultivated.[68]

As for the other cereals, which have to be grouped together from the pollen evidence (wheat, barley and oats), well over half of the pollen sequences covering the Iron Age indicate local cereal production, stretching from Dorset to southern Scotland, and from East Anglia to west Wales. By the Roman period cereal cultivation had become even more widespread, with cereal pollen recorded at more than three-quarters of the sites.

Pollen of many other possible crops, such as legumes and root vegetables, cannot be separated into cultivated and wild types. Apart from cereals, the main crops that can be identified from their pollen grains are hemp and flax, although identification of the former can be difficult.[69] Hemp (*Cannabis sativa*) was used in pre-modern times in fibre production, and its pollen may be abundant in lake sediments due to the practice of 'retting' – soaking the hemp in water to soften

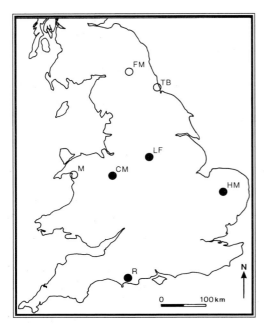

Distribution of hemp pollen in the Iron Age and Roman periods: filled circles indicate presence in both periods; open circles indicate presence in the Roman period only. FM - Fozy Moss, TB - Thorpe Bulmer, LF - Leash Fen, CM - Crose Mere, M - Moel y Gerddi, HM - Hockham Mere, R - Rimsmoor

it during processing. Hemp has been recorded in Iron Age deposits at Crose Mere, Leash Fen, Hockham Mere and possibly Rimsmoor.[70] Records for the Roman period are more frequent, including all of the sites with Iron Age records plus Moel y Gerddi in Wales and Thorpe Bulmer and Fozy Moss in northern England.[71] Macroscopic remains of hemp are rare. They have been recorded from Roman York, but do not necessarily reflect local cultivation.[72]

Flax (*Linum usitatissimum*) is another fibre plant, used for linen, which also provides linseed oil. Like hemp, flax is soaked in water during fibre production, so it is surprising that it is rarely recorded in pollen sequences from lakes. There are no records of its pollen in securely dated Roman deposits, but macroscopic remains are quite frequent from the Neolithic period onwards. Roman examples are widespread, including several sites in Oxfordshire, such as Barton Court Farm, Thornbrough in Northumberland, and Collfryn in mid-Wales.[73]

EVIDENCE OF CROPS FROM MACROSCOPIC PLANT REMAINS

Charred plant remains are common on Romano-British sites, but their systematic collection and study has only recently been undertaken. The number of sites with detailed reports on the botanical remains is, therefore, small. Waterlogging provides another means of preservation at some sites, particularly in wells and ditches. Assemblages from such contexts often illustrate rather different aspects of the economy to those indicated by charred material. We have seen, for example, that they provide evidence for the nature of local grassland communities, while charred remains tend to be biased towards the products of arable fields, which were likely to have been exposed to charring during processing.

Mixed with the crop plant remains are often a variety of weed seeds, which presumably grew in the fields with the crop and were gathered with the harvest. These weeds can provide information on the type of land being cultivated, and also on the time of sowing and method of harvesting. While many of the weeds of Roman fields were native plants, there are a number of species that may represent Iron Age or Roman introductions, including the corn marigold (*Chrysanthemum segetum*) and the cornflower (*Centaurea cyanus*).[74]

In addition to crops and weeds, remains of a range of native plants can be found on archaeological sites, but these are unlikely to provide an accurate indication of the character of the surrounding landscape. Their presence on the site may reflect their growth within the confines of the settlement, or they may have been brought there because they were useful, or by accident. Hazelnuts are a common find, presumably because they were used for food, while a range of other trees and shrubs are represented in charcoal assemblages from hearths and as structural remains from waterlogged sites (see chapter 2). Again, these plants will have been selected in relation to their use for specific purposes and need bear little relation to the composition of any local woodland. So, plant remains from archaeological sites provide more information on methods of crop production, processing and consumption, and on the utilization of natural resources, than on the general character of the landscape. For this reason plant remains from archaeological sites are not given the same detailed treatment here as was applied to study of pollen sequences in chapter 2.

Especially large assemblages of crop remains have been found in towns, such as York and London, and military sites, such as South Shields on Hadrian's Wall, but many such finds may represent imports from abroad to supplement British crop production.[75] For example, a military warehouse dating from AD 70–120 in York contained a mixture of spelt wheat (*Triticum spelta*), barley (*Hordeum vulgare*), and rye (*Secale cereale*) remains, with several exotic species of weed.[76] The grain was infested with insect pests, several of which were again non-native, suggesting that the grain had been imported.[77] Such finds have no clear bearing on agricultural systems in Britain, although they might suggest increasing pressure on the land to the point where demand could no longer be met by local production. Smaller assemblages from less romanized sites also need not reflect local cereal cultivation, as cereal was clearly traded within Britain.

Some attempts have been made to identify 'producer' and 'consumer' sites from the weed seeds associated with the cereal grain, and from the level to which the cereal has been processed. However, the results of different methods are often conflicting in terms of whether or not a specific site was a producer.[78]

This raises an important issue in the interpretation of crop remains. Much evidence for the presence of specific crops consists of small assemblages from isolated features that need not contain a typical sample of the crop plants reaching the site. The crop remains and associated weeds may have been preserved at one of a number of stages of crop processing, such as threshing, winnowing or sieving, and at each stage the composition of the assemblage is altered by successive removal of unwanted elements.

Before considering crop cultivation in Roman Britain it is necessary to begin by examining the nature of Iron Age agriculture. Many of the agricultural developments of the later Iron Age persisted into the Roman period, and indeed many supposed Roman innovations are increasingly being found to date back to the Iron Age.

IRON AGE CROPS

Several Iron Age sites have produced large quantities of charred grain, particularly from pits apparently used for storage, as at Ashville, Abingdon and Danebury, Hampshire.[79] Such features are not found on sites in the north and west, probably because the soils are unsuitable, and in these areas grain was probably stored in raised timber structures (four-post granaries). The absence of obvious storage pits from western Britain has meant that few large crop assemblages have been recovered, although recent study of a range of settlement sites in northern Britain has revealed charred plant remains in various other features, such as ditches and hearths.[80]

During the Iron Age the main crops were spelt wheat (*Triticum spelta*) and hulled six-row barley (*Hordeum vulgare*), both of which can be grown on a range of soils.[81] In hulled barley the grain is tightly enclosed within a casing (the hulls or husk), which needs to be removed before the grain can be used for food. This can be done by exposure to heat (parching), making the hulls brittle so that they break away during threshing. This contrasts with 'naked' barley, where the grain is not enclosed and is 'free-threshing'. In view of the extra effort required to process hulled barley it is, perhaps, surprising that later prehistory saw an increase in cultivation of this type. Animals will eat the hulled grain, however, and it has been suggested that the increased use of the hulled form reflects its role as animal fodder in the Iron Age and Roman periods.[82]

During the Iron Age there was also some cultivation of emmer wheat (*Triticum dicoccum*), a legacy from the Bronze Age, which is best suited to light soils, and bread/club wheat (*Triticum aestivo-compactum*),[83] a crop best suited to heavier silt/clay soils, which was to become of key importance in the first millennium AD. Bread wheat, in contrast with spelt and emmer, is free-threshing, so does not require parching. This tends to cause it to be under-represented in the crop record, as it would have been less likely than the other wheats to have been exposed to charring. Oats (*Avena* sp.) and rye (*Secale cereale*) also appear in the Iron Age crop record, although it is uncertain whether they were deliberately grown as crops or represent contaminants. Evidence for other crops is limited, although the site at Hengistbury Head has provided evidence of peas (*Pisum sativum*), Celtic bean (*Vicia faba*), and flax from the late Iron Age.[84]

Weed assemblages from this period provide indications of the use of a range of soil types for crop cultivation that would today be considered marginal. For example, the late Iron Age and early Roman settlement at Thorpe Thewles, near Durham, produced an assemblage dominated by weeds, particularly the heath-grass (*Danthonia decumbens*), with some cereal grains and chaff, mainly of spelt wheat and barley.[85] Similar assemblages came from the late Iron Age sites at Stanwick and Rock Castle, North Yorkshire,[86] and from late Iron Age deposits at Cefn Graeanog, north Wales, where spelt chaff was also found.[87] Heath-grass is today predominantly a plant of damp acid soils, and the abundance of this and other perennial weeds could reflect the use of former pasture for arable, or the minor disturbance of the soil involved in ploughing with an ard.[88]

Similarly, evidence both from these sites and from several in the south, particularly the Upper Thames Valley sites of Farmoor and Ashville,[89] indicates expansion of cultivation onto wet soils. Common spike-rush (*Eleocharis palustris*), a plant of damp or waterlogged soils, often occurs with cereal remains, suggesting that it was a weed of crops. Occasional records of stinking chamomile (*Anthemis cotula*) from Iron Age sites, again as at Ashville, may suggest the cultivation of heavy clay soils, associated with an increase in the evidence for artificial drainage of fields.[90] As mentioned in chapter 2, weed species found in Iron Age crop assemblages from southern Britain also suggest that soil nitrogen was becoming depleted.

ROMAN CROPS

Much of the evidence for Roman crops comes from excavations of corn-driers from sites in southern England[91] and granaries from town and military sites, as discussed above. As for the Iron Age, intensive sampling in a few areas (notably at the Upper Thames Valley and northern English sites, referred to earlier) has revealed crop remains from a wider range of other contexts.

The main crop species grown in Britain continued to be spelt wheat and barley, but increasing use appears to have been made of bread wheat, rye and oats.[92] It has already been mentioned that bread wheat is suited to fertile clay and silty soils, and its increased exploitation might suggest further expansion in the use of such soils for arable, when they may previously have been used predominantly for grassland. In contrast with bread wheat, oats and rye are tolerant of a much greater range of soil conditions and could have been grown on soils that were becoming depleted by prolonged cultivation. Martin Jones has suggested that the parallel increase of these three crops in the Roman period may reflect an increasing economic disparity between wealthy farmers, intensively cultivating the fertile loams, and poor farmers, working increasingly nutrient-depleted soils.[93]

The evidence for the cultivation of bread wheat is patchy, however, and it is uncertain when it became the dominant crop. In the south it may have become significant in the late Iron Age at some sites, as at Barton Court Farm, Oxfordshire, while the earliest record from northern England is from a terminal Iron Age context at Rock Castle, near Stanwick, North Yorkshire.[94] At many other sites it appears not to have become significant until the Anglo-Saxon period.[95]

In addition to the staple cereal crops, the Roman period saw increased use of a variety of other plants for culinary purposes.[96] Some, such as the olive (*Olea europaea*) and fig (*Ficus carica*), represent imports, but at many sites there is evidence for a range of culinary herbs, including dill (*Anethum graveolens*) and coriander (*Coriandrum sativum*), and other plants, which may have been grown in gardens, as at Fishbourne.

There has been some debate over whether or not grapes (*Vitis vinifera*) were grown in Britain.[97] Grape pips are quite frequently found in Roman towns, as in London, Silchester and York, and sometimes from villas, as at Gorhambury, near St Albans, and Winterton, Lincolnshire.[98] In these contexts they are usually accompanied by a range of exotic food plants, and presumably reflect imported raisins. However, an area of ditches excavated at North Thoresby in Lincolnshire has been suggested to represent a vineyard, and more convincing evidence has recently come from Wollaston, Northamptonshire, where grape pollen was found in a series of planting trenches.[99]

Returning to the evidence for more usual crops, where detailed sampling has been undertaken on both Iron Age and Roman deposits from the same site it is possible to examine changes in agricultural economy that may reflect the process of romanization. This can be illustrated by two sites in the Upper Thames Valley: Ashville and Barton Court Farm. The former produced a rich assemblage of plant remains from a series of pits, ditches, post-holes and wells.[100] Spelt wheat and barley were predominant, with a little emmer and club wheat. The cereals grown during the occupation do not seem to have changed significantly, but, as mentioned above, there is evidence that during the late Iron Age local drainage was improved by ditch digging. A contrast is provided by Barton Court Farm, where late Iron Age and early Roman enclosed settlements were succeeded by a villa towards the end of the third century.[101] Plant remains were preserved charred in corn-driers and pits, while a range of waterlogged remains was again recovered from a well. Here the variety of crops grown in the Roman period was more diverse than at Ashville, including spelt wheat, bread wheat, emmer wheat, barley, flax and Celtic bean. Thus, even within this one region, differences in the degree of romanization between sites are strongly reflected in the crops grown.

ANIMALS

Animal bones have been recovered from many Roman-period sites, principally in southern Britain. The acid soils that predominate in the uplands of the north and west lead to poor bone survival, so that the evidence for animal husbandry is again biased to the villa landscape. As has been discussed in relation to some crop assemblages, the animal bones from a site need bear little relation to the local farming system, since animals and their products were widely traded. Bone remains mainly provide information on dietary preferences, butchery and disposal practices, and use of animal products other than meat, such as hides and horns.[102] These aspects are beyond the scope of this book. All that will be mentioned here is general trends in livestock over the Roman period and how these might relate to landscape use.

The three main animals that provided food in the Roman period were cattle, sheep and pigs, although remains of pigs are much less abundant than the other two at most sites.[103] Goats were also kept, but their bones cannot always be separated from those of sheep, so the relative proportions of these two animals is usually uncertain.[104] Throughout the Roman period there was a trend towards increasing numbers of cattle at the expense of sheep, apparently reflecting a Roman dietary preference for beef. This trend is most marked at the most romanized sites, such as forts, towns and villas, while many native settlements seem to have continued the Iron Age pattern of a predominance of sheep.[105]

Some local variations in this pattern occur in relation to local soil/pasture conditions. Sheep are not suited to low-lying sites prone to flooding because of the likelihood of infection by liver fluke. Sites with pasture close to rivers, as at Farmoor, therefore tend to have greater numbers of cattle bones.[106] Sheep are best kept on well-drained downland sites, and in some instances villas in such areas seem not to have followed the general trend towards increased cattle husbandry, but to have concentrated instead on sheep. An example is Barnsley Park, Gloucestershire, where the bone assemblage shows high frequencies of sheep throughout the occupation of the site from the late second until at least the late fourth century.[107] Wool production may have been an important part of the economy at such sites. However, not all sites in this area show a similar predominance of sheep. Cattle were more abundant in samples from Cirencester, leading King to suggest that the inhabitants of Barnsley Park had an unromanized diet, while living in the romanized context of a villa.[108]

A further factor that must be taken into consideration when comparing bone assemblages from different sites is that, as with crop remains, different sites played different roles in the economy. A distinction should be drawn between producer and consumer sites, and Noddle has pointed out that the latter tend to have a higher proportion of cattle than the former.[109] This factor may be reflected in the Cotswold examples discussed above, as sites like Barnsley Park would probably have supplied the town at Cirencester.

In the Roman period both sheep and cattle often seem to have been killed at a greater age than in the Iron Age, perhaps suggesting a shift in emphasis from the production of meat to that of milk, wool and hides.[110] Large supplies of leather were required by the army, and the waterlogged conditions at the fort at Vindolanda have preserved many examples of its use, including shoes, horse tack and tents.[111] King suggested that farmers who kept their animals long into maturity may have been relatively wealthy, since keeping the animals for longer would have put increased pressure on pasture.[112] This may also be linked to the introduction of hay production, which would have provided fodder for cattle that were kept stalled in winter.

Mature cattle may also have been kept to provide traction for ploughs, and to pull carts for the transport of the crop. The increasing importance of cattle during the Roman period has been linked by Grant to a greater emphasis on arable cultivation, especially on heavier soils.[113]

Pig bones tend to be particularly abundant at military, town and villa sites, as at Fishbourne, and seem to be a reflection of a high–status romanized diet.[114] Further evidence for the consumption of pig meat is again provided from Vindolanda, where the waterlogged wooden writing tablets refer to pork, pork fat and pig's trotters.[115] References are also made to venison, and both pig and deer (red, roe and fallow) bones have been found on the site.[116] Deer bones are also frequent from both villas, such as Shakenoak, and native settlements in the later Roman period, perhaps reflecting an interest in hunting,[117] although deer may also have been important in providing antler as a raw material.[118]

It has been suggested that greater numbers of pig and red deer bones in later Roman deposits may reflect an increasing use of woodland,[119] but neither of these animals requires woodland. Red deer may live in both open moorland and wooded environments. Pigs have traditionally been assumed to reflect the presence of woodland because of the medieval practice of pannage, in which pigs were released into oak woods to feed on the acorns, but they could just as easily have been fed in other ways, such as on the waste products of cereal processing.[120] Maltby has suggested that pigs may have been kept in individual households in towns such as Winchester and Dorchester, again a common practice in the medieval period.[121]

CONCLUSION

The Roman occupation might be expected to have triggered an immediate change in agriculture in Britain, due to the sudden increase in population and large military presence, combined with the influx of new crops, techniques and equipment. Evidence for an immediate impetus to agriculture is fairly limited, however, and seems confined to the native landscape. The existence of both arable and pastoral agriculture in this area from the Iron Age means that the necessity for importation of large quantities of grain from further south may not have been as great as previously thought. Local production could have supplied at least some of the army's needs, although demand may have outstripped the ability of the local population to supply in the early stages of the occupation. Several of the pollen sequences from the area suggest an increase in clearance in the early Roman period, presumably at least partly to provide further agricultural land.

In the villa landscape the pollen evidence that most of the land was already being exploited for agriculture prior to the Roman period is supported by the widespread existence of major prehistoric field systems, many of which apparently continued in use into the Roman period. In this area there seems to have been little scope for expansion in the amount of land for agriculture, since most woodland had already been cleared by the end of the Iron Age. Increased production may have been achieved by the more intensive use of existing land, as suggested by the evidence for manuring and crop rotation, by conversion of some areas of grassland to arable, and by drainage of wetland areas such as the Fens. Thus, the construction of the villa landscape may have involved little change in the extent of farmland, as it was established in an existing agricultural landscape. Output, therefore, had to be enhanced by more intensive, rather than extensive, farming.

CHAPTER 6

URBAN
AND INDUSTRIAL
LANDSCAPES

INTRODUCTION

The Romano-British economy was not entirely based on agriculture, and the Romano-British landscape was not entirely a patchwork of greater and lesser farms, forts, their cemeteries, and the churches and temples used by their inhabitants. Two other aspects of the landscape of Roman Britain require special attention, and these will be considered separately here. Such treatment is to assist in discussion, not because either was separate from most other aspects of its contemporary landscape. These two landscapes are what we will refer to as the 'urban' and 'industrial' landscapes of Roman Britain.

Urban landscapes developed around both large (or 'public') and small towns.[1] Industrial landscapes were smaller sub-areas within the native and villa landscapes that were made distinctive by the extraction of raw materials or mass-production, targeted at non-local markets.[2] These landscapes are associated with potteries, tileries, iron-working, glass manufacture, salting and mining, although these activities also took place on a smaller and more local scale without producing such landscapes.

Industrial landscapes were frequently centred on small towns, especially along the boundary of the native and villa landscapes.[3] This is not to say that there were no industrial landscapes away from towns, or away from this zone, nor that all small towns were closely connected with industry, but at the transition from the native to the urban landscape there seems to have been an 'industrial zone': from what is today south Lancashire to the West Country.[4]

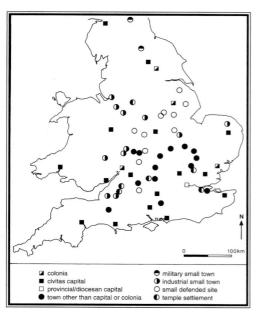

Urbanism in Roman Britain. Distribution map of walled large and small towns, and small towns with specialized functions (based on Burnham and Wacher 1990)

THE URBAN LANDSCAPE

The urban landscape of Roman Britain has seldom been the subject of detailed study in its own right, although there has been much archaeological work on towns. Archaeologists have often neglected the hinterland of towns while working on the 'townscape' within their walls.[5] There are important exceptions to this generalization, of course, notably studies of the hinterlands of Roman London and York, and the large-scale programme of research on the environs of Wroxeter.[6]

In urban hinterlands the needs and activities of town life brought about distinct forms of landscape, not the result of agricultural societies and of farming activities. Such landscapes linked town and country, but they did so by bringing the concerns of the towns – their need for food, the burial of their population, their temples, their defences, and even their residential areas – outside town walls and urban limits. The town 'came out to meet the country', even when the country ran up to the town walls.

CHARACTERISTICS OF THE URBAN LANDSCAPE

Consequently, the urban landscape was derived from the characteristics of the town itself, and interaction of the town and its surroundings. This was a situation romanized from its inception, because urban landscapes were the product of the establishment of romanized towns, and so formed patches of intense romanization even when the surrounding agricultural landscape was not especially romanized, as at Carmarthen.[7]

The occupation of towns spread beyond their walls to form (sometimes large) suburbs, as at Southwark, immediately south of London.[8] These could represent the growth of towns after the construction of walls, or the result of including only part of the built-up area inside their circuit. The structures and activities found in such areas often resemble those within the towns, but major buildings were probably rarer in such 'extramural' settlements, if not entirely unknown, as the discovery of both a possible *mansio* and a possible military guild-building in Southwark suggests.[9]

Urban hinterlands also included cemeteries (as at Lankhills and Poundbury) and access roads.[10] Large towns could also have elaborate water supplies, comprising water leats (dug water-supply channels) or aqueducts (raised channels providing them with water), as at Leicester and Dorchester.[11] Some towns had extramural amphitheatres, as at Silchester, and temples were often to be found outside large towns, as at St Albans and London, sometimes as part of elaborate religious complexes, as at the Gosbecks site outside Colchester.[12] Everyday activities also affected the urban hinterland, as at Cirencester, where a range of urban-related features included an amphitheatre, cemeteries, and quarries which were used as rubbish tips when disused.[13] Quarries might have been among the most striking features of the immediately extramural zone. For example, Wacher has suggested that Cirencester's streets alone required 150,000 cubic metres of material, potentially representing a quarry of 50 by 100 metres in diameter and 30 metres deep in the urban hinterland.[14]

Both small and large towns also caused alterations in the rural settlement patterns around them. Towns were often surrounded by greater numbers of villas than elsewhere in their area,[15] although not all towns had such groups of villas. For example, there is no group of villas surrounding Silchester,[16] and, in general, these groups seem less common in the north of Britain. Neither York nor Aldborough, for example, seem to have had such an encircling cluster of villas, while some large southern towns, such as Cirencester and St Albans, had many villas in their hinterland.[17]

Villa clusters are especially common around small towns, which may have been more closely integrated into the economy and society of the surrounding countryside than larger urban

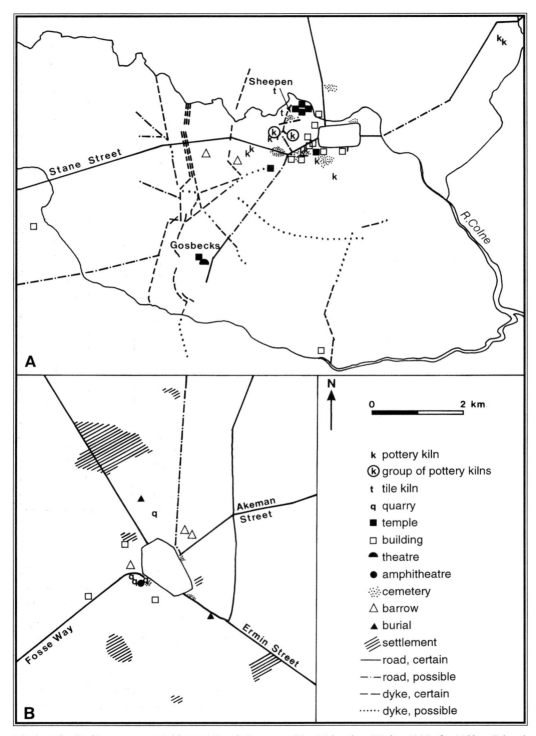

The hinterlands of large towns at Colchester (A) and Cirencester (B). (A based on Wacher 1995 after Niblett, B based on Darvill and Gerrard 1994)

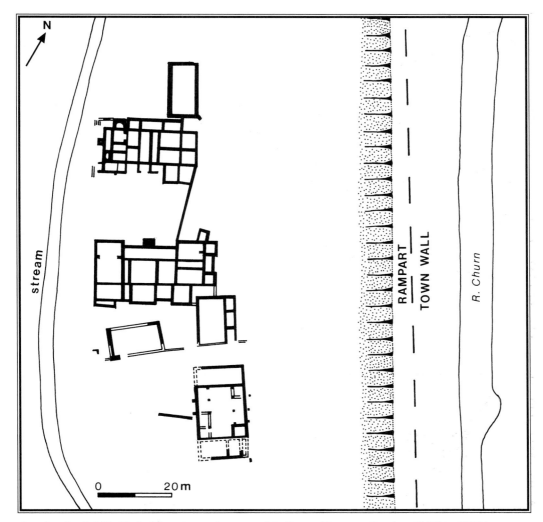

An urban farm? Villa-like buildings close to the town wall in Roman Cirencester (based on McWhirr 1986a)

centres. Some scholars have argued that the large towns at Cirencester and Silchester were also closely linked to their hinterlands, as large villa-like buildings have been discovered inside their town walls, and agricultural implements and corn-driers have been found at town sites.[18] The function of these structures is not beyond doubt, however, and their villa-like plans may simply tell us that villa houses were also erected outside agricultural rural contexts to express the status or rural affinities of their owners.

Corn-driers in urban contexts might represent the secondary processing of crops brought to urban centres from the surrounding countryside, while agricultural implements could have been manufactured or repaired in towns, or brought to them for religious reasons, as scrap or in payment of debts. Nor are there gates, tracks or paths directly linking those urban structures claimed as farms to the exterior. So, while it is possible that farming took place inside Romano-British towns, the evidence for this, and for the function of the relevant structures, remains uncertain.

Reconstruction of a mansio. *(Painting of the* mansio *and bath-house in the Roman town at Chelmsford by Frank Gardiner, reproduced by permission of Chelmsford Museums Service)*

London provides an example of another widespread aspect of the hinterland of large towns: an increasing number of small roadside settlements, perhaps mostly villages, as one approaches the town by the Roman roads linking it to other urban sites. Such Romano-British settlements have been found at many of the medieval village sites along the London–Dover and London–Chichester roads in what is today Greater London. Examples are at Staines, Putney, Streatham, Croydon and Ewell.[19] Others may have existed in the proximity of other medieval and later villages, as the recent discovery of a Romano-British settlement at Tulse Hill suggests.[20]

These roadside settlements probably provided services to travellers, although a more formal system of roadside and urban hostels for government officials (*mansiones*) was established throughout Britain.[21] These were primarily for people on official business, so probably took on the temporary character of administrative buildings when officials were resident. *Mansiones* were found both in large towns – as at Silchester – and small towns – as at Wall – but probably served the same function in each, and presumably catered for non-governmental travellers also.

Small farming settlements were often located close to towns, as at Allington Avenue near Dorchester in Dorset, and during the course of the Roman period new types of extramural site were established.[22] Christian cemeteries and churches were founded outside towns during the Roman period, as at Colchester, and at St Albans such a cemetery included a *martyrium* containing the burial of the martyr St Alban.[23] The urban landscape can, however, be understood as extending from the centre of a town to the limits of its hinterland as a continuous gradual transition from the urbanized core. The gradualness of this transition was punctuated by barriers – walls, ditches, etc. – acting as boundaries, and within towns the physical structure of the urban community was provided by its property-divisions, walls, gates and streets.[24] These shaped the

Silchester Roman town. Aerial photograph showing the line of the town walls and cropmarks of parts of the street plan and internal buildings, including (approximately in the centre of the wallled area) the forum/basilica complex. (Cambridge University Collection of Air Photographs: copyright reserved)

urban form, but they did not shape all towns in a similar way, and could be replanned in the course of the Roman period.[25]

There seems not to have been a set plan for the layout of town walls, gates, and streets in Britain. At the more formally organized large towns, street plans could be very regular – with street-grids and gates at equally spaced intervals – or much less so, without clear evidence of grids; even London probably had a somewhat irregular street pattern.[26] The principal physical focus of larger towns was the forum/basilica complex, a combined town hall and market area.[27] This gave large towns a clear-cut centre, which became a major factor in the distribution of activities within them. The town centre was often further emphasized by the erection of other public buildings, such as large baths and market halls.[28]

Domestic buildings within the town were set along, and often back from, the streets and were constructed of both timber and mortared stone, often with tiled or slate roofs.[29] In large early Romano-British towns, big houses, analogous to villas, are frequently found, but there were also many lesser buildings, some almost certainly shops and houses, as in London and St Albans.[30] Later Roman towns also contained many large and well-appointed romanized houses, but these may have been wider spaced and more often set back from the streets, as if in gardens or yards.[31] The well-known plans of Silchester and Caerwent probably represent the fourth-century state of these towns, illustrating this sort of development.[32]

THE PROBLEM OF THE 'DARK EARTH'

The character of late Roman large towns in Britain is complicated by the existence of a widely found, but enigmatic, deposit known as the 'dark earth'.[33] Our understanding of the late Romano-British townscape and its relationship with the urban hinterland depends on how this layer is interpreted. Dark earth occurs over the latest early Roman town layers in many – perhaps most – Romano-British towns, including London, Lincoln, York and Gloucester. This junction is at a stratigraphical, not horizontal, level, a point well illustrated at many sites in London, but this horizon is different chronologically at different sites.[34] Immediately above the dark earth deposits at these towns there is usually the earliest evidence of Anglo-Saxon occupation. This is also clearly demonstrated at many sites in London. Seldom, if ever, are there more Roman layers above the dark earth.

The dark earth deposit consists of a charcoal-rich soil containing late Roman, and sometimes Anglo-Saxon, artefacts.[35] These may include coins, pottery, building materials, animal bone and metal (especially iron) slag. Dark earth varies in detail from site to site in exact composition, the specific range of finds, its colour, and the degree to which it seems to have differences within it. Some contains 'tip lines', sloping layers of deposit as if thrown down, and features such as wells or pits seem to have been cut from within this deposit at a few sites.[36]

There are essentially four views on what dark earth represents:

1.   Disuse:[37] the deposit is no more than an accumulation of soil on derelict sites.
2.   Gardens/farms:[38] the deposit is composed of soil deliberately dumped in order to grow vegetables for food, with towns turned into farms, or to 'landscape' towns to resemble parks, within which were set the houses of the rich.
3.   Rubbish tips:[39] the soil derives from occupation, and represents the result of rubbish disposal onto neighbouring vacant plots.
4.   Occupation:[40] the deposit is the remains of occupation of some type that left no obvious structural remains. The key possibilities are turf- or mud- (cob) walled houses, or timber-framed buildings. The deposit would derive from the collapse, rebuilding, and post-depositional modification of these and associated occupation layers. This view might be compatible with both 2 and 3 above.

The evidence for 1 is the lack of obvious buildings, the overall similarity of the deposit, its long period of formation, and perhaps that analysis of the soil shows that it contained animal dung.[41] Against it, the finds, and the fact that underlying deposits seldom show much evidence of plough damage (which might be expected on fertile disused land), weigh heavily. The evidence for 2 is very similar, and might relate the occupation of large, more widely spaced, buildings to these (apparently) open spaces. Gardens might also explain the lack of ploughing and the dung (for fertilizer), although the quantity of finds still presents serious problems.

Evidence for 3 is the combination of finds with the above and one specific sequence from York (at Wellington Row) in which dark earth seems to fill a disused building.[42] It runs into problems in explaining the large areas of dark earth found in many locations in London, and probably originally covering the entire area encompassed by large urban excavations, as at Milk Street and Newgate Street.[43]

Option 4 has in its favour that it explains the finds and the charcoal very well, and it suggests why there is so much dark earth at previously densely populated sites. It also explains the animal dung, as this might be brought in by accident with turf, and was often used deliberately in mud-brick construction as a binding agent. Dung was also used in wattle-and-daub panels, which might have been present in such buildings (e.g. as doors). Against it there are two general objections: the lack of any obvious remains of such buildings and the inclusion of Anglo-Saxon finds in several dark earth deposits. There is also the more specific case of Wellington Row in York.[44]

The general objections need not be considered as formidable problems. The former is answerable by examining evidence of medieval and later cob- and turf-walled buildings. If these survive as surface features at all, it is as little more than low linear mounds of soil, but usually they are reduced to soil layers, like those of the dark earth. The latter is easily explained either by a continuous process of dark earth formation extending beyond the Roman period, or by the redeposition of finds by worm- and root-action.[45] The Wellington Row sequence presents more problems for this view, but is readily explicable if we allow that some excavated dark earth deposits represent redeposited dark earth, or associated occupation debris, rather than material that has formed *in situ*.[46]

The possibility that the dark earth represents structural activity is reinforced by the discovery of stake-holes, as if for parts of buildings, in the latest pre-dark earth deposits at several sites. These might be taken as evidence of structures within the dark earth, and at least one set of such features is literally within this deposit – cut into and covered by dark earth. This suggests that they cannot, if taken together, be dismissed as earlier features covered by this deposit by chance, and the existence of these features casts serious doubt on the 'rubbish tip' interpretation.

If the dark earth deposits represent buildings, then this may explain the tip-lines as resulting from the collapse and redeposition of earth-built structures. This view is supported by the usual lack of dark earth inside buildings and why, at some sites, the deposit ends to leave a street visible.

Finally there is some important evidence to bring into the discussion from outside the urban landscape: the discovery of dark earth at rural and military sites, as at Hayes Farm in Devon and at Pevensey.[47] The rural context of Hayes Farm makes the dark earth at that site unlikely to represent garden soil, while Pevensey Castle was plainly not disused while this deposit formed. There are also some types of site where dark earth never occurs, despite post-Roman disuse. For example, it is absent from all Romano-British temple sites, suggesting that simple disuse of Romano-British stone buildings did not cause it to form. At other towns, as at Wroxeter, periods of well-attested late Roman disuse are not associated with any dark earth. Nor is dark earth exclusively found in Britain or in Roman-period contexts, as it occurs, for example, in a Viking Age town at Birka in Sweden. So, a unique set of late Roman circumstances cannot be used to explain it.

Consequently, the most convincing view of dark earth may be that it represents dense occupation rather than disuse. As we shall see, this may have occurred in towns that show increased evidence of labour-intensive manufacturing, so high densities of low-status population might be anticipated on other grounds. At rural settlements, such as Hayes Farm, the deposit may represent the spread of an urban building style to a rural context. The occurrence of the dark earth at forts, as at Pevensey, is also easily explained in terms of intensive occupation.[48]

SOCIAL AND ECONOMIC ASPECTS OF THE URBAN LANDSCAPE

The towns at the centre of urban landscapes must lie at the heart of its explanation in social and economic terms. Many aspects of the urban landscape of large towns are unrelated or, more accurately perhaps, peripherally related to the agricultural communities of their surrounding countryside. Among these aspects can be included facilities for mass entertainment, water supply, burial and the accommodation of townsfolk who did not want, or were unable, to live within the walls. In small towns there is much more evidence of a close relationship between the town and the surrounding rural community.

Both types of town were dependent for their existence on the maintenance of the urban population and on their continuing needs for the specific services represented. So, extramural areas were not so much a part of the countryside, in social or economic terms, as part of the town. This relationship was reinforced by the physical similarities between extramural areas and intramural areas which have already been mentioned.

This, of course, begs the question of the form of that social and economic landscape. In the case

Reconstruction of a large Romano-British town. (Painting of Canterbury c. AD 300, by Ivan Lapper, on display in Canterbury Heritage Museum ©)

of most towns, the surrounding countryside was part of the villa landscape, so it is not surprising that villa-like buildings were constructed in towns, as at Silchester and Cirencester. In large towns, at least, these buildings were probably not, however, performing the same economic function as they did in the rural landscape. They are, perhaps, best compared to the many well-appointed 'town houses' (of ultimately Mediterranean plan) that occur at the same sites.[49] Like villas, these buildings might have had baths, courtyards, corridors, sculptured architectural elements, mosaics and painted wall-plaster.[50] Walthew has argued that there are many similarities between the more elaborate Romano-British town houses and villas, supporting the interpretation of a social, economic or cultural relationship between their owners.[51] Of course, one way in which this could have happened is for élites to have had both town and country houses.

Textual evidence also suggests that in Britain, as elsewhere in the Empire, the rural élite was tied into the network of towns by strong social and economic links, which were formalized by participation in the town council (*curia*) and by the erection of monuments symbolizing élite patronage of the arts and of local communities.[52] In Britain, direct evidence exists for most of these aspects of urban life. Inscriptions and other textual sources make it clear that the Roman imperial system of tribal *civitates* was established in the province from the first century onward.[53] All *civitates* had their own capitals (like modern British counties have 'county towns'), and the locations of the British *civitas* capitals are known: all are what we would describe as 'large towns'.

The physical setting of this system of local government was the provision of the forum-basilica complex already mentioned, enabling meetings to be held to conduct administration and to dispense justice.[54] The forum was able to accommodate the meetings of the *curia* in a specially designed council chamber and held offices for local government workers. Here, too, may have been the offices of legal firms, conveniently located to advise and represent local people on Roman law, and perhaps of scribes to assist in drafting legal and other documents.[55] The forum 'square' probably functioned as a market area. In Britain such areas have been shown on excavation to have heavily worn, patched or replaced paving. Direct evidence for a possible *curia* chamber has been identified at Caerwent, located in one of the rooms around the forum and apparently furnished with benches and a rostrum.[56]

Direct textual evidence detailing the functioning of local government in Roman Britain is lacking, but there is one piece from fifth-century Britain that probably preserves information about this subject.[57] In describing his childhood, St Patrick (who grew up in Britain) recalled that his father had served on the *curia* of a neighbouring town, although they had lived in what he called a *villula* (a 'little villa') in the hinterland of another smaller centre, probably what we would call a small town. This sounds very much like the relationship between villas, small towns, and large towns described above, and, if so, hints at the possible relationship between the rural élite and the *curiae* of the large towns, even at the very end of the Roman period.

It would be a mistake, however, to suppose that rural and urban societies were indistinguishable. Some towns probably contained élites unconnected with the countryside. These may have included officials of provincial and local government, religious leaders, intellectuals, those educated into professions (such as the law and medicine), and wealthy artisans and traders. Such people could easily be represented in the archaeological record of towns by elaborate town houses and high-status burials. Although inscriptions and textual sources make it clear that these groups existed in Britain,[58] it is unclear how they were distributed throughout the province or how, in detail, they relate to the known archaeology of urban sites. Although one might associate them with larger urban centres, some of the more developed small towns, such as

Water Newton and Ilchester, might have provided a range of professional and religious services to their surrounding communities and could have contained such groups.[59]

On these grounds, then, it is possible to envisage an urban élite that was partially different from that of the countryside. It is also possible to see large towns as much more socially differentiated communities, if only due to the increased range of opportunities for the acquisition of wealth.[60] Of these, trade and crafts-activity are at the fore in the archaeological record. The evidence for trade in most of the large towns of Roman Britain is impressive. It is clear that some large towns, such as York and London, were important nodes in the early Roman trading system across the Empire.[61] Trade probably also ensured that such towns remained the most cosmopolitan civilian communities in Roman Britain.[62]

While it has been argued by Dixon and Reece that all Romano-British towns were little more than élite settlements with appended servants' quarters, this overstates the case for the élite domination of even early Romano-British towns.[63] Many of the known structures are élite in character, but many are not, and economic functions out of character for a romanized élite are widely evidenced, as in St Albans and London.[64] So there is no doubt that towns, especially large ones, contained élite populations, but to describe them as élite settlements is perhaps misleading.

Overall, the commercial and service aspects of early Roman towns required that they contained substantial non-élite populations. This is true of both large and small towns, which encompass some similar buildings, although the grander end of the scale of urban architecture is principally found in Britain in large towns.[65] The 'strip-houses' and lesser town houses of the *civitas* capitals and small towns alike are usually seen as residences of the non-élite population.[66] Although, as Wacher has pointed out, it must be remembered that by no means all commercial and low-status activities took place in connection with such structures,[67] many of these buildings may have been shops, and there is no reason why people could not have been living 'over the shop' in the upper storeys of such buildings. In small towns the provision of shops seems consistent with the view that these were local market centres, also providing opportunities for local rural populations to purchase manufactured and other 'traded' items, and to gain access to services unavailable in the countryside. In large towns, both rural and urban populations could have provided customers to maintain a variety of commercial activities.

Consequently, social and economic factors worked together to make large towns focal places in the Romano-British landscape and maintain them as centres of population, and of social, cultural and economic diversity.[68] The economic opportunities of these towns, and perhaps the attractions of large population concentrations and services unavailable in the countryside, promoted their rapid establishment as major centres for social and economic activities.[69]

It may be that there were other attractions to large towns for the rural poor, including greater personal freedom, a more varied, sophisticated or cosmopolitan atmosphere, and an ability to enter more fully into romanized culture than was possible in a rural setting. Whether or not these people were aware of the health hazards of living in such population concentrations, with the local germ-pool swelled by new strains brought by ship, is unclear. Although Romano-British towns seem to have been cleaner than their medieval successors, there are the first records from Britain of several urban environmental problems. These include the presence of black rats, the carrier of bubonic plague, in York and London,[70] and cases of tuberculosis discovered in human skeletal remains from Ashton in Northamptonshire and Dorchester in Dorset.[71] The towns of Roman Britain may not have been healthy places, a feature that the increasing use of mud- or turf-built low-status dwellings in the late Roman period may have aggravated. These problems may have had their own consequences for the landscape: if death rates were higher in towns than in the countryside, yet towns were perceived as attractive residential locations, then a constant influx of population may have offset increased mortality rates.

Both large and small towns can be seen as taking in human and material resources, providing services and producing wealth. Some of this wealth could have diffused, through kinship linkages and the return of temporary workers, to the countryside, promoting rural wealth. Urbanism might, therefore, have acted as a stimulus to general economic growth, but not only because of its trading aspects. Towns did not merely generate wealth; they also dispersed it more widely among social groups. In the course of urban-based contacts, romanization may also have spread among the British population, again promoting rural change.

Large towns may also have directly controlled their rural hinterlands. Although no direct evidence demonstrates that British towns had urban-administered hinterland zones (*territoria*) extending around them, most scholars have agreed that these probably existed.[72] If this is so, whatever regulations or restrictions existed within the *territoria* plainly did not exclude farming and farms, which are found right up to the walls of Romano-British towns. Likewise, different regulations seem to have governed the areas within the walls compared with the *territorium*. For example, there is the well-known Roman legal prohibition of adult burial inside town walls.[73]

It seems unlikely that all aspects of such arguments can be applied to small towns: that at Shepton Mallet had two cemeteries within it.[74] Although some of these towns, as at Ilchester and Kenchester,[75] did have walls, there is no evidence to support the interpretation that small towns had *territoria*, and the different relationships between these sites and their hinterland may suggest that they had a different form of legal and administrative relationship with it.[76] In administrative terms their role may be more easily seen in relation to the *pagi* (or civil parish-level divisions) of the Empire, which lay beneath those of the *civitates*, than to the *civitates* themselves.[77] The uneven distribution of small towns precludes the view that each *pagus* had a small town as its administrative core, replicating the large town:*civitas* relationship already discussed. Small towns seem, therefore, much more a response to local requirements, especially local social and economic needs, and religious practices, than to the structures of provincial or imperial government.[78]

There is, however, evidence to suggest that small and large towns were closely interlinked.[79] Both types of settlement relate to, and were vehicles for, economic activities and romanization in their localities, and both were probably a market-place for, and consumers of, rural agricultural products. So, it seems that these were complementary, not conflicting, forms of urbanism, and parts of the same social and economic system. A key aspect of this system was mass-production, and a consequence of mass-production was the industrial landscape.

THE INDUSTRIAL LANDSCAPE

The industrial landscape of Roman Britain is distinguished by including any of several distinctive features: tips of waste from mass-production (such as large slag tips), workshops for large-scale production processes, large quarries or groups of mine shafts, and a communications network (roads, rivers or ports) serving the needs of mass-production and regional or imperial distribution.[80] Obviously, such landscapes occurred where the industries that formed them were located, and different activities involved in specific industries resulted in differences in the exact shape that these landscapes took in any locality. Although other large-scale industries may have produced industrial landscapes, pottery-making and iron-working will be taken here as examples, being the most extensively studied.

POTTERY PRODUCTION

The manufacture of pottery by specialist potters for local communities was established before the Roman Conquest,[81] but the scale of this changed as a result of the incorporation of Britain into the Empire. In the early Roman period, pottery was both imported in large quantities, especially from Gaul, and manufactured in Britain.[82] The imports were widely used – samian ware is one of the most common finds on British archaeological sites – but local products, such as Severn Valley ware, also supplied a large domestic market, both military and civilian.[83] This domestic market led to the establishment of many local Romano-British potteries, as in south-east Wales, Kent and the East Midlands.[84] Most of these early Roman pottery types continued (in romanized form) pre-Roman ceramic traditions, as in the case of black-burnished ware type 1 (BB1).[85]

British suppliers could also obtain distant markets, especially through the supply of the Roman army,[86] and the military also organized their own production and supply of pottery and other materials.[87] These changes in the scale of production and the marketing of products beyond the locality were, therefore, significant impacts of the inclusion of Britain into the Roman Empire.[88] These impacts are most visible in terms of artefacts, however, and have left only slight traces in the landscape. These include an increased number of kilns and a new longevity in their use, alongside new potting sites. The establishment of large kiln complexes, with a major impact on local landscapes, is a feature of the late Roman period in Britain, rather than earlier.[89]

In late Roman Britain, as the work of Fulford, Swan and others has demonstrated, the scale of production of the British kilns increased dramatically.[90] A few of these large suppliers managed to obtain a major share of the British market, as was the case for Oxfordshire ware, New Forest ware and Crambeck ware.[91] British products were now the mainstay of ceramic use in Britain, and the amount of imported ceramics decreased proportionally, to become only a minor part of late Roman pottery assemblages found in excavation.[92]

This increased scale of production was also associated with the concentration of production in fewer and larger clusters of kilns.[93] These comprised local groups of kilns, operated from many juxtaposed sites, which produced a very similar range of products, as in the New Forest and Oxfordshire.[94] These similarities enable the analysis of each group of kilns as a separate production centre, but how production was organized is a matter of debate.

These large clusters of kilns could result in local landscapes that were primarily given over to mass-production. For example, the Alice Holt kilns gave rise to a local topography of large mounds of waste material resulting from potting.[95] Such dumps could spread out for hundreds of metres around the kiln sites, growing in extent as potting progressed.

The kiln sites formed groups of functionally related, and to some extent similar, sites in the local landscape. These might be served by roads and connected with dwellings and storage spaces. So, the surroundings of these sites differed from those of the rest of the villa landscape in which they were set, and occupied large areas of ground.

When such industrial areas were closely spaced in the landscape so as to form distinctive zones, these can be called 'industrial landscapes'. These landscapes were common in late Roman

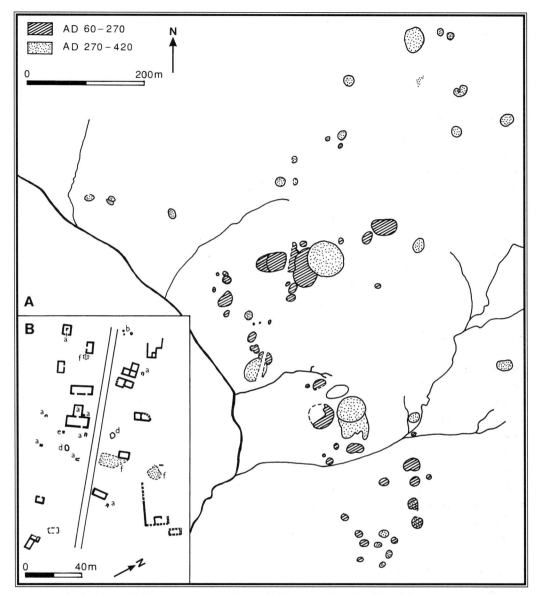

Pottery production sites and effects on their surroundings. A: The waste tips of the Alice Holt pottery production site in Hampshire (based on Lyne and Jefferies 1979). As an inset (B), another pottery production site (extensively excavated in the nineteenth century) at Normangate Field, Castor: a - ovens, b - grinding stones, d - prepared clay, e - well, f - paved areas. (Based on Artis 1828, reproduced in Swan 1984)

Britain, being produced by each of the major pottery producers: Oxfordshire ware, Nene Valley ware, black-burnished ware, New Forest ware, and probably Crambeck ware.[96]

The most vivid illustration of this comes from the hinterland of the small town at Water Newton, at the heart of the Nene Valley ware pottery industry.[97] Water Newton was plainly a wealthy late Roman town, probably with aspirations to large town status. Immediately to its west

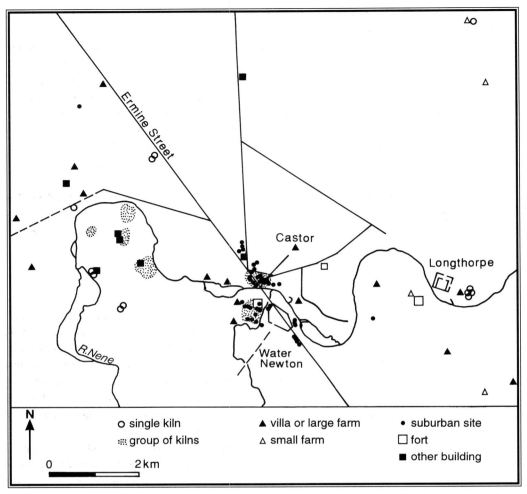

Pottery production and other activities in the hinterland of the small town at Water Newton (based on B. Jones and Mattingly 1990)

was a remarkable landscape of kilns and related buildings associated with the production of Nene Valley ware. The lack of excavation in their environs has prevented the discovery of extensive dumps of waste material, but these must surely have existed here, as at other kiln sites. This complex was only the heart of a wider area with many kilns stretching more than 4 kilometres from the town. The total area encompassed by these kilns, as recently mapped by Jones and Mattingly, is greater than that of the town itself.[98]

To the north of Water Newton, a Roman road departed from the main pattern of routes (linking towns) to serve a single, palatial villa terraced into the hillside and commanding wide views.[99] This was in the parish of Castor, after which Nene Valley ware used to be called 'Castor ware' by archaeologists. Some scholars have likened this villa to a modern stately home,[100] but perhaps the most pertinent analogy is with the grandiose dwellings of eighteenth- and early nineteenth-century industrialists. Unless the complex was built for official administrators, for which there is no other evidence, then the most likely source of exceptional status/wealth in this area is likely to have been pottery production.

It might be expected that pottery production would also have produced significant landscape change by causing a reduction in the extent of woodland due to fuel requirements. Whether or not this occurred could be assessed from pollen sequences in areas of pottery production, but only one such sequence is available. This is from Sidlings Copse, in the centre of the production area of Oxfordshire ware and close to the pottery-producing villa at Headington Wick.[101] This shows that woodland was already sparse in the Roman period, although willows may have been planted locally as a fuel supply. As discussed in chapter 2, woodland was probably scarce in many parts of the villa landscape in the Roman period, and it was conserved by management practices, such as coppicing.

There were, of course, much smaller-scale pottery producers catering for the local market throughout the Roman period, and not all pottery production – even in late Roman Britain – can be seen in terms of mass-production.[102] Nor were potteries the only type of mass-production to have had a significant impact on the landscape.

IRON-WORKING

Whereas potteries probably only produced industrial landscapes in the late Roman period, early Roman Britain was not without landscapes of this sort. Iron-working gives an example of this, and the development of large-scale iron production was a major economic and technological change of the Roman period. This did not affect every site or area equally, and in the native landscape the pre-Roman pattern of domestic iron-working seems to have been maintained during and beyond the Roman period. In the villa landscape, and in the towns of Roman Britain, a large new market existed for iron. This was expanded by the requirements of the Roman army, with its iron spearheads, sword blades, tools and so on.

To meet this demand, iron works were established in the early Roman period in several parts of Britain where ores were available.[103] These included the Weald and the Forest of Dean. These iron producers were similarly spaced in the landscape to the pottery-producing sites, although they were established at an earlier date.[104] Like potteries, although such iron-producing sites comprised many physically separate foci, we must not underestimate the scale of activity involved.

In the Weald, Roman-period iron-working furnaces outnumber those of all later periods until the Industrial Revolution.[105] The size of the Roman furnaces, where excavated, has also been shown often to have been larger than those of the later Middle Ages, with which they are juxtaposed in the modern landscape. It must be remembered that the later medieval furnaces were part of an industry that supplied medieval England with a major part of its iron: even in the sixteenth century there were still fewer and smaller furnaces in the Weald than in the Roman period.[106]

Although the scale of Roman-period iron-working in the Weald compares favourably with that of the Middle Ages, this was not the largest concentration of Roman-period iron works. Two other areas had very large clusters of such works: the Forest of Dean and the East Midlands.[107] The former was clearly the larger of these two production areas, but the details of this activity are less clearly understood than its counterpart in the Midlands. An indication of the scale of production in the Forest of Dean, and of its potential environmental impact, can be gained from early research. This identified Romano-British slag tips extending over some 120

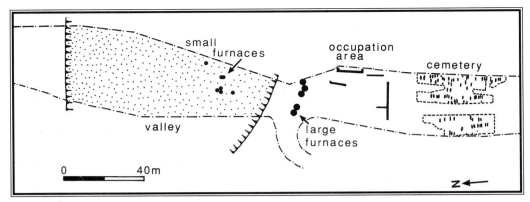

A Romano-British iron-working site at Laxton, Northamptonshire. Slag and waste from the furnaces was deposited in the valley (stippled). (Based on Jackson and Tylecote 1988)

hectares, so large an area that mining them for the remaining ore became an industrial operation itself in the Industrial Revolution.[108]

The Northamptonshire sites could also have had major impacts on their local environment. At Laxton the iron works consisted of a cluster of furnaces and the scale of their production is again attested to by the size of the waste tips that they produced.[109] A poorly defined area of iron waste extends over 400 metres around the furnaces, with slag tips extending for 450 metres, but more striking is the fact that a 100-metre wide river valley adjacent to the furnaces was filled with iron slag.

Furnaces were accompanied by attendant buildings, often, it seems (as at Beauport Park and Garden Hill), including bath houses – presumably for the employees. They could be associated with villas, as we have seen was the case for some pottery-producing sites.[110] Furnaces formed, therefore, similarly distinctive local landscapes to the pottery-production areas, and, like them, these can be termed 'industrial landscapes'. Unfortunately, it is not possible to use pollen analysis to assess the impact of the major iron industries on woodland resources, since there are no detailed pollen sequences available from such areas.

It must, of course, be remembered that there were other industries in the landscape, such as tile and brick production, stone quarrying and lead smelting, which had major impacts on their environments.[111] However, many Romano-British industries did not result in industrial landscapes at all, due either to their character or to the scale of activity, such as pewter production.[112] Others only produced such landscapes on rare occasions, when local circumstances permitted unusually large-scale activity, as in Essex (where salting produced an industrial landscape of waste tips – the Red Hills – along the coast) and at Droitwich, where salting supported an industrial small town, with an associated villa adjacent to it.[113]

LESSER FEATURES OF THE INDUSTRIAL LANDSCAPE

The principal types of subsidiary features associated with this landscape were those connected with the management of water: water-mills and aqueducts. There are few certainly industrial instances of aqueducts in Britain, and that at Dolaucothi seems to be the best documented. This was associated with Roman gold mining, but the complexity of the evidence at Dolaucothi, where medieval and other features complicate understanding of the Roman activity at the site, makes it less instructive than might be hoped.[114]

There is much evidence that water-mills were widely used in the Romano-British countryside, both in military and civilian contexts, and both in the villa and native landscapes.[115] The use of water-mills in industrial production in Roman Britain is, as yet, uncertain, however, although a trip-hammer connected to a water-mill is known from Kent.[116]

A much more problematical area is the way in which products were transported. Plainly, the siting of bulk producers, such as the Nene Valley potteries, by rivers may imply that water transport played a role in this, but the extent is unclear.[117] Work by Fulford and Hodder,[118] much of it in the 1970s, suggested that marketing patterns could be reconstructed from pottery distributions in relation to towns, roads and waterways. Recent work in Roman economic history[119] has made it clear that water and road transport costs in Roman Britain were probably analogous to those of eighteenth-century England.[120] So, either form of transport might have been employed, but water was probably favoured for bulk transport. Recent work has also shown that large sea-going vessels were common in the Roman world, and regular long-distance maritime transport was commonplace.[121]

This coincides well with evidence for the supply of northern garrisons by water along the west coast, bringing BB1 from Dorset to, for instance, Hadrian's Wall.[122] It suggests that the rivers and natural harbours of Roman Britain formed important routes whereby products were delivered to retailers and customers from large-scale producers, whether under civilian or military control. Presumably this also implies either that large producers had their own ships, capable of long sea journeys, or that a flourishing shipping business existed.

This is complicated, however, by the military organization of army supplies. The Roman army (and navy) manufactured their own pottery and operated other state-owned production to fulfil their logistic requirements when these could not be catered for by local producers.[123] Thus, it is possible that some military supplies were from unusually distant, but unusually well-organized, producers with privileged access to transport, and even rights to unhindered transit along the road network. The part played by water transport in supplying the Roman army in the north has been a source of recent controversy, and although this has been effectively resolved, it has prompted renewed interest in the role of water transport in Roman Britain.[124]

It has been suggested that both the Roman army and Romano-British civilian producers employed canals for shipping large quantities of bulk materials.[125] There is, however, no convincing evidence for the construction of Roman canals in Britain. In this context it is important to recall that the long-established interpretation of the Car Dyke (a Roman-period artificial waterway) as a canal is no longer tenable. As Simmons has made clear, this view is undermined by the existence of causeways taking Roman roads across the Car Dyke.[126] Excavation of these, as at Dowsby, has shown that it was not a continuous waterway capable of use for long-distance shipping, and the reconstructable system of artificial channels in the Fens closely resembles those known from medieval and later drainage schemes. This would have facilitated agriculture, taking advantage of fertile silts around the Fen-edge, and assisted salting.

SOCIAL AND ECONOMIC INTERPRETATION OF THE INDUSTRIAL LANDSCAPE

There are two main interpretations of the economic and social context of the industrial landscape. The first, and most usually employed, explanation is that (excepting a few cases where military supply was the purpose) all industrial production was a minor aspect of an essentially agricultural economy.[127] In this interpretation, Romano-British industry was no more than the 'off-season' activity of farmers, who produced pottery and other manufactured items to offset low points in the agricultural year. There is a small amount of evidence to support this view, and some industrial production was probably organized in this fashion, such as quern production at Lodsworth.[128] There are also structures of uncertain function, and corn-driers, at a few pottery-production sites.

While small-scale production may have been widespread within the context of single farms or of local communities,[129] it was not necessarily the only way in which production was organized in Roman Britain. The alternative 'proto-industrial' interpretation of Romano-British industry is that there was a greater degree of industrialization, with some communities earning their living primarily through mass production, catering for regional markets. A proto-industrial economy is not fully industrialized, but nor is industry simply a seasonal sideline in all cases. There are two key pieces of evidence to support a proto-industrial interpretation. First, calculations of production time (based on experimental and anthropological data) suggest that it is impossible for all known Romano-British pottery – even that of any single type of the major late Roman finewares – to have been produced by part-time work, unless a very large workforce was involved.[130] Second, the number and scale of Romano-British mass-production sites in several industries exceeded those of similar late medieval industries, located in the same or similar areas, which textual evidence shows were organized on a proto-industrial scale. This view is also supported by the lack of direct evidence for seasonality (which has been archaeologically detected elsewhere) at Romano-British industrial sites. The existence of small towns apparently supported by large-scale production, as at Charterhouse, is another strong piece of evidence against the interpretation that all Romano-British industry was a seasonal activity undertaken by farmers.[131]

If one adopts a proto-industrial view of Romano-British industry, these aspects of the industrial landscape are more easily interpreted. Mass-production throughout the year, and the year-round exploitation of raw materials on a large scale, must have involved large groups of employees, because these were labour-intensive activities in a pre-mechanized period. Such a workforce could have formed the basis for small towns linked to industry, while elsewhere a more dispersed form of production was possible, or had been chosen, depending on the products involved. Pottery, glass, salt and worked-shale products could be produced at many small juxtaposed locations, but large-scale iron-working and mining required populations to be concentrated in larger communities. This is not to say that pottery-making or other activities could not produce the wealth to maintain such communities, as may have been the case at Water Newton and Droitwich, nor that manufacturers of other commodities might not have taken advantage of the existence of an 'industrial small town' to provide their own workforce. Likewise, diversification by producers could also have produced communities where industrial production generally, rather than a specific industry, was the means of support. So, it is unsurprising to find evidence of small towns with diversified large-scale production as their means of support, as seems to be the case at Wilderspool.[132]

It must be stressed that this interpretation does not imply that industry, however diversified, was the only basis for the economy of any of these towns, or that most Romano-British 'industries' were organized on such a large scale. Merely it suggests that year-round large-scale production was an important part of the economic support of some urban communities. In other towns, where industry was probably only a minor part of their late Roman economy, what may be large-scale production centres are also found that date to the fourth century. The late Roman refurbishment of disused basilicas as industrial workshops, as at Silchester and Caerwent, and the similar re-use of the legionary headquarters (*principia*) at York, may be explained in this way.[133] Large-scale urban-based production may have to be set alongside much smaller-scale production (and craftwork, such as jewellery making) in the towns[134] and rural industries, ranging in size from mass-producers to local occasional production sites, not necessarily involving any structures at all.[135]

Ownership in this landscape is also hard to assess. It is usually assumed that each kiln site represents a different workshop and owner, but the emergence of villas at industrial sites (as at Droitwich and Ashtead) hints at single ownership of several sites, or possibly even of entire industries.[136] The villa adjacent to, and on the same hilltop as, the Romano-British quarry at Ham Hill may also be an example of this. If so, it shows that even the large-scale extraction of raw materials might have proved very profitable.[137] In this case the market may also be visible, as Ham stone was used for construction in many neighbouring Romano-British villas.

If juxtaposed, but physically separate, kiln sites were collectively owned, this would explain the degree of standardization found in the forms and decoration of pottery made by large-scale producers. It would also explain the lack of wealth apparent at the majority of excavated potteries in comparison to farms in the surrounding countryside, and may be supported by comparison with textually attested industries elsewhere in the Empire.[138] The implication of the emergence of villas in conjunction with industries is that a single individual or kin-group was benefiting disproportionately from the fruits of the labour of others. This may imply both a ranked structure of production and the employment of craft-workers by a (non-producing?) owner. That such owners may have displayed wealth and social rank in the form of a villa may suggest the assertion of social superiority as well as economic control.

The leading civilian customers for manufactured goods of this type, such as fine pottery, are to be found among the inhabitants of the villa landscape and towns. There, British-made mass-produced products are common, even in low-status urban settings. This level of production was, therefore, for the mass-market, not only the élite or the army, although the army could both use such products and, as we have seen, organize its own large-scale supply.[139]

It must, however, be recalled that, throughout the Roman period, production on this scale co-existed with much smaller-scale, and more localized, manufacturing. This could have involved farmers, and may have had seasonal aspects, but it did not result in an 'industrial landscape'.

THE ORIGINS OF THE INDUSTRIAL AND URBAN LANDSCAPES

The origins of these two types of landscape can be considered together, and were probably closely related. Both industrial and urban landscapes came into existence with the Roman Conquest and its consolidation, and nothing resembling them preceded this.[140] Both were established within the first century of Roman rule: examples of each have been identified in Britain before AD 100, for instance at Colchester and Holt.[141] By the end of the second century, all parts of Roman Britain, excepting the north-west of Wales and, perhaps, western areas of the *civitas* of the Dumnonii, had these types of landscapes. From the third century onwards, industrial landscapes may have been present from Cornwall (where there were, at present only poorly understood, tin mines) to Kent, and from southern Dorset to the quarries of Hadrian's Wall.

There is evidence suggesting Iron Age production at some, but not all, Romano-British 'industrial' sites.[142] The urban landscape also often developed from the urbanization of late Iron

Age political centres (*oppida* and probable royal residences), among them Silchester, Winchester, Colchester and St Albans.[143] Probably not all – or even all important – Romano-British towns (including the three largest: London, Cirencester and Wroxeter) originated in this way.[144] Some towns, as at Wroxeter, and at least some of the industries established in the Roman period, as at Holt, almost certainly resulted from Roman military occupation.[145] The origins of London, which eventually became the capital of Roman Britain, are currently uncertain but may lie in either military activities or civilian trade, possibly a combination of both.[146] Thus, some Romano-British towns and industrial sites had Iron Age predecessors but others did not.

Small towns also seem to have originated due to both civilian and military reasons,[147] some beginning as military *vici*, others for official administrative purposes at Iron Age centres (probably without intervening Roman military use), and others probably due to industrial specialization, as we have already seen. Although, like large towns, some of those with civilian origins seem to have developed from Iron Age secular sites, Iron Age religious centres also preceded several Romano-British small towns. This led to sites that may be classified either as 'small towns' or as 'temple settlements', as at Springhead, Nettleton, and even Bath,[148] although there are some small towns that seem predominantly secular in the Romano-British period yet were located at Iron Age religious sites, as at Heybridge.[149]

In the case of large towns, the location of major foci of Roman imperial administration at important Iron Age centres after the Conquest may have been partly for reasons of propaganda and as a legitimation of imperial rule. The extent to which local people took part in, or became fully assimilated into, romanized urban life in Britain has been a matter of some debate, often closely connected with the discussion of the origins, or the end, of towns.[150] However, it seems difficult to argue against the view that large towns played a major role in administration and commerce, and the case that they were population concentrations seems somewhat stronger than has sometimes been claimed.

As for industrial sites, pre-Roman production centres may have hinted at economic opportunities for Roman-period civilian entrepreneurs and business people. Alternatively, local manufacturers may have taken advantage of larger, more accessible or more profitable markets after the Conquest. Investment by the Roman army, as we have seen, almost certainly promoted growth in some such centres, and led to the establishment of new industries and production centres.

Consequently, urban and industrial growth both coincided with, and originated from, similar factors, at least to some extent, although large industries were often rurally located. Urbanization and the impact of large-scale industries on their surroundings may be among the most important landscape consequences of the Roman Conquest.

CHAPTER 7

THE END OF THE ROMANO-BRITISH LANDSCAPE

The whole of the Romano-British landscape did not 'end' simultaneously. Different landscape components outlasted the end of Roman Britain to different extents and, as this varied regionally, the different landscape types that we have described came to an end at different times.

THE ANGLO-SAXON 'INVASION'

When the Roman Empire officially withdrew from Britain in the early fifth century, local ('sub-Roman') people formed their own independent kingdoms. In most of what had been the east of Roman Britain this period of independent sub-Roman rule was relatively short-lived, as a mixed group of Germanic barbarians (the Anglo-Saxons) migrated into this area from across the North Sea. Although the details are unclear, the Anglo-Saxons probably had complete political control of eastern England by c. AD 600, and their migration resulted in the occupation of many areas of what had been Roman Britain by people living in a style (and with a technology) similar to that of the pre-Roman Iron Age.

The Anglo-Saxon 'invasion' was probably not, however, the reason why Roman Britain came to an end: the Anglo-Saxons migrated from continental north-west Europe to eastern Britain in the wake of the imperial collapse, rather than before it.[1] When this occurred is unclear, as controversy surrounds the dating of the earliest Anglo-Saxon groups in Britain, and it is difficult to distinguish between migrants living within late Roman society and the earliest independent settlers. On archaeological grounds, however, it appears that people culturally connected with the Anglo-Saxons of the second half of the fifth century were probably arriving in Britain as early as the first decades of that century.[2] These seem mostly to have been men serving in the Roman army, where the use of barbarian irregular troops was common by the late fourth century.[3] These troops may also have been accompanied by women, as is evidenced by the discovery of characteristically Germanic jewellery at several late Roman sites, as at London and Dorchester-on-Thames.[4] Whether or not there is a direct relationship between such groups and the Anglo-Saxons who settled in eastern England later in the fifth century is, however, unclear, not least because it was these groups (among others) that such soldiers were in Britain to fight.

The situation is much clearer for the mid–late fifth century, however, as recent work by Böhme, Hines and Scull has shown.[5] There is extensive archaeological evidence, mostly from graves, that between AD 450 and 500 a large part of eastern England was settled by communities using 'Anglo-Saxon' (that is, Germanic) artefacts and practising Germanic styles of burial. So we can say on much firmer grounds that the Anglo-Saxon period probably began in the quarter century 450–475, even if some 'Anglo-Saxons' were to be found in earlier fifth-century Britain.

The result of this political and cultural transformation was that part of the Romano-British landscape passed under Germanic occupation, whereas part remained under the control of 'Britons' whose culture and society derived from that of the Romano-British past.[6] It is central to understanding the end of the Romano-British landscape to recognize this fundamental division.

The division of late Roman Britain into five Roman provinces is also important in providing a framework that can be used to understand these changes.[7] Using the fourth-century provincial structure of Britain, the Anglo-Saxon political takeover was (prior to *c.* AD 500) an event that occurred principally in only one of the five provinces. In this province, *Flavia Caesariensis* (the East Midlands), the cessation of activity at Romano-British settlements may have taken place in the fifth century, although even this is in doubt, but in many other areas this did not occur until much later.[8]

In two, or perhaps three, of the areas of Britain that had been other late Roman provinces there were up to some 150 years of independent ('Dark Age') Britain, before the Anglo-Saxons permanently became the dominant political, military, cultural and economic group.[9] It is in the context of two post-Roman political and cultural regions – one 'British' (that is, sub-Roman), one Anglo-Saxon – that the end of the Romano-British landscape must be placed.

THE END OF THE VILLA LANDSCAPE

There is no convincing evidence that villas in those areas that passed initially into Anglo-Saxon control were occupied after the mid-fifth century, although villa sites were re-used for settlements in the sixth century and later.[10] Many villas, however, show evidence of so-called 'squatter occupation' of immediately post-Roman date.[11] This is an outmoded term for the refurbishment of villas using lower technology than that used to build them, such as patching mosaics with stone slabs and propping-up roofs with posts cut through mosaic, tessellated, or cement floors. This squatter occupation shows a remarkable consistency from site to site, as if part of a common architectural style.[12] There is also a similarity in the dating of these changes. Where villas lasted until *c.* AD 400 (and not all did), they seem to exhibit such changes at a date following the latest datable Roman artefacts. This date is conventionally placed in the early fifth century, but (given the available evidence) may be later in that century.[13]

In the Anglo-Saxon east of Britain, small farming settlements of Anglo-Saxon rectilinear timber buildings were founded at (or near) villas, as at Barton Court Farm,[14] but there is no strong evidence of occupational continuity between the villas and the Anglo-Saxon settlements on any of these sites. Although the Anglo-Saxon settlements at villas may also have been farms, no certain links are visible in terms of construction techniques, cultural background, artefact types, or technological developments between them and the villas that had occupied the same sites. These farms are unlikely to have been those of an Anglo-Saxon élite equivalent to villa owners, and there is some doubt as to whether any such group was present in early Anglo-Saxon society.[15] So, it seems implausible that these settlements represent a transformation of villas into Anglo-Saxon farms, as is occasionally argued.[16]

While James, Marshall and Millett have pointed to similarities between early Anglo-Saxon architecture in general and Romano-British rural buildings,[17] and these have been stressed more strongly by P.W. Dixon and P.H. Dixon,[18] this cannot provide a specific connection between villas and Anglo-Saxon farms, rather than a general connection between Anglo-Saxon and Romano-British architecture. This may be explained by the employment of forced labour to construct Anglo-Saxon buildings, or by the fusion of rural Romano-British and Anglo-Saxon populations through intermarriage or peaceful co-existence. If Britons constructed Anglo-Saxon settlements, those involved are more likely to have been from lower-status British groups than the villa-dwelling élite.

The general lack of evidence of violent destruction at Romano-British rural settlements, and the textually-attested British refugee population overseas from the fifth century onward, may suggest that the inhabitants often fled prior to the arrival of the new landowners. The majority of villas probably did not, however, survive as British farms into the mid-fifth century. Most were abandoned, perhaps as a result of social upheavals, in the early fifth century and a large minority of fourth-century villa sites had already fallen into disuse prior to AD 400.[19]

There are a few exceptions to this general pattern of fifth-century discontinuity at villas. In the area around London and St Albans a few villa sites (as at Latimer) show evidence of timber buildings, possibly belonging to the later fifth or sixth century.[20] Their distribution is of special interest as it is in this area (alone in what is today eastern England) that there may have been an independent British kingdom in the fifth and sixth centuries, analogous to those which existed in the west and north of Britain at this time.

In west (especially south-west) Britain, where part of what had been the villa landscape was under British control, a few sites have evidence that seems to suggest use in the later fifth or sixth century, but it is unclear how we should interpret this.[21] The correlation between seventh-century churches and monasteries and some of the villas of this area has suggested to Pearce that they represent a sequence well known from fifth- and sixth-century Gaul.[22] There, as Percival and others have shown, villa owners entering monastic life would sometimes turn their villas into monasteries.[23] That this sequence may hold true for at least some sites in south-western Britain is suggested by fragmentary evidence from several sites, including Banwell and Frocester. This sequence is, however, most clearly evidenced in south Wales, where equivalent hints have long been known.[24] Recent work at Llandough shows that a large 'sub-Roman' cemetery developed at a villa site subsequently used for an eighth-century and later monastery, the medieval phase of which partly overlay the villa.[25]

The end of late Romano-British villas was, therefore, not a single event. It was a long process occupying a timespan from c. AD 350 to c. 500, and some sites probably continued in use as monasteries into the sixth century and later in the West Country and south-east Wales. The peaceful co-existence of Anglo-Saxons and Britons in eastern England is also suggested in the fifth and sixth century by several sources of evidence. Throughout eastern Britain there is a widespread scatter of slight evidence for continued occupation at Romano-British rural settlements in the fifth and sixth centuries, and some cemeteries established in the Roman period seem to continue into this period, as at Queensford Mill.[26]

Although the so-called 'Romano-Saxon' pottery once claimed to show the transition from Roman to Anglo-Saxon ceramics has proved illusory, there is a small amount of credible evidence for interaction between the producers of Romano-British and Anglo-Saxon pottery, and perhaps even of 'Romano-British' kilns functioning into the later fifth or sixth century.[27] Many Anglo-Saxons also seem to have acquired Romano-British objects that were treasured sufficiently to be placed in their graves, perhaps indicative of some affinity with the Romano-British past, or of contact with the remaining British population.[28]

All of this evidence suggests, rather than proves, that there was a considerable British population remaining in what had been the eastern part of the villa landscape in the fifth and sixth centuries, and that this population lived peacefully (and perhaps at first independently) alongside the Anglo-Saxons.[29] It is difficult to recognize sites belonging to this population due to two factors. First, Romano-British rural settlements are largely recognizable because it is possible to date them using coins and mass-produced objects. When new coins were no longer minted and mass-production ceased, similar sites, if they existed, would be very hard to date. Second, the difficulty in recognizing British sites of the fifth and sixth centuries in areas where the British retained political control might suggest caution when placing importance on their apparent absence in the Anglo-Saxon east,[30] although settlements of earlier periods are also more difficult to date in the west and north.

So, occupation may have continued at some, perhaps many, non-villa rural settlements in parts of the villa landscape within the Anglo-Saxon area of fifth- and sixth-century Britain, even if direct evidence for this is sparse. This need not have involved a continuation of Romano-British settlement forms or locations, however, and we should not assume that activity continued at all such sites. Patterns of site-abandonment and reorganization are indicated from the Roman period, and we can assume that sites were abandoned for various reasons during this period as well. As already mentioned, there were also Britons who themselves migrated at the end of the Roman period. There is strong textual evidence for a mass-migration from southern Britain to Brittany in the fifth and sixth centuries, and of migrations to other parts of what are today France, Spain and, possibly, Ireland.[31] The potential impacts of these population movements must be allowed for when discussing the end of the Romano-British landscape, but their scale and consequences are unclear: they could have resulted in widespread desertion, but we do not know where or when this occurred.

In western parts of the villa landscape, more continuity of non-villa rural settlement may be anticipated. Evidence for this is scattered and somewhat ambiguous, but may indicate widespread settlement continuity in areas under British control.[32] For example, organically-tempered pottery (sometimes called 'grass-tempered pottery') dating from the fifth and sixth centuries has been found at many rural non-villa Romano-British settlement sites in the West Country.[33]

Other components of the villa landscape show a similar variation in the dating of their final phases. Temples, for example, seem to have been completely out of use by the second decade of the fifth century, with the sites at Uley, Maiden Castle and Nettleton apparently demonstrating a sequence of initially drastic decline followed by replacement with what are probably Christian religious sites.[34] Other temples went into decline in the fourth century and had passed out of use by AD 400. Again, their sites were sometimes apparently used for Christian religious sites, as in Gaul, and this re-use may also be related to widespread social upheaval and attendant religious changes in the first decade of the fifth century.[35]

Unsurprisingly, therefore, pagan mausolea and walled cemeteries also ceased at this time, although a new, Christian, British élite may have employed small rectangular mausolea to commemorate its members.[36] These sites may attest, in archaeological terms, to a widespread religious change among the élite, also perhaps identifiable in textual sources.

These, along with monastic sites and probably increasing numbers of rural churches, led to the formation of a distinct sub-Roman landscape across Britain, which was to survive for centuries in the British-controlled west and north. In the Anglo-Saxon east this was partially swept away, still in the process of formation, although to what extent is as yet unclear. Most of western and northern Britain had never been part of the villa landscape, and this landscape shows a different pattern of change.

THE END OF THE NATIVE LANDSCAPE

The native landscape was left unaffected by the Anglo-Saxon settlement of eastern Britain in the fifth and sixth centuries. It was only in the seventh century that most of this area was taken over by Anglo-Saxons, and then only slowly. In this area, non-military secular settlements, as at Trethurgy in Cornwall and Ty Mawr in Wales, did not dramatically change form until at least the seventh century, when enclosed sites appear to have been abandoned in favour of unenclosed farms.[37] The farming systems supporting them also operated through the fifth and sixth centuries without disruption, as discussed below.

Consequently, large tracts of the native landscape did not transform radically with the end of Roman Britain, but changed only gradually. These changes seem to have been further hindered by the tendency to conservatism found throughout Roman Britain, which may have been most strongly expressed in the native landscape. Apart from the absence of Roman military sites, the landscape of much of the west of Britain in AD 500 probably differed only slightly from the same region in AD 400, although there are hints of increased productivity and wealth among low-status farms.[38] The exception to this rule may have been northern Britain, where evidence from pollen analysis, discussed later in this chapter, suggests that dependence on the military economy may have caused severe problems for the agricultural system when this ceased to operate.

The farms and hill-forts of much of the native landscape seem likely to have continued in use, much in their Roman form, into the fifth and sixth centuries, at least where these were not closely connected with the military. It is only the military sites (and the pagan shrines, which we see replaced by new Christian centres as the area was converted to Christianity in the fifth century), that show much evidence of change. Remarkably, no pagan shrine in western Britain shows evidence for activity after the early fifth century, like the temples of the villa landscape, suggesting widespread and similar religious change at this time.[39] This similarity is supported by the re-use of pagan religious sites in the native landscape, as probably at Capel Eithin, for Christian religious sites, and especially for cemeteries, in the sixth and seventh centuries.[40]

Like the villa landscape, the native landscape also shows other evidence of widespread religious change at, and immediately following, the end of Roman Britain. Monasteries and rural churches were founded in the sixth century, if not the later fifth, at sites such as St Kew in Cornwall, and Caldey Island in south-west Wales. Many early Christian cemeteries sprang up across the region, as at Cannington, Tintagel Church, Plas Gogerddan, and Bayvil.[41] These formed a new 'sub-Roman' landscape closely related to its Romano-British predecessor, but newly Christianized by the establishment of ecclesiastical centres and cemeteries. This landscape was established early enough to be 'exported' by British missionaries from Wales to Cornwall before the early sixth century, beyond Hadrian's Wall to Whithorn by the sixth century, and to Ireland in the later fifth and sixth centuries.[42] Change in the native landscape was not, however, restricted to this rapid emergence of Christian monasteries, churches and cemeteries in the fifth and sixth centuries.

The large number of modern excavations at Roman forts has clarified the final phases of these sites throughout the native landscape. Roman forts usually show disuse before AD 410 (the formal end of Roman political control) and no evidence of fifth- or sixth-century use.[43] This aspect of the native landscape changed, therefore, throughout the region, as the Roman army withdrew in the fourth and early fifth century. Unsurprisingly, this seems to have been associated with the reassertion of local leadership, and notably tribal kingship centred on hill-forts, which themselves had often been used in the Roman period as secular élite settlements.[44] Such sites include Dinas Emrys and Degannwy in Wales, and Tintagel and Chun Castle in Cornwall.[45]

In northern Britain an exception to this general rule seems to have occurred, as a group of forts (once part of the late Roman military command of the *Dux Britanniarum*) was apparently re-used for secular élite settlements, similar to those found in hill-forts, and their enclosing walls were refortified.[46] This group of sites seems to have been afforded special attention because it was on the line of Hadrian's Wall and its approaches to the south. In re-using these forts, British kings could redefend the line of the Wall against hostile neighbours to the north. Casey has recently argued that environmental evidence and textual indications suggest that this was merely the continuation of the units stationed on the Wall under sub-Roman rule.[47] This is, however, implausible both on textual grounds and (crucially) because environmental data, discussed below, show major discontinuity in the agricultural activity in this area.[48]

Alternatively, the Wall may have been garrisoned by tribal British war-bands – groups of élite warriors under the leadership of the king.[49] Such war-bands would not have required the same supply system or food production as a late Roman garrison, and may have been more dependent on pastoral (rather than arable) production than the Roman army had been.[50]

Much more drastic change in the fifth century can be seen when we examine the industrial and urban landscapes. These aspects, closely linked to each other and the imperial system, might, like military sites, be expected to provide a reflection of broader imperial political and economic transformations.

THE END OF THE INDUSTRIAL LANDSCAPE

The industrial landscape ended when the Roman industries ceased production. This is usually supposed to have occurred rapidly in the early fifth century, but recent work suggests a slower decline, through localized production, lasting throughout that century, and perhaps even beyond in some cases.

The Oxfordshire ware potteries were in production late enough to use early Anglo-Saxon pottery stamps on at least one of their products, and Nene Valley ware was produced late enough for one of its forms to be copied in local early Anglo-Saxon pottery.[51] The recent re-dating by Böhme and Hines of the Anglo-Saxon invasion to the mid–late fifth century, rather than the early fifth, suggests that we must place these products in the mid–late fifth century also.[52] The discovery of a complete Anglo-Saxon pot of the sixth century in the flue ashes of a Romano-British pottery kiln in Lincolnshire suggests at least some local manufacture into the sixth century but, soberingly, this kiln apparently made wares superficially indistinguishable from late fourth-century pottery.[53]

If the localization of production permitted pottery kilns to operate into the fifth and even sixth centuries, similar hints are seen in other industries. Droitwich, for instance, gives us an example of sixth-century salt production, while the Roman tin mines of Cornwall may also show evidence of sixth-century exploitation.[54] This was apparently on a sufficient scale to allow eastern Mediterraneans to refer to tin as 'the British metal' at this time, and for Mediterranean merchants to visit Britain to obtain it.[55]

Yet, despite evidence of localized production and small-scale continuity, this was insufficient to maintain a proto-industrial level of production, or to prolong the industrial landscape of Roman Britain in its fourth-century form.[56] The landscape was now no longer modified by the continued accumulation of slag tips from iron-working or heaps of waste products from potting, although such tips remained as (disused) features in it.

These aspects of the Romano-British industries came to an end when mass-production on a proto-industrial scale ceased in the early fifth century.[57] It can, therefore, be claimed that the Romano-British industrial landscape came to an end in the early fifth century, even if Romano-British industries did not cease as abruptly as was once supposed.

The rapid decline of mass-production has been seen by many as clearly linked to the end of urban life. This raises the question of the end of the urban landscape, which, more than any other aspect of the Romano-British landscape, has excited the attention of scholars seeking continuity between Anglo-Saxon England and Roman Britain.

THE END OF THE URBAN LANDSCAPE

The end of Romano-British urbanism has been a controversial problem for archaeologists and historians alike. While extreme views of urban discontinuity within the Roman period, as proposed by Reece,[58] are probably no longer tenable, there is a range of contrasting alternatives for what was happening inside towns at the end of Roman Britain, and in the centuries that followed. There has been far less attention, however, placed on examining these questions in relation to their hinterlands: the urban landscape surrounding them.

Hints of 'sub-Roman' activity in such urban landscapes have, for example, been found at St Albans, London, Silchester and Caerwent, where urban territories were arguably maintained into the fifth and sixth centuries.[59] In the Anglo-Saxon areas of the east, this activity shows as gaps in the distribution of early Anglo-Saxon cemeteries, as at Silchester, and may be supported by evidence for boundary dykes surrounding the town, if these in fact belong to this period.[60] The name of one British kingdom, Gwent, can be translated as the 'territory of *Venta Silurum*' (Caerwent), implying the survival of a political unit dependent on the town.[61]

At St Albans the evidence is of a different character, with traces of the survival of the *martyrium* established at St Alban's tomb in the late Roman period as a religious centre through the sixth and seventh centuries, as Gildas and Bede seem to suggest.[62] In the town, 'sub-Roman' (or undated, but probably sub-Roman) occupation has been found in most of the larger areas excavated.[63]

Bassett has drawn attention to strong textual evidence for the survival of ecclesiastical dioceses based on late Roman *civitates* (in this period, 'administrative places') in the British west, and even parts of Anglo-Saxon England.[64] These may have helped to preserve urban territories with which they may have been coterminous, as at Wroxeter. If so, then as this seems a widespread pattern, the likelihood of aspects of the urban landscape surviving into the sixth century is great.

There is much scattered evidence suggesting that some sort of activity was taking place inside western British towns in the fifth and sixth centuries, as at Cirencester, Dorchester and Gloucester.[65] The difficulties of interpreting occupation associated with few surviving artefacts, and reusing pre-existing structures, are, however, considerable and they are not simplified by the problems in dating material from the fifth and sixth centuries. There is very much more undated and miscellaneous evidence, which might date from the fifth or sixth century, to support the datable and better-known instances of such activity. So, these datable instances of occupation, as at the amphitheatre outside Cirencester, or at Gloucester, may represent the visible 'tip of an iceberg' of occupation. Evidence from Wroxeter, where the town centre contained large sub-Roman timber buildings, has shown how ephemeral the traces of substantial sub-Roman British structures might be, and how difficult it may be to date even extensively excavated and well-preserved structures in such contexts.[66]

Even if there were far more people in British towns in the fifth century than is usually supposed, this does not, however, mean that the urban landscape or the social and economic system surrounding it survived. Towns may have been political and episcopal centres in sub-Roman western Britain, but this cannot be taken to suggest that the urban landscape continued to exist in its late Roman form. In a sense it may still have operated, on a far reduced scale, but changes had taken place in the character of towns making them 'not as they once were'.[67]

This is far from claiming that the urban landscape did not survive in some form and in some places, especially in western and northern Britain, into the fifth or even, in part, the sixth century. But if so, we must imagine a pale reflection of what that landscape was once like. The existence of continuing settlement in suburbs in western Britain, for instance, is attested to at Poundbury, where a sub-Roman settlement was sited on, and re-used structures from, a late Roman cemetery.[68] At Allington Avenue, a suburban domestic settlement continued in use into the fifth or sixth century.[69]

The difficulty in identifying low-status sites of the fifth to seventh centuries in Britain, and their lack of 'diagnostic' artefacts, limits our ability to recognize this pattern more generally. There are other hints of the survival of such urban landscapes in a sub-Roman form in the British-controlled zone, however, as at Caerwent.[70] There, we may see the extramural cemetery of the urban community maintained into the sixth century, and possibly later. Even in the British zone, this pattern of urban landscape continuity was, however, apparently terminated by settlement-shift in the fifth or sixth century. At some towns this may have involved the re-use of hill-forts nearby (perhaps to become settlements similar in character to late Roman small towns) as at South Cadbury and possibly Cannington.[71] It must be stressed that most towns did not develop in this way: this is a pattern which may be exhibited at a few western British towns, but where the Britons no longer held political control, town life dwindled and disappeared in the fifth century.[72]

The early Anglo-Saxons were unused to towns, which did not fit into their society and economy.[73] Such people had no use for urban political centres, nor were they Christians who might hope to maintain earlier Christian churches and other sites. In the early Anglo-Saxon areas the urban landscape ended, therefore, in the later fifth century or before, apart perhaps from some pockets of British survival (including Lincoln).[74] In the British zone the urban landscape ended, in part, at approximately the same time. There may have been shifts to successor-sites in some towns, but elsewhere some former towns may have remained centres of local importance due to the survival of episcopal centres. These centres, on rare occasions, survive today, albeit seldom as the seats of bishops. An example is the church of St Andrew's, Wroxeter, seemingly the direct successor of a sub-Roman predecessor.[75]

This survey of the end of the Romano-British landscape, stressing discontinuity in the Anglo-Saxon east and relative continuity in the British west, can be compared with evidence for continuity and change in the general character of the environment provided by pollen analysis.

POLLEN EVIDENCE FOR LANDSCAPE CONTINUITY AND CHANGE

The end of Roman Britain, in environmental terms, has usually been seen as having been accompanied by widespread woodland regeneration following the abandonment of agricultural land. This view has been based on vegetation changes apparent in a handful of pollen sequences, mostly from northern England and Scotland. These led Turner to the conclusion that 'the majority of pollen diagrams indicate a regenerated forest and a lower proportion of arable and pasture land . . . Some show no change and only a very small proportion indicate a higher level of activity than in the Iron Age.'[76] This limited evidence for post-Roman woodland regeneration was seen as generally applicable, suggesting that large areas of land were abandoned after Roman withdrawal, a view challenged by Bell.[77]

The recent increase in the number of radiocarbon-dated pollen sequences spanning both the Roman period (discussed in chapter 2) and the post-Roman period has provided the opportunity to reassess this issue.[78] Examination of all pollen sequences covering the period AD 400–800 from Roman Britain and Scotland reveals an interesting pattern. Less than half of the sequences show signs of reduced intensity of land use, and half of these are in the extreme north of England, near Hadrian's Wall. Of the seven Welsh sites, only three show evidence of reduced activity, the others indicating continuity or increased agricultural activity. It is, therefore,

clear that Roman withdrawal did not generally result in wholesale abandonment of agricultural land and woodland regeneration.

The consistent pattern of land abandonment near Hadrian's Wall is, however, a striking exception to this pattern and, ironically, is in direct opposition to previous interpretations of the pollen evidence from part of this area. Turner argued for continuity of farming until at least the sixth century in north-east England, followed by woodland regeneration after that date.[79] This suggestion was based on radiocarbon dates apparently associated with woodland regeneration phases in the pollen sequences, but at some of the sites, including Fellend Moss and Steng Moss, regeneration began before the radiocarbon-dated level.

Examination of the pollen sequences discussed by Turner, and the others that have subsequently become available, provides no supporting evidence for her hypothesis of initial continuity.[80] All sites in the Hadrian's Wall area show evidence for the abandonment of agricultural land and woodland regeneration coinciding with Roman withdrawal.[81] This pattern may reflect the collapse of agricultural

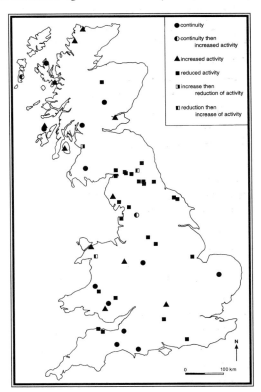

Pollen evidence for landscape continuity and change at the end of the Roman period (based on S.P. Dark 1996 with additions)

systems that had previously supplied the Roman forces based on, and around, Hadrian's Wall. As mentioned above, this makes the often-stated view, reiterated by Casey,[82] that fort communities along the Wall 'stayed put' after the end of Roman rule, unlikely.

In contrast, many sites in the rest of England and in Wales show continuity of landscape use, or even intensified activity, in the immediate post-Roman period. Outside the villa landscape, for example, in north-west Wales, this may reflect a lack of integration into the imperial economy, so that Roman withdrawal had little negative impact. The general picture of increased activity or continuity in Scotland, again, presumably reflects the lack of integration of the area into the Roman economy. Evidence for continuity in more romanized regions, such as south-east Wales and Dorset, suggests that economic change did not generally result in widespread landscape discontinuity even in these areas.

Unfortunately, too few sequences are available from areas where the villa economy was well developed to enable more than tentative conclusions to be drawn about the environmental consequences of its end. The current evidence is somewhat ambiguous: the pollen sequence from Sidlings Copse, Oxfordshire, indicates post-Roman agricultural expansion in such an area,[83] while the site of Snelsmore in Berkshire suggests some abandonment of land.[84] Clearly, more pollen evidence is required to establish general trends (if any) in southern and eastern England.

As the climatic evidence discussed in chapter 2 suggests that the end of Roman Britain coincided approximately with a phase of climatic deterioration, it is worth examining the pollen evidence to see whether climate change may have played a part in the changes of land use seen at some of these sites. The overall picture of continuity or increased activity, both within the former area of Roman Britain and into the far north of Scotland, suggests that the deterioration of climate was not significant enough to have a major detrimental effect on agriculture across the whole of Britain. It is notable, however, that most of the sites where there is evidence for reduced human activity are at higher altitudes (more than 150 metres), while sites where there was continuity or increased activity are mainly at lower altitudes.[85] This could be taken to suggest that climatic deterioration caused land abandonment in some areas that were already marginal for agriculture. Several high-altitude sites show continuity or increased activity, however, so it seems unlikely that the deterioration of climate was significant enough alone to cause the abandonment of upland areas.

Clearly both the pollen and settlement evidence suggest that some elements of the landscape survived after Roman withdrawal, and this brings us to the final section of this chapter. To what extent did the Romano-British landscape survive into the Middle Ages, and how much of it survives today?

THE MEDIEVAL SURVIVAL
OF THE ROMANO-BRITISH LANDSCAPE

The medieval landscape differed drastically from that of the Roman period – most of the characteristic site types of the Romano-British landscape had disappeared completely by AD 700. Villas, temples, Roman-style forts and Roman industrial sites, for instance, had all ceased to exist long before the end of the sixth century. The seventh century brought further changes, even where the Britons retained political control. In eastern Britain, monasteries and rural churches, on the medieval continental European rather than the late (or sub-) Roman model, were introduced following the Conversion of the Anglo-Saxons. Monasteries became common aspects of the British landscape by AD 700 in both the Anglo-Saxon and British zones.

The regeneration of urbanism and of long-distance trade in middle Saxon England in the seventh and eighth centuries led to the rapid growth of towns and trading places, which also derived from contemporary continental European practices rather than the Roman past.[86] Later still, in the tenth and eleventh centuries, we can see the origins of most later medieval English villages, perhaps linked in some fashion to the development of the state or economy.[87] The Norman Conquest, too, brought in its aftermath new types of sites rare, or absent, from even late Anglo-Saxon England: castles, manor houses, moated sites, and windmills.[88] So, by AD 1100 there were very few aspects of the British landscape that derived from the Romano-British past.

New types of field system and land management had replaced Roman modes of rural economy, and in some areas it seems that the extent of woodland exceeded that of the Roman period.[89] The scale of industrial production was not to reach that of the fourth century until the late Middle Ages, or possibly later, showing that the changes involved did not always represent technological development. For instance, medieval rural sites were seldom as commonly served with window glass, mortared stone walling or well-made covered floors as were those of the fourth century, and hypocausts were unknown, although structurally there is much in common between the more modest villas and medieval manor houses.

In these terms, not much of the landscape of Roman Britain survived into the thirteenth century, yet it is vital not to overlook important continuities where these existed. Some of these seem trivial today, for example the observation that medieval Britain must have contained far more standing ruins of Roman date than do modern England or Wales. The east gate of Lincoln provides an example of a major standing Romano-British structure used in the medieval period, and later, but it was by no means unique in this respect.[90] The countryside may have contained many more such buildings, and medieval pottery has frequently been found within Romano-British structures and beneath the collapsed remains of roofing, but this is a topic little studied.

The usual ascription of 'robber trenches' to the immediate post-Roman period is implausible, as neither Britons nor Anglo-Saxons habitually built in stone until after the seventh century.[91] Some robbing certainly occurred from then on, as re-used stone in Anglo-Saxon buildings attests, but much Roman masonry seems to have been standing to be used as quarries in the Middle Ages. Thus, Roman stone and other building materials found their way into many medieval buildings, sometimes in large quantities.

The re-incorporation of Roman fort and town walls into medieval *enceintes* provided another form of continuity, while Roman-period boundaries and locations were preserved in many field systems.[92] Medieval boundary lines often seem to have employed Romano-British features, presumably because they were the principal physical constraints on action in many areas. The re-use of Roman sites for medieval castles, towns and churches was accompanied by the use of Roman road-lines as the standing for those of later centuries. So, although in an unsystematic and piecemeal way, elements of the Roman landscape survived as features, or major constraints on boundaries, into the Middle Ages.

The extent to which such re-used boundary lines represent more than the pragmatic utilization of ruins is difficult to assess. They may have held a symbolic importance in medieval society, as evidenced, for instance, at the Roman fort at Segontium, but they may simply have been convenient standing features without complex meanings in the medieval period. There is no evidence to indicate that continuity of occupation is implied by this.

It would be incorrect, therefore, to claim that the landscape of Roman Britain formed the usual structure of the medieval landscape, but it is true that it formed part of its basis – a partial skeleton of boundaries and site locations. This was amplified in specific cases where associations of sites were remembered in the Middle Ages, as at St Albans. Some Roman towns could, therefore, retain a role as political or religious central places without direct continuity being implied.

This is not to say that no cases of continuous use existed, as the example of St Albans may indicate, but this was the exception rather than the rule. In western Britain there seems to be a stronger case than in the eastern (what were, in the sixth century, Anglo-Saxon) areas for continuity of use of farms, albeit with shifting locations, as Leech has convincingly argued in west Somerset and Dorset.[93] Yet these cases seldom appear to represent the same settlement surviving on a single site over centuries, rather small (family?) communities that shifted in location over long periods of time.

What we lack, apart from these instances of the 'communal' survival of farming settlements and the rare cases of ecclesiastical sites showing long-term continuity of use, is clear evidence that functions and uses of the landscape continued into the Middle Ages. The pattern is more strongly marked by discontinuity than continuity, and the contrast between locational and boundary continuity and functional continuity may be salutory. This suggests that the medieval landscape was not an 'organic' consequence of the Romano-British landscape but the product of religious, social, cultural, political or economic changes affecting the physical layout of rural life. These changes seem apparent in both the British and the Anglo-Saxon areas, and their causes may not be uniform or contemporary.

In Anglo-Saxon England, farms established on villa sites were, for instance, usually deserted in the seventh century, while in the same century evidence for rural settlement continuity in social and economic terms ends in western Britain.[94] The medieval village seems to have formed not with the Anglo-Saxon invasion as once supposed, but many centuries later, in the late Saxon period.[95] In Wales the medieval landscape appears to have come into existence during the period between c. AD 600 and c. 800 to judge from, albeit scanty, textual evidence.[96] Onto this 'late Saxon', or more properly 'early medieval', landscape was imposed a Norman pattern of feudal castles and manorial sites. Thus, by AD 1100, if not before, there was no direct link at the vast majority of sites between Romano-British and medieval site-use, unless mediated through the survival of ecclesiastical centres.

This pattern of widespread landscape discontinuity discredits the view that the medieval and modern countryside is − in its fundamentals − derived from that of the Roman or prehistoric periods. It suggests that there have been at least two fundamental transformations in landscape structure following the Roman period, the first in the seventh century and the second in the Norman period, with a further change in England in the tenth to eleventh centuries. So, medieval British landscapes were not 'older than we think' − they were the product of post-Roman changes.[97]

THE MODERN SURVIVAL OF
THE ROMANO-BRITISH LANDSCAPE

If it is clear that (generally) the Romano-British landscape came to an end in the seventh century or before, it is also clear that Roman innovations in site locations still influence the modern landscape, as they did in the Middle Ages. The most obvious of these are the patterns of town sites and roads ultimately based on those of Roman Britain. Many, although not all, modern

British cities have Roman origins: London, York, Gloucester, Cirencester, Carlisle, Lincoln, Canterbury, Cambridge and Exeter, to name but a selection.[98]

Moving beyond this level, it is still possible to recognize both rural and urban churches with probable or possible Romano-British (or at least sub-Roman) origins, as already noted, while many cathedrals are on, or close to, Romano-British Christian episcopal centres.[99] This religious continuity is one of our most striking inheritances from Roman Britain.

The medieval transformation of the landscape also gave us a large number of castles on Roman fort sites: as at Pevensey, Portchester, Caernarvon and Neath. Such sites frequently employed Roman defensive circuits in their own baileys, preserving not merely the site but also the stonework. As many of these castles have survived as important military, symbolic, civil or judicial places into the nineteenth or twentieth centuries, and today frequently play a role in our own landscape of heritage and tourism, they can be claimed as among the inheritance of the Romano-British landscape. While these examples represent what are, in most cases, medieval uses of Roman sites, one might claim that excavated Roman sites today have again become part of our landscape. The display of sites such as Fishbourne and Bignor villas, for example, creates places of interest and representations of Roman Britain that receive large numbers of visitors.

It is, however, noteworthy that most aspects of the Romano-British landscape have passed altogether from our settlement pattern, surviving, if at all, only as historic sites and minor landscape features. For instance, the Romano-British farmsteads of the north and west are, for the most part, not on what are today occupied locations. Villas rarely have modern secular buildings on their sites, and temple sites have almost always been replaced by fields in the modern countryside. This in itself may tell us about how the Romano-British landscape ended, and about the fundamental discontinuities, as well as continuities, that mark its partial survival.

NOTES

CHAPTER 1

1. Suggested by Scott 1990, 1991. Deliberate killing has now been confirmed by palaeopathological methods by Mays (1993)
2. Rivet and Smith 1979
3. Percival (1988, pp. 25–30) reviews the relevant evidence
4. Bowman and Thomas 1983, 1987, 1991; Bowman, Thomas and Adams 1990; Bowman 1994
5. For these the starting point is Collingwood and Wright 1965
6. Sedgley 1975
7. For example, J.T. Smith 1978b, 1982, 1987
8. For some examples of how the Romans depicted the countryside outside Britain see Percival 1988, pp. 21–5
9. Milne 1985; Miller et al., 1986
10. For identification of pollen and interpretation of pollen data see Moore et al., 1991
11. Stuiver and Pearson 1993
12. For an introduction to the archaeology of Roman Britain see Collingwood and Richmond 1969; Frere 1987; B. Jones and Mattingly 1990
13. Wider issues of residuality and the associated problems examined below are discussed in K.R. Dark 1995, chapter 2
14. For example, at Gadebridge Park (Neal 1974)
15. See Barker 1986 for examples
16. See K.R. Dark 1995 chapter 2 for this point and the following paragraph
17. *Ibid* for a discussion of how archaeologists have approached this problem
18. Gaffney and Tingle 1989
19. For examples, R.K. Morris and Roxan 1980
20. For example, the site at Cherhill (P. Johnson and Walters 1988; Walters 1996, p. 158)
21. Potter 1996
22. On research patterns in Romano-British archaeology see Hingley 1991
23. Kelly 1990
24. For example, the data reviewed in Scott 1993a
25. For recent surveys of the British Iron Age see Cunliffe 1991; Fitzpatrick and Morris 1994; Champion and Collis 1995. For surveys of the prehistoric sociopolitical background see Bradley 1984, 1991; Champion 1994

26. Sellwood 1984
27. Frere 1987, pp. 27–33; Millett 1990, pp. 17–21; B. Jones and Mattingly 1990, pp. 43–7
28. Millett 1990, pp. 17–20
29. Van Arsdell 1989; Haselgrove 1993. For a recent discussion of the possible relationship between these coins and ritual see Creighton 1995. On the even more problematical 'currency bars' see Hingley 1990
30. Sellwood 1984
31. Champion 1994; Collis 1994, pp. 138–40; Millett 1990, pp. 18–20
32. Haselgrove 1988; Dent 1982, 1983b; Millett 1990, pp. 35–8
33. Downey et al. 1980; Drury 1980; Wait 1985
34. Fitzpatrick 1984
35. Cunliffe (1991) reviews the entire archaeology of Iron Age Britain. See also J.D. Hill 1995b, pp. 54–62
36. The precise function of these kiln-like structures is uncertain. Analysis of charred grain from 'corn-driers' by Veen (1989) suggested use both for roasting germinated grains to produce malt, and parching/drying prior to consumption and storage
37. Reynolds 1979, 1981, pp. 97–122
38. Collis 1994, pp. 127–30; Henderson 1992
39. J.D. Hill 1995b, especially pp. 54–60
40. Rivet and Smith 1979; Millett 1990, pp. 17–20
41. For a review of the range of settlement locations in Britain during this period and later see C. Taylor 1983
42. For example, Crumley 1974
43. Hogg 1975, 1979
44. *Ibid*
45. K.R. Dark 1994b
46. Cunliffe 1984c, 1991, 1994a
47. For example, Haselgrove 1986; Stopford 1988; Bowden and McOmish 1989; Sharples 1991b; J.D. Hill 1995a, 1995b, pp. 67–9
48. Cunliffe 1984a, 1984b; Cunliffe and Poole 1991a, 1991b; Sharples 1991a, 1991b
49. Dent 1983b
50. Potter and Johns 1992, pp. 43–5
51. Wait 1985
52. Potter and Johns 1992, pp. 19, 44
53. P. Crew 1983, 1984a
54. K.R. Dark 1990, final report in preparation
55. G.J. Wainwright 1979
56. Coles 1987
57. Cunliffe 1987. See also Cunliffe 1988

58. Macready and Thompson 1984; Fitzpatrick 1985. On the cultural and political consequences of this trade see Haselgrove 1984; Trow 1990; Woolf 1993b
59. Rippon 1996, p. 24
60. Coles and Minnitt 1995
61. Morrison 1985
62. Hunn 1992; Clifford 1961; Wacher 1995, pp. 302–4
63. Wheeler 1954; Haselgrove, Turnbull and Fitts 1991; Welfare *et al.* 1990; Haselgrove, Lowther and Turnbull 1991
64. By such sites we mean what have also been called 'territorial *oppida*' rather than hill-fort-sized settlements, sometimes classifed as 'enclosed *oppida*'. For the terminology see J.D. Hill 1995b, p. 70. For the sites see Collis 1984; Millett 1990, pp. 21–9; Cunliffe 1991. See also Woolf 1993a
65. Frere 1987, pp. 31–2; B. Jones and Mattingly 1990, pp. 42–55; Potter and Johns 1992, pp. 33–5
66. Frere 1987, pp. 34–5; Potter and Johns 1992, pp. 33–4; Millett 1990, p. 48. On Colchester see also Fitzpatrick 1986
67. Crummy 1980. See also Wacher 1995, pp. 112–14
68. D. Miles and Palmer 1995, p. 378
69. Sellwood 1984
70. Burgess 1980
71. On the reasons for this, its history and Roman perceptions of Britain see G. Webster and Dudley 1965; G. Webster 1980, 1981; Millett 1990, pp. 40–64; Stewart 1995. A useful chronological table (with maps) of the relevant events is provided by Millett 1995, pp. 13–17
72. *Ibid*; Todd 1984a, 1984b, 1985
73. For a clear example of the latter situation see Hanson and Campbell 1986. See also Millett 1990, pp. 54, 68
74. Millett 1990, pp. 65–85
75. Haselgrove 1984; Millett 1990, pp. 29–35; Trow 1990. For comparison see also Fulford 1985, Haselgrove 1987b
76. On romanization see Millett 1990; Hanson 1994. See also Trow 1990; Woolf 1992, 1993c. On the destroyed houses at London and St Albans see Perring 1987, pp. 147–51. See also Niblett 1993, especially pp. 85–6
77. King 1990. However, on religion before the Conquest see Fitzpatrick 1984, 1991
78. Frere 1987, pp. 281–2
79. A. Birley 1979, pp. 28, 107–14
80. A. Birley 1979 *passim*
81. Evans 1987
82. For this and other examples see Gelling 1988
83. J.D. Hill 1995b. On the diversity of tribal groups see Rivet and Smith 1979

CHAPTER 2

1. Randsborg 1991, p. 23
2. Lamb 1981; Lamb 1995, p. 165
3. Dansgaard reproduced in Lamb 1995, p. 93
4. Lamb 1995, p. 167
5. Leemann and Niessen 1994
6. *Ibid*
7. Matthews and Karlen 1992
8. Karlen 1991
9. Baillie 1995, p. 31
10. Rothlisberger reproduced in Lamb 1995, p. 166
11. Baillie 1995
12. Baillie and Munro 1988
13. Baillie 1994
14. Baillie 1995, p. 81
15. Baillie 1995, p. 85
16. Dugmore *et al.* 1995; Pilcher and Hall 1996
17. Barber 1981
18. J. Turner 1964; Dickinson 1975; Barber 1982; Stoneman quoted in Barber *et al.* 1994, p. 33
19. Tipping 1995a, p. 80
20. Dickinson 1975; Blackford and Chambers 1991
21. Tipping 1995a, p. 79
22. C.P. Burnham 1989, p. 14
23. Akeroyd 1972
24. C. Thomas 1985, pp. 17–34
25. *Ibid*, p. 34
26. Waddelove and Waddelove 1990
27. Boon 1980
28. Akeroyd 1972
29. The regression ('Tilbury V') is dated by radiocarbon dating of organic deposits, giving a result centred on 1750 BP (Devoy 1979)
30. Godwin 1943
31. Discussed in Boon 1980, pp. 25–6
32. Hibbert 1980
33. Caseldine 1986, p. 78; 1988 p. 56; Housley 1988, pp. 79, 82
34. Housley 1988, pp. 79, 82
35. Rippon 1996, p. 22
36. For Rumney Great Wharf see J.R.L. Allen and Fulford 1986; Fulford, Allen and Rippon 1994. For Oldbury Flats see J.R.L. Allen and Fulford 1992
37. J.R.L. Allen and Fulford 1987
38. Summarized in D. Hall and Coles 1994
39. Godwin 1978, pp. 106–7
40. Shennan 1986
41. For example, Salway 1970, pp. 8–9; Godwin 1978, p. 79
42. D. Hall and Coles 1994, p. 92
43. *Ibid*, p. 105
44. Flooding in the third century was first suggested by Bromwich (1970) and Churchill (1970), and supported by Potter (1981). More recent evidence is presented by D. Hall and Coles 1994, p. 114
45. Waller 1994
46. Bidwell and Holbrook 1989, pp. 1–2
47. *Ibid*, pp. 50–1
48. Graham 1978
49. The various aspects of the nature of the Thames in the first century AD are summarized in Milne *et al.* (1983) and Milne (1985, pp. 79–86)
50. Macklin and Needham 1992; Macklin and Lewin 1993

51. See review by Moore 1993

52. Boardman 1992

53. Bell 1992

54. M.J. Allen 1992

55. R. Jones, Benson-Evans and Chambers 1985

56. M. Jones 1978

57. Lambrick 1992, p. 99

58. For example, Moore 1968

59. J. Turner 1979

60. J. Turner 1981

61. Each site must also have at least two samples from the Roman period, and from the Iron Age if deposits of this date are present. Two samples are obviously inadequate to enable changes in vegetation during the Roman period to be reconstructed, but can give an 'averaged' picture which enables a broad comparison between the Roman-period and Iron Age vegetation. Use only of sites with greater temporal resolution would reduce the data set drastically. As it is, some sequences that have previously been employed in discussions of the Roman period have been excluded, such as Neasham Fen, Durham (Bartley *et al.* 1976), due to poor temporal resolution (samples approximately three hundred years apart)

62. Comparison of information between the sites is complicated by differences in data presentation by different authors. Pollen data are usually given as percentages – each pollen type is expressed as a percentage of all the other types present, but variations from this method occur. For peat sites many workers attempt to exclude plants that may have been growing on the peat surface (e.g. heather and sedges) from their calculations to enable a reconstruction of vegetation on dry land. Unfortunately, this can be a problem where similar plants grow on the peat and in the surrounding area, as with members of the grass family, where the pollen cannot generally be separated into different species. In lakes, local plant growth is less of a problem since the pollen of most aquatic plants can be identified quite closely, and the basis for calculation is then total pollen, excluding that of aquatics. Some workers include the spores of ferns on the grounds that they occur in both wetland and dryland environments, while others exclude them.

For the purpose of comparing the vegetation at different sites it is necessary to adopt a standard 'pollen sum' as the basis for calculations. The sum adopted here is total pollen and spores excluding those of aquatic plants and *Sphagnum* moss. This means that pollen assemblages from some peat sites may be biased by growth of local plants, but this is a factor that is discussed where necessary, rather than introducing the subjective element of attempting to separate plants likely to have been growing on peat surfaces.

63. A.P. Brown 1977; I.G. Simmons, Rand and Crabtree 1983, 1987; K. Smith *et al.* 1981

64. J. Miles 1988

65. For example, Tinsley and Smith 1974

66. J. Turner 1979

67. G. Davies and Turner 1979

68. Dumayne and Barber 1994

69. It is not possible to establish a certain relationship between construction of the Wall and vegetational change at any of these sites because the pollen sequences are dated by radiocarbon dating, which gives an age range for the dated event. For a discussion of this problem see Dumayne *et al.* 1995

70. Dumayne and Barber 1994

71. *Ibid*

72. *Ibid*, p. 170

73. Tipping 1995a, 1995b

74. Davies and Turner 1979

75. A.M. Donaldson and Turner 1977; Roberts *et al.* 1973; Bartley *et al.* 1976

76. Bartley *et al.* 1976

77. *Ibid*

78. Rowell and Turner 1985

79. S. Johnson 1989, pp. 19–21; McCarthy 1986

80. Crew 1991b

81. Mighall and Chambers 1989, 1995

82. Crew 1989, 1991a

83. Chambers and Lageard 1993

84. Kelly 1988; Chambers and Price 1988

85. Elner and Happey-Wood 1980

86. Watkins 1990

87. Chambers 1983

88. J. Turner 1964

89. Mackay and Tallis 1994

90. Huckerby *et al.* 1992

91. Summarized in I.G. Simmons *et al.* 1993

92. Atherden 1976

93. I.G. Simmons and Cundill 1974

94. Waton 1982

95. For Sidlings Copse see Day 1991, 1993. For Headington Wick villa see Jewitt 1851

96. Waller 1994

97. *Ibid*, pp. 124–33

98. *Ibid*, pp. 259–63

99. *Ibid*, pp. 288–95

100. O. Rackham 1990, pp. 63–70

101. For example, J. Turner 1965

102. For example, the Neolithic hurdle track from Walton Heath and early Bronze Age Eclipse track; Coles and Orme 1977; O. Rackham 1977; Coles *et al.* 1982

103. Coles and Orme 1978

104. Meiggs 1982, pp. 261–8

105. Godwin 1975, pp. 276–7. Charcoal probably of chestnut has been identified from the iron-making villa of Chesters, at Woolaston, Gloucestershire (Figueiral 1992)

106. Lambrick and Robinson 1979, pp. 81, 122

107. For Sidlings Copse see Day 1991, 1993

108. Robinson 1986

109. Lambrick and Robinson 1979, p. 81

110. Hanson 1978a

111. Summarized in Milne 1985

112. D. Goodburn 1991

113. Perring 1991a, pp. 74–7, 80–1

114. Miller *et al.* 1986

115. Hillam and Morgan 1986
116. McCarthy 1991
117. Huntley 1991
118. Groves 1991
119. A.R. Hall and Kenward 1990, pp. 338–9
120. McCarthy 1995
121. McDonald 1988
122. Lambrick and Robinson 1988
123. Lambrick and Robinson 1979 pp. 118–19
124. Greig 1988
125. Girling and Straker 1993, pp. 250–2
126. A.R. Hall and Kenward 1990, pp. 360, 400–4
127. *Ibid*, pp. 351, 361, 403, 418
128. A.R. Hall, Kenward and Williams 1980, pp. 128, 133; A.R. Hall and Kenward 1990, pp. 341, 413–14
129. *Ibid*
130. Nye and Jones 1987, pp. 323–4

CHAPTER 3

1. For general studies see Rivet 1964, 1969b; Todd 1978b; Percival 1976, 1982, 1988; Black 1987b; Hingley 1989. A catalogue of possible villas is given by Scott 1993a
2. Percival 1976, pp. 13–15, 25–30
3. A point especially argued by Reece 1988
4. For surveys of the broader issues of Roman rural organization and agriculture see K.D. White 1977; Greene 1986
5. Millett 1990, pp. 82–3, 91–2
6. For example, Collingwood and Richmond 1969, pp. 133–4
7. Sumpter 1988; Wrathmell and Nicolson 1990; Rawes 1991
8. Millett 1990, p. 154
9. Millett 1990, p. 92
10. K.R. Dark forthcoming; the following two paragraphs are based on that analysis
11. For general discussions see Collingwood and Richmond 1969, pp. 134–49, 151–2; Frere 1987, pp. 261–3; Hingley 1989, pp. 35–54
12. Collingwood and Richmond 1969; Richmond 1969
13. A. Saunders 1962; Branigan 1982, pp. 82, 84
14. J.T. Smith 1963
15. A.M. Williams 1909; Colllingwood and Richmond 1969, pp. 145–9; King and Potter 1990; J.T. Smith 1964
16. Philp 1984; Black 1982, 1987b, pp. 24, 49, 52–3, 57–8, 60, 67, 73; Radford 1936; Gascoigne 1970; C.M. Bennett 1962; Brodribb *et al.* 1968–78
17. Neal 1976
18. For Woodchester see G. Clarke 1982. For Bignor see Frere 1982; Aldsworth and Rudling 1996
19. Mackreth 1978
20. J.T. Smith 1978a, 1987b; Millett 1990, pp. 199–200. See also Black 1987b, pp. 26–7
21. For King's Weston see Collingwood and Richmond 1969, pp. 136–7. For Wraxhall see Branigan 1976a, pp. 47, 90. For Chew Park see Rahtz and Greenfield 1976
22. Hingley 1989, pp. 45–6

23. For Iwerne see Branigan 1976a, p. 81. For Holcombe see Pollard 1974. For Lufton see Hayward 1953, 1972
24. For Sparsholt see Johnston 1988, pp. 31, 37. For Barton Court Farm see D. Miles 1986
25. Tomalin 1987, pp. 19–28
26. McWhirr 1986b, pp. 97–9
27. Black 1987b, pp. 51, 53–4; Blagg 1996; Bidwell 1996; Liversidge 1955, 1969
28. Bidwell 1996, p. 27
29. Clifford 1954
30. Meates 1979; Black 1987b, pp. 73–4
31. For Ditchley see Radford 1936. For Hambleden see Cocks 1921. For Norton Disney see Oswald 1937
32. Walters 1996, pp. 159, 161
33. For Frocester see Gracie 1971; Gracie and Price 1980; Price 1993. For Fishbourne see Cunliffe 1971a, 1971b
34. Detsicas 1983, pp. 120–6
35. For example, Dawson 1994. For the context see Black 1987a
36. Meates 1979; Philp *et al.* 1991; R. Goodburn 1981
37. D. Miles and Palmer 1990
38. On the temples and their religions see M.J.T. Lewis 1966; Drury 1980; Horne 1981; Henig 1984; King 1990. On temples 'in the Romano-British landscape' see Blagg 1986
39. D.R. Wilson 1975; Muckelroy 1976. For continental analogies see Horne and King 1980. See also Quinnell *et al.* 1991
40. Lewis 1966, p. 135
41. R.J. Williams *et al.* 1996
42. Margary 1973; Chevallier 1989, especially pp. 158–9
43. Corder and Kirk 1932; Ramm 1988, pp. 84–7; D. Miles and Palmer 1990
44. Cunliffe 1973, pp. 101–2
45. Holleyman 1935; Burrow 1981, pp. 78, 80, 192, 235
46. Wheeler 1932, 1943
47. K.R. Dark 1993a, p. 137
48. *Ibid*, pp. 138, 142
49. Hartridge 1978
50. For the sites see R.F. Smith 1987, pp. 260–1. On their interpretation see K.R. Dark 1993a
51. Potter 1989, pp. 153–5, 160–9; 1996
52. Hallam 1964; Hanley 1987
53. McOmish 1993; Entwistle *et al.* 1994, especially pp. 7–17, although the settlement plan may have changed in the course of this occupation, and at least part of the trackway may have passed out of use by the end of the Romano-British occupation
54. Wedlake 1982
55. Clay 1985; Hingley 1989, pp. 102–3
56. For Chalton see Cunliffe 1977. For Grandford see Potter and Potter 1980, 1982
57. Eagles and Swan 1972
58. Potter and Potter 1980, 1982
59. On this and the broader context see D.J. Thompson 1987; Todd 1989a

60. Leech 1982a; Ellis 1984

61. Anon 1995. Our thanks to the Canterbury Archaeological Trust for providing further information about this site

62. Stead 1980; Ramm 1988, pp. 81–3; Hayfield 1988, pp. 114–16; Powlesland 1988, pp. 140–4

63. For what seems to be a clear-cut southern example at Frilford villa see Hingley 1985, 1989, p. 103

64. Whitwell 1988, pp. 54–9

65. Whitwell 1988, pp. 51–4

66. May 1996

67. W.G. Simpson 1966, p. 21

68. Cunliffe 1973, pp. 100–1

69. Rawlings and Fitzpatrick 1996

70. R.A. Chambers 1976; Hinchliffe and Thomas 1980; Hanley 1987, pp. 21–2

71. R.F. Smith 1981, 1987; Hands 1993

72. Rawes 1985

73. For 'river-ford' sites see R.F. Smith 1987

74. Ramm 1978, 1980; Hartley 1980; Faull and Moorhouse 1981; Manby and Turnbull 1986; Spratt and Hartley 1993; P.R. Wilson 1995

75. Hayfield 1988

76. Raistrick and Holmes 1962. See King 1986 for the local context

77. Didsbury 1988, p. 24

78. Inman 1988

79. Hayes 1988; Spratt and Hartley 1993, pp. 160–1

80. Stead 1972

81. See Spratt and Hartley 1993, pp. 155–8, 161 for some dating evidence

82. Dent 1982, 1983a, 1983b

83. Whitwell 1988, pp. 50, 65

84. See Hallam 1970; Todd 1973; Potter 1981; Simco 1984; G. Webster 1991

85. Todd 1973, pp. 4, 6, 7, fig. 4, 8, 109–10

86. Simpson 1966, pp. 15–20

87. Todd 1973, pp. 98–9

88. Ibid

89. Garton 1988

90. Simco 1984, pp. 24–5; Dix 1981

91. Mackreth 1988; Pryor 1984; Fulford 1992, pp. 27–9, 36

92. Brooks and Bedwin 1989, pp. 12–16

93. G. Webster 1991, pp. 15, 104–7

94. Dunnett 1975, pp. 109–10

95. Ibid, p. 110

96. Todd 1973, pp. 99–100; Dunnett 1975, p. 109

97. For this section see D. Miles 1982a; Young 1986; Fulford 1992; Lambrick 1992

98. Bowen and Fowler 1966, p. 46

99. Ibid, p. 48

100. Lambrick and Robinson 1979

101. Parrington 1978

102. R.F.J. Jones 1975, 1987a, pp. 828–30

103. Lambrick 1990

104. Fowler 1967

105. D. Miles and Palmer 1990; Lambrick 1992, pp. 99–102

106. Bowen and Fowler 1966; Branigan 1976b; Leech 1976, 1982b; Leech and Leach 1982; McWhirr 1986b; D. Miles 1984

107. Wainwright and Davies 1995; RCAHMW 1976

108. Burrow 1979, 1981. Note especially his observation that the deposition of coin hoards in hill-forts may suggest their disuse, pp. 143–4

109. Burrow 1981, especially pp. 78–9, 139, fig. 29, 142–5, 227–8, 290, fig. 42, 291–3

110. On this see K.R. Dark 1994b

111. Ibid, p. 87

112. Field 1965

113. Wacher 1978, pp. 128–9

114. McKinley and Heaton 1996

115. Leech 1981

116. For the site see Green 1987; Farwell and Molleson 1993

117. K.R. Dark 1994a, Mawer 1995

118. Buteux 1990; Leach 1991a, 1991b

119. West 1976

120. For Bagshot see Cole 1994. For Wells see Rodwell 1980a, 1982

121. C. Thomas 1981

122. Fowler 1968, 1970

123. Jarrett and Wrathmell 1981

124. RCAHMW 1976, pp. 48–9, 57–8

125. Rawes 1981

126. McWhirr 1986b, pp. 66–7, 70

127. Cunliffe 1973; Detsicas 1983; Williamson 1984; Branigan 1985

128. Cunliffe 1973, pp. 98–9; Rudling 1982b, p. 284; Bell 1977; Drewett et al. 1988, p. 212

129. Philp 1973

130. Wolseley et al. 1927; Cunliffe 1973, pp. 96–8; Drewett et al. 1988, pp. 205–6

131. Drewett 1982; Rudling 1982a, p. 84; Drewett et al. 1988, pp. 206–12. See also Black 1987b, pp. 96–7

132. Neal 1989; Clay 1985

133. Wedlake 1982; Hingley 1982

134. D. Miles and Palmer 1982, 1990; D. Miles 1983; Hingley 1988

135. D. Miles and Palmer 1990

136. T.G. Allen et al. 1993

137. Rahtz 1951. See also Rahtz and Watts 1979

138. ApSimon 1965

139. Isserlin 1994. See also Henig 1984a, 1984b

140. For late Roman legal restrictions on society and economy see A.H.M. Jones 1964

141. Horne 1981

142. Neal 1976

143. Black 1994

144. Ward-Perkins 1938

145. Black 1987b, pp. 98–101; Hadman 1978

146. Black 1987b, pp. 11–18

147. Cunliffe 1971a, 1971b. See also Drewett et al. 1988 pp. 217–20

148. For a discussion of the origins of these villas see Black 1987b, pp. 11–19

149. For the villa sites see Black 1987b, 1994

150. B. Jones and Mattingly 1990, pp. 56; Niblett 1992; Crummy 1992

151. Haselgrove 1982, 1987a; Sellwood 1984; B. Jones and Mattingly 1990, pp. 50–5

152. Jessup 1962; Philpott 1991

153. Haselgrove 1982, 1984. See also Trow 1990

154. Fitzpatrick 1985

155. Potter and Johns 1992, p. 87

156. Millett 1990, p. 69

157. On imperial relations with non-Roman élites generally see Hassall 1987

158. On their scale and relative simplicity see Black 1994

159. Branigan 1982. See also Black 1987b, pp. 90–5

160. Although it is frequently discovered in extensive modern excavations, as at Faversham (Philp 1968)

161. Neal et al. 1990

162. Downey et al. 1980; King and Soffe 1991; France and Gobel 1985

163. King 1990

164. Clack 1982

165. For the interesting, but disputed, suggestion that Gallo-Roman settlers can be identified in Gloucestershire see Branigan 1973

166. Trow and James 1989; Trow 1988

167. Black 1994, although he envisages a larger role for such groups in the first century also

168. Frere 1982; Drewett et al. 1988, pp. 220–7; Aldsworth and Rudling 1996

169. Wilson and Sherlock 1980

170. G. Clarke 1982

171. Walters 1996

172. Neal 1974; Philp 1996; Down 1979

173. Potter and Johns 1992, pp. 201–3

174. K.R. Dark 1996a

175. Fulford 1989; Millett 1990, especially p. 169

176. Potter and Johns 1992, pp. 201, but see their doubts on p. 212

177. K.R. Dark 1994a, pp. 25–7

178. For a classic study of villa society see Rivet 1969a. For more recent views see Todd 1978a; Percival 1976; Rippengal 1993; K.R. Dark 1994a, pp. 25–30

179. Millett 1990, p.198

180. E.G. Turner 1956

181. Millett 1990, p. 203

182. Todd 1989a, especially p. 16

183. Stevens 1966. For Smith's views see J.T. Smith 1964, 1978a, 1978b, 1982, 1985, 1987

184. Applebaum 1966

185. Especially in Hingley 1989

186. D.L. Clarke 1972a

187. Coles and Minnitt 1995

188. S. Clarke 1990

189. For Winterton see Stead 1976a. For Rockbourne see RCHME 1984. For Gorhambury see Neal et al. 1990

190. Neal 1989

191. Stead 1976a

192. McWhirr 1986b, pp. 94–5; Hanworth 1968; Drewett et al. 1988, pp. 227–8

193. RCHME 1984

194. P. Morris 1979

195. Philp et al. 1991

196. For comparison see Drinkwater 1981

197. Black 1982, 1987b, pp. 57–60, 83

198. Johnston 1978, p. 74

199. On the relationship between coin and food rents in Gaul see Drinkwater 1981

200. Oswald 1937, 1949; Philp et al. 1991

201. Collingwood and Richmond 1969, p. 147

202. Hadman 1978

203. M. Jones 1986; Neal et al. 1990. For a summary of such attempts and brief evaluation, see D. Miles 1989, p. 123

204. Finberg 1955

205. The fullest published account of Redlands at the time of writing is Keevill 1996

206. For Barnsley Park see G. Webster 1982; G. Webster and Smith 1983; G. Webster et al. 1986. For Brading see Tomalin 1987, pp. 19–28

207. Branigan 1989. See also Goodall 1972

CHAPTER 4

1. Philpott 1991. See also Whimster 1977, 1981

2. Based on Branigan and Dearne 1992

3. K.R. Dark 1994a, pp. 44–9

4. See below and Nash-Williams, 1969; J.L. Davies 1980, 1991b

5. Fox and Ravenhill 1966, 1972; Collingwood and Richmond 1969, pp. 15–70. See also S. Johnson 1983

6. Salway 1980; Sommer 1984; J.L. Davies 1991a

7. Sommer 1984

8. On this see G.D.B. Jones 1984

9. For the problems of military supply and the consequences of military occupation see Manning 1975; Hanson 1978a; Birley 1981a; Breeze 1984, 1985; J.L. Davies 1984; Anderson 1992

10. Daniels 1980; Welsby 1982; S.T. James 1984; K.R. Dark 1994a, pp. 44–9. For an interesting discussion of changes in the deployment of cavalry units see Breeze 1993

11. Casey and Davies 1993

12. Maxfield 1980; Griffith 1984; Manning 1988; B. Jones and Mattingly 1990 pp. 97–101, 131–4

13. Casey and Davies 1993

14. For discussions of military–civilian relations see Casey 1982; Blagg and King 1984; J.L. Davies 1984; S. Johnson 1989, pp. 81–100; Hanson and Macinnes 1991; Higham 1982, 1989

15. Breeze and Dobson 1987; Bruce 1978; Breeze 1982, pp. 73–96, 1989, pp. 37–46; S. Johnson 1989; Ordnance Survey 1989. See also Breeze and Dobson 1985; Daniels 1989. On frontiers and their functions see Hanson 1989

16. For excavations at Castle Nick see Frere 1986, pp. 378–81. For Poltross Burn see Breeze and Dobson 1974

17. For example, Woodfield 1965; Charlesworth 1977. See also Bishop and Allason-Jones 1988

18. On possibilities of their use for signalling see Donaldson 1986, 1988

19. Haigh and Savage 1984

20. Breeze and Dobson 1969, 1974 discuss the range of fort types and the possible significance of variations in this. For *vici* on the Wall see Sommer 1984; Snape 1991

21. For examples see Bidwell 1985; R. Birley 1977; Wilmott 1995, 1996; Bidwell and Speak 1994; Crow 1995. For preliminary results of the analysis of the waterlogged texts ('Vindolanda tablets') describing life on the Wall, found in the course of these excavations at Vindolanda, see also Bowman and Thomas 1983; Bowman 1994

22. Hanson *et al.* 1979; Bishop and Dore 1988; Burnham and Wacher 1990, pp. 51–62; Bidwell and Holbrook 1989

23. Collingwood and Richmond 1969, pp. 172; Richmond and Gillam 1951; Gillam and Daniels 1961

24. Jarrett 1976; G.D.B. Jones 1976, 1979, 1982, 1991; Potter 1979, 1980; Breeze 1982, pp. 83–4; Bellhouse 1989. See also the summary of the evidence from the Wall in B. Jones and Mattingly, pp. 109–19. For an important critical evaluation of this evidence see Daniels 1990

25. Daniels 1980; S. Johnson 1989, pp. 109–11; Bidwell 1991. See also S.T. James 1984

26. Kilbride-Jones 1938

27. Ordnance Survey 1969; Robertson 1979; Keppie 1975, 1982; Breeze 1982, pp. 97–124; Hanson and Maxwell 1983. See also Mann 1988

28. Keppie and Walker 1981; Hanson 1979

29. Gillam 1975; Hanson 1979; Keppie and Walker 1981; Maxwell 1985; Breeze 1989, pp. 46–52

30. Breeze 1975, 1982, pp. 118–24; Daniels 1991. See also Speidel 1987

31. Breeze 1982, pp. 138–9, 145, 156

32. Charlton and Mitcheson 1984

33. This has been greatly clarified by the work of Jobey, Robertson and Maxwell: Jobey 1974, 1982a, 1982b; Robertson 1970, 1975, 1978, 1983; Maxwell 1983a, 1989

34. On the settlements of this zone and their civilian and military context see Hartley 1972; Jobey 1974, 1982a; M.J. Green 1978; Hanson 1978b; Breeze 1979; Miket and Burgess 1984; Robertson 1970, 1983; Maxwell 1980, 1983a; Keppie 1989; Hanson and Macinnes 1991

35. On the general characteristics of Romano-British civilian settlements in this region see Jobey 1960, 1963, 1964, 1965; Clack 1982. See also Higham 1982, 1986, 1989; Higham and Jones 1976, 1983, 1985; Bewley 1994

36. R.A. Webster 1972

37. Kilbride-Jones 1938; W.G. Collingwood 1908, 1909

38. Jobey 1960; Clack, 1982 p. 380

39. Jobey 1960; Clack 1982, p. 380

40. Charlton and Day 1978; Clack 1982, p. 380

41. Jobey 1978b

42. Jobey 1970, 1973

43. Jobey 1960; Clack 1982, p. 380

44. Coggins and Fairless 1980

45. Jobey 1959

46. Higham and Jones 1983, 1985, pp. 95–7

47. Hodges 1991, pp. 74–7

48. Higham and Jones 1983, 1985, pp. 96–7

49. For surveys of settlement in this region see Hogg 1966; C.A. Smith 1974, 1977; Mytum 1982; Lloyd-Jones 1984, pp. 47–9; Crew 1984b; Kelly 1990

50. *Ibid*

51. Longley 1988

52. C.A. Smith 1986, 1987, 1988

53. RCAHMW Anglesey 1937; Savory 1961; Lloyd-Jones 1984, pp. 49–50

54. Lloyd-Jones 1984; Blockley 1991

55. Gardner and Savory 1964

56. O'Neil 1937; Musson 1981; Britnell 1989; Britnell and Musson 1985. See also Musson *et al.* 1991

57. For general surveys see H. James and Williams 1982; G. Williams 1988

58. G.J. Wainwright 1971; H. James and Williams 1982; G. Williams 1985, 1988

59. Avent 1973, 1975

60. G. Williams 1985, 1988

61. Benson, Evans and Williams 1990

62. G.J. Wainwright 1967; Boon 1988

63. Grealey and Jones 1972

64. For general surveys see C. Thomas 1966a; N. Johnson and Rose 1982; Quinnell 1986

65. *Ibid*

66. S.J. Simpson *et al.* 1989; Masson Phillips 1966; Todd 1987, pp. 227–8

67. Quinnell 1986, p. 120

68. Christie 1993; Fowler 1962; A. Saunders and Harris 1982; Harris 1980; Guthrie 1969; Christie 1978; Quinnell 1986, pp. 115–18, 120

69. C. Saunders 1972

70. H. Miles and Miles 1973, 1974; Quinnell 1986, pp. 126–30

71. Fox, Radford and Shorter 1950

72. Peacock 1969

73. For a recent discussion of this see Maxfield 1995

74. For a claimed example of a stone-built Romano-British shrine in this area see S.I. White 1981, 1982. Note, however, that this interpretation is far from secure: see H.J. James 1992

75. Dudley 1967; C. Thomas 1985, pp. 163–4

76. Rivet and Smith 1979

77. H. James 1993; Wacher 1995

78. B. Jones and Mattingly 1990, pp. 43–5, 154. See also K.R. Dark 1994a, pp. 97–102

79. K.R. Dark 1994a, pp. 99–100; B. Jones and Mattingly 1990, p. 44

80. However, some types of villas seem to be especially common in specific *civitates*, and such identities might have been expressed in other terms, such as differential use of artefacts or different religious beliefs. See Millett 1990, p. 200 for such a villa group

81. H. James and Williams 1982, pp. 297–9; Scott 1993a, p. 57

82. Branigan 1980; Clack 1982, pp. 381–5

83. Scott 1993, p. 48

84. Jobey 1978a; Charlton and Mitcheson 1984; extensively illustrated for the area south of the Wall by Welfare and Swan 1995

85. Daniels and Jones 1969; Welfare and Swan 1995

86. This is implied in Gildas' *De Excidio Britanniae* Book 1. On the date of Gildas and his geographical knowledge see K.R. Dark 1994a, pp. 258–66

87. R.C. Turner and Scaife 1995, especially Turner, pp. 204–20

CHAPTER 5

1. For a detailed account of Roman agricultural tools see Rees 1979

2. See, for example, Frere and St Joseph 1983, pp. 201–17

3. Discussed in Gaffney and Tingle 1989, pp. 210, 224–5

4. Williamson 1987

5. Fleming 1988

6. 'Celtic field' is a term loosely applied to fields of regular shape laid out prior to the Anglo-Saxon period: see Bowen 1961, p. 2

7. Bowen 1978

8. Ford 1982

9. Cunliffe 1977

10. Drewett 1982, pp. 97–104

11. For Rookery Hill see Bell 1976b. For Thundersbarrow Hill see Drewett 1978, pp. 72–3

12. Bowen and Fowler 1966, pp. 57–61

13. Ford *et al.* 1988; Bowden, Ford and Mees 1993

14. Entwistle *et al.* 1994

15. Riley 1978, 1980

16. Hayfield 1988, pp. 116–18

17. T.G. Allen *et al.* 1993, pp. 187–91

18. Fowler 1986

19. Benson and Miles 1974

20. Parrington 1978; Lambrick and Robinson 1979

21. Lambrick 1992, p. 99

22. C.A. Smith 1977

23. Higham and Jones 1983

24. Higham 1983

25. Higham 1978

26. Frere and St Joseph 1983, pp. 216–7

27. Higham and Jones 1985, pp. 91–3; Higham 1986, pp. 203–6

28. Frere and St Joseph 1983, pp. 214–16

29. Fowler 1983, p. 155

30. Frere 1988, p. 434

31. Haigh and Savage 1988, pp. 67–8

32. Guthrie 1969

33. N. Johnson and Rose 1982, p. 174, fig. 12.3

34. Fowler 1985, p. 81

35. Lambrick and Robinson 1979, pp. 121–2

36. For Silchester see Reid 1903, p. 426. For York see A.R. Hall, Kenward and Williams 1980, pp. 143–4. For London see Armitage, Locker and Straker 1987, p. 273

37. Cunliffe 1971a, p. 128

38. Lambrick and Robinson 1979, p. 127

39. Instances where box was used to line Roman coffins are given by Godwin 1975, p. 175

40. For Usk see Rees 1979, p. 45. For Coygan Camp and others see *ibid*, pp. 54–5

41. Fowler 1978, pp. 83–8

42. Lambrick 1992, pp. 97–9

43. Hartridge 1978

44. Rees 1979, pp. 59–61

45. For Latimer see Branigan 1971, pp. 47, 60–2, 180. For Gadebridge Park see Neal 1974, p. 42, fig. 22. For Newhaven see Bell 1976a. For Rudchester see Gillam *et al.* 1973

46. For Denton Burn see Frere 1988, p. 433. For Throckley see J. Bennett 1983. For Carrawburgh see Breeze 1972

47. Fowler 1983, pp. 153–4

48. *Ibid*, pp. 154–5

49. Topping 1989a, 1989b

50. Topping 1989b, p. 162; Frere 1984, pp. 278–9

51. Rees 1979, p. 57

52. For Rumney see J.R.L. Allen and Fulford 1986; Fulford, Allen and Rippon 1994. For Oldbury Flats see J.R.L. Allen and Fulford 1992

53. Fulford, Allen and Rippon 1994, p. 207

54. J.R.L. Allen and Fulford 1987, p. 274

55. Salway 1970, pp. 10–12

56. Frere and St Joseph 1983, pp. 213, 215

57. Discussed in Applebaum 1972, pp. 97–102

58. Frere and St Joseph 1983, pp. 212–14

59. B.B. Simmons 1979

60. M. Jones 1978, p. 109

61. Drewett 1982, pp. 104–5

62. M. Jones 1981, p. 113

63. Rees 1979, vol. 2, p. 474

64. *Ibid*, pp. 475–6

65. *Ibid*, p. 477

66. For York see A.R. Hall and Kenward 1990, pp. 412–14, 417–18. For Carlisle see Goodwin and Huntley 1991, pp. 59–60

67. For Rimsmoor see Waton 1982. For Hockham Mere see Sims 1978. For Hadrian's Wall see Dumayne and Barber 1994

68. Chambers 1989

69. It is not always possible to separate hemp pollen from that of the hop (*Humulus lupulus*), which is in the same family (Cannabaceae) and occurs naturally in fen environments. See Godwin 1967; French and Moore 1986

70. For Crose Mere see Beales 1980. For Leash Fen see Hicks 1971. For Hockham and Rimsmoor see note 67

71. For Moel y Gerddi see Chambers and Price 1988. For Thorpe Bulmer see Bartley *et al.* 1976. For Fozy Moss see Dumayne and Barber 1994

72. Hall, Kenward and Williams 1980, p. 143

73. For Thornborough see Veen 1992, p. 46. For Collfryn see G. Jones and Milles 1989, microfiche pp. 76, 81

74. Greig 1991, pp. 306–7

75. For London see Straker 1984, pp. 323–29. For South Shields see Veen 1992, pp. 47–50, 154–5

76. D. Williams 1979, p. 62

77. Kenward 1979, p. 71

78. Hillman 1981; G. Jones 1984, 1987. For comparison of these models in analysis of crop assemblages from northern England see Veen 1992, pp. 91–9

79. For Ashville see M. Jones 1978. For Danebury see M. Jones 1984

80. Veen 1992

81. M. Jones 1981; Greig 1991, p. 306

82. Veen, 1992, pp. 74–5

83. Club wheat (*Triticum compactum*) is a form of bread wheat (*T. aestivum*) that cannot usually be separately identified from archaeological material

84. Nye and Jones 1987

85. Veen 1992, p. 42

86. *Ibid*, pp. 42, 45

87. Hillman 1981, p. 146

88. Veen 1992, pp. 137–8; Hillman 1981, p. 147

89. For Farmoor see Lambrick and Robinson 1979. For Ashville see M. Jones 1978, p. 109

90. M. Jones 1978, p. 109

91. Veen 1989

92. M. Jones 1981; Greig 1991, p. 309

93. M. Jones 1989, p. 133

94. For Barton Court Farm see M. Jones and Robinson 1986, microfiche chapter 9. For Rock Castle see Veen 1992, p. 45

95. M. Jones 1981, p. 107

96. *Ibid*, p. 97; Greig 1991, p. 312

97. Evidence for the cultivation of grape available up to the mid-1970s is discussed by Williams 1977

98. For London see Willcox 1978; Tyers 1988, p. 448; Pearson and Giorgi 1992, p. 165. For Silchester see Reid 1903, p. 427. For York see Greig 1976; Hall and Kenward 1990, p. 407. For Gorhambury see A. Wainwright 1990, p. 218. For Winterton see D. Williams 1977, p. 331

99. D. Webster, Webster and Petch 1967; Meadows 1996

100. M. Jones 1978

101. M. Jones and Robinson 1986

102. King 1989, pp. 51–2; 1991, p. 15

103. For reviews of bone assemblages from Roman-period sites see King 1978, 1984, 1991; Maltby 1981; Luff 1982; Noddle 1984

104. Maltby 1981, pp. 159–60

105. King 1978, pp. 211–16; 1984, pp. 187–218; 1989, pp. 53–4

106. B. Wilson 1979, p. 133

107. Noddle 1986

108. King 1989, p. 59

109. Noddle 1984, pp. 110–11

110. *Ibid*, pp. 111, 115; Maltby 1981, pp. 175, 179–82

111. Van Driel-Murray 1993

112. King 1989, p. 55

113. Grant 1989, p. 138

114. King 1978, p. 216

115. Bowman 1994, pp. 68–70

116. Hodgson and Smith 1985, microfiche VIII; Seaward 1993, pp. 112–13

117. King 1978, p. 216

118. Grant 1981, pp. 210–11

119. King 1978, p. 216

120. See, for example, Biddick 1984

121. Maltby 1994, p. 98

CHAPTER 6

1. Wacher 1995; Burnham and Wacher 1990

2. Millett 1990, pp. 165–76

3. K.R. Dark 1996a

4. *Ibid*

5. Four important overviews of work on Romano-British towns have recently been published: Burnham and Wacher 1990; Greep 1993; Wacher 1995; A.E. Brown 1995. This section naturally leans heavily on the data summarized by these scholars. See also G. Webster 1988

6. Perring 1991b, pp. 44–6; Ottaway 1993, pp. 12, 20–1. On the first stages of the Wroxeter project see Ellis *et al.* 1994

7. Wacher 1995, pp. 391–4; H. James 1990, 1993

8. Esmonde Cleary 1987. For Southwark see Wacher 1995, pp. 105–7

9. Cowan 1992; Wacher 1995, pp. 105–7

10. Wacher 1995, pp. 89, 127, 305 provide clear examples

11. Stephens 1985a; Wacher 1995, pp. 46, 349–52, 327–8. For their military equivalents see Stephens 1985b

12. Wacher 1995, pp. 112–3, 127–8

13. Darvill and Gerrard 1994, pp. 57–86, especially p. 60

14. Wacher 1995, p. 308

15. Millett 1990, pp. 189–95; Burnham and Wacher 1990, p. 44

16. Boon 1974, p. 255

17. Burnham and Wacher 1990, p. 44

18. McWhirr 1976; Millett 1990, pp. 135–6; Wacher 1974, 1995, pp. 287, 317–16. Note his scepticism about the most celebrated urban farm of this sort, at Cirencester, p. 318

19. Perring 1991b, pp. 44–6

20. Greenwood and Maloney 1995

21. A thorough study of *mansiones* in Britain is provided by Black 1995, on which this paragraph is based

22. S.M. Davies *et al.* 1985

23. Potter and Johns 1992, pp. 206–7

24. For examples see Fulford 1993; Crummy 1993; Niblett 1993

25. For example, M.J. Jones 1985

26. Wacher 1995, p. 89

27. Wacher 1995, pp. 37, 39, 42–3

28. Mackreth 1987; Blagg 1991, pp. 3–7

29. Perring 1987; Blagg 1991

30. Perring 1987; Wacher 1995, pp. 63, 66–7, 95, 221–2, 230–1, 234–5

31. For example, at St Albans: Niblett 1993, pp. 88–91

32. Fulford 1993; Brewer 1991. For the view that these plans are essentially fourth century see Esmonde Cleary 1989, p. 77

33. For a recent general discussion K.R. Dark 1994a, pp. 15–19. The following is based on that – fully referenced – survey unless otherwise referenced here

34. Yule 1990, p. 623

35. The fullest recent discussion of its composition and variations is Macphail 1994. Comments here are based on that discussion unless otherwise referenced

36. Yule 1990, pp. 623–4

37. Reece 1980

38. P.W. Dixon 1988, 1992

39. Ottaway 1993, pp. 112–14

40. K.R. Dark 1994a, pp. 15–17

41. Macphail 1994, pp. 32–4, 36

42. Ottaway 1993, pp. 112–14

43. Yule 1990, pp. 261–4

44. Ottaway 1993, pp. 112–14

45. Discussed by Yule 1990, who views all dark earth as the outcome of such modification

46. Ottaway 1993, pp. 113–14

47. Simpson *et al.* 1989; Fulford and Rippon, 1994 pp. 4, 7; 1995 pp. 8–10

48. On the broader context of occupation in late Roman forts see Southern and Dixon 1996, especially pp. 83–6, 127–41

49. Perring 1987

50. *Ibid*; Wacher 1995, pp. 46, 49; P. Johnson 1993; Ling 1993

51. Walthew 1975

52. Wacher 1995, pp. 36, 38, 40, 42

53. Rivet and Smith 1979

54. Wacher 1995, pp. 42–3

55. Such as the legal text found in London relating to land in Kent: see Perring 1991b, pp. 47–8

56. Brewer 1991, p. 82, 1993, pp. 63–4

57. K.R. Dark 1993b

58. A.R. Birley 1979, 1981b

59. Burnham and Wacher 1990, pp. 62–70, 81

60. Wacher 1995, pp. 63, 66–8

61. Wacher 1995, pp. 88–111, 167–88. On Britain and imperial trade see Fulford 1984, 1989. See also Fulford 1991

62. For the diversity of the Romano-British population see A.R. Birley 1979, 1981b

63. P.W. Dixon 1988, 1992; Reece 1980

64. Wacher 1995, pp. 66–8

65. Perring 1987; Burnham 1989; Burnham and Wacher 1990, pp. 15–23

66. Burnham and Wacher 1990, pp. 18, 20

67. Wacher 1995, pp. 66–8

68. For a general discussion of Romano-British ('large') town life see Wacher 1995, pp. 33–81

69. On town/country economic relations see Fulford 1982; Millett 1990, pp. 195–7, Whittaker 1990

70. J. Rackham 1979; Armitage, West and Steadman, 1984

71. Stirland and Waldron 1990

72. Wacher 1995, pp. 19, 36, 38. See also Millett 1991

73. Collingwood and Richmond 1969, p. 166

74. Buteux 1990; Leach 1991a, 1991b

75. Burnham and Wacher 1990, pp. 62–76

76. Wacher 1995, pp. 19, 36, 38

77. Wacher 1995, p. 40

78. Millett 1986; Hingley 1989, pp. 111–20

79. St Patrick's account implies interlinkage between large and small towns: see K.R. Dark 1993b

80. Greene 1986, chapter 3

81. Henderson 1992, p. 112

82. Fulford 1984, 1989, pp. 178–80, 185–6

83. For samian ware in Britain see P.V. Webster 1987. For Severn Valley ware see P.V. Webster 1972, 1977a, 1977b; Rawes 1983; Timby 1990

84. P. Webster 1991; Monaghan 1987; Griffiths 1989. In general see Swan 1984, 1988

85. Farrar 1973; Swan 1984, p. 54

86. Gillam 1970, 1976. See also P. Webster 1991

87. For an excavated military pottery-production depot see Dannell and Wild 1987. See the discussion by Middleton 1979; Greene 1986

88. Fulford 1984, 1989, 1991. See also Hingley 1982

89. Swan 1984

90. Fulford 1975, 1989, pp. 192–5; Swan 1984

91. Young 1977; Fulford 1975; P.R. Wilson 1989

92. Fulford and Bird 1975; Fulford 1977

93. On the scale and methods of Romano-British pottery production in its imperial context, and in relation to comparative anthropological data see Peacock 1982

94. Fulford 1975; Young 1977

95. Lyne and Jefferies 1979

96. Swan 1984; Millett 1990, pp. 165–74

97. Burnham and Wacher 1990, pp. 81–92. See also B. Jones and Mattingly 1990, pp. 172–3, 209–10

98. B. Jones and Mattingly 1990, p. 209, fig. 6.27. See also Burnham and Wacher 1990, pp. 86–7

99. Wild 1978 for the site and its local context, Burnham and Wacher 1990, p. 87. See also Mackreth 1984

100. De la Bédoyère 1991, p. 98

101. For Sidlings Copse see Day 1991, 1993. For Headington Wick villa see Jewitt 1851

102. For a brief review of all the relevant evidence see Fulford and Huddleston 1991, especially pp. 38–40

103. B. Jones and Mattingly 1990, pp 180–1, 192–5

104. Cleere 1974; Cleere and Crossley 1986

105. Hodgkinson and Tebbut 1985; Cleere and Crossley 1986; Gardiner 1991

106. Crossley 1981a

107. B. Jones and Mattingly 1990, pp. 193–5

108. K.R. Dark 1996a

109. Jackson and Tylecote 1988

110. Branigan 1989; Cleere 1974; Money 1977

111. For examples of these see McWhirr 1979a, 1979b; McWhirr and Viner 1978; Rudling 1986; Soffe *et al.* 1989; Dunning 1949; G. Webster 1953; Elkington 1976; Whittick 1982

112. Beagrie 1989

113. Sealey 1995; Burnham and Wacher 1990, pp. 211–17; Fawn *et al.* 1990; Woodiwiss 1992

114. On this problematical site see Boon and Williams 1966; G.D.B. Jones and Lewis 1971; Burnham and Burnham 1993; Greene 1986, pp. 143–6; Bick 1988; Bick and Boon 1993; Annels and Burnham 1986; B. Jones and

Mattingly 1990, pp. 181–4; G.D.B. Jones and Maude 1991a, 1991b; Burnham, Burnham and Walker 1992

115. Spain 1985

116. Spain 1985. Publication of the site at Ickham, Kent, is forthcoming

117. Swan 1984 p. 6

118. Fulford 1977; Fulford and Hodder 1975; Hodder 1972, 1974, 1979; Hodder and Hassall 1971; Hodder and Millett 1980

119. Especially that by Duncan-Jones 1982. See also the archaeological discussion by Greene 1986

120. K.R. Dark 1996a

121. Greene 1986, p. 25

122. See B. Jones and Mattingly 1990, p. 211. For BB1 in the west see J.R.L. Allen and Fulford 1996

123. Swan 1984, pp. 8, 19, 87–9. On state-owned manufacturing for military supply in the late Roman period see S.T. James 1988

124. For the start of this controversy see Selkirk 1983; and for its resolution see Anderson 1992

125. For example, in Selkirk 1983. See also N.A.F. Smith 1978

126. B.B. Simmons 1979

127. Esmonde Cleary 1989

128. Peacock 1987

129. For a possible example, wherein such a community may have signalled some facet of group identity, see Quinnell 1993

130. K.R. Dark 1996b for this and the following two paragraphs

131. Burnham and Wacher 1990, pp. 209–11; Todd 1994

132. Hinchliffe *et al.* 1992; Strickland 1995

133. K.R. Dark 1996a

134. Richmond 1966

135. For example, see Leech 1977

136. Burnham and Wacher 1990, pp. 211–17; Woodiwiss 1992; Lowther 1930

137. Gray 1930; Burrow 1981, pp. 141, 198–202

138. K.R. Dark 1996a

139. *Ibid*; Greene 1986; Peacock 1982

140. On the most specialized Iron Age industry see Henderson 1992. For other examples see E. Morris 1994a, 1994b; Ehrenreich 1985, 1994

141. For Colchester see Crummy 1993. For Holt see Grimes 1930

142. Manning 1979

143. For general views see Crummy 1982; Todd 1987; Webster 1988. For individual towns see Fulford 1993; Qualmann 1993; Crummy 1993; Niblett 1993

144. Milne 1993; G. Webster 1993; Wacher 1995, pp. 28–31, 82–3, 88–90

145. Grimes 1930

146. Milne 1993; Wacher 1995, pp. 88–91

147. Discussed by Burnham and Wacher 1990, pp. 7–24, on which the following paragraph is based

148. Burnham and Wacher 1990, pp. 188–92, 192–8, 165–6. On the problems of classification and the enigmatic walled site at Bath see K.R. Dark 1993b

149. Denison 1994, p. 2

150. For example, see Reece 1980; R.F.J. Jones 1984, 1987b

CHAPTER 7

1. Esmonde Cleary 1989; K.R. Dark 1994a chapters 1 and 7

2. Hawkes 1989

3. Southern and Dixon 1996, pp. 46–52

4. Wacher 1995, pp. 108–9; Burnham and Wacher, 1990, pp. 121–2

5. Böhme 1986; Hines 1990; Scull 1992, 1993

6. On this see K.R. Dark 1994a

7. *Ibid*, pp. 8–9

8. On the spread of Anglo-Saxon burial customs and political control see K.R. Dark 1994a, pp. 218–19. The evidence from the East Midlands is discussed by Hines 1984, 1992; Scull 1992; Carver 1992; Williamson 1993, pp. 49–58

9. K.R. Dark 1994a

10. K.R. Dark 1993b

11. For a recent discussion see Dark 1993b

12. Esmonde Cleary 1989, pp. 172–3

13. For a discussion of the problem see K.R. Dark 1994b, pp. 93–5, 98

14. D. Miles 1986. Also discussed by Lewit 1991

15. Scull 1993

16. As by Lewit 1991

17. S. James *et al.* 1984

18. P.W. Dixon 1982; P.H. Dixon 1993

19. Potter and Johns 1992, pp. 212–3

20. K.R. Dark 1994a, pp. 86–9 on which the following paragraph is based. See also Wingfield 1995; Branigan 1971

21. K.R. Dark 1993b

22. Discussed in K.R. Dark 1994a, pp. 160–2, on which the observations in this and the following paragraph are based

23. Percival 1988, chapter 9

24. K.R. Dark 1983

25. Thomas and Holbrook 1996. See also Davies 1982, pp. 189–90

26. Burnham and Wacher 1990, p. 121. For a similar site at Wasperton, in the West Midlands, eventually used by people employing Anglo-Saxon burial customs, see Wise 1991

27. K.R. Dark 1996b

28. R. White 1988

29. A major research project directed by Heinrich Härke is currently examining this question. For preliminary results see Härke 1995

30. As pointed out by Higham 1992

31. Fleuriot 1982

32. K.R. Dark 1996b. See also Leech 1982

33. For dating and distribution see K.R. Dark 1994a, pp. 123–5, 1996b. Further examples, including sherds from Chisenbury Warren (Entwhistle *et al.* 1994), have been found since 1994

34. Woodward and Leach 1993, pp. 316–27. See also

K.R. Dark 1994a, chapter 2

35. Discussed in K.R. Dark 1994a, chapter 2

36. On the continuation of these types of burial into the sixth century in western Britain see H. James 1993; K.R. Dark 1994a, pp. 119–21

37. K.R. Dark 1996b

38. See below and K.R. Dark 1996b

39. K.R. Dark 1994b, chapter 2

40. H.J. James 1992

41. Olson 1989; Edwards and Lane 1992a; K.R. Dark 1994b, chapter 2

42. P. Hill 1987, 1988

43. K.R. Dark 1992

44. K.R. Dark 1994a, chapter 3

45. K.R. Dark 1994b, chapter 3

46. K.R. Dark 1992

47. P.J. Casey 1993

48. See also K.R. Dark and Dark 1996

49. K.R. Dark 1992

50. K.R. Dark 1992; K.R. Dark and Dark 1996

51. K.R. Dark 1996b

52. Böhme 1986; Hines 1990

53. K.R. Dark 1996b

54. *Ibid*

55. Wooding 1996

56. K.R. Dark 1996a

57. *Ibid*

58. Reece 1980

59. K.R. Dark 1994a

60. Wacher 1995, pp. 418, 420

61. K.R. Dark 1994a, pp. 84–5

62. K.R. Dark 1994a, p. 88

63. *Ibid*; Niblett 1993, pp. 89–90

64. For example, Bassett 1990, 1992

65. K.R. Dark 1994b, pp. 94–5

66. R. White 1990

67. Gildas *De Excidio Britanniae* Book 1

68. C.S. Green 1987

69. S.M. Davies *et al.* 1995

70. Edwards and Lane 1988, pp. 35–8

71. K.R. Dark 1996a, pp. 164–9

72. Brooks 1986, 1988. See also Wacher 1995

73. For a recent view of early Anglo-Saxon society and economy see Scull 1993

74. M.J. Jones 1993, 1994

75. Bassett 1990

76. J. Turner 1981, p. 71

77. Bell 1989

78. The following discussion summarizes the results of S.P. Dark 1996

79. J. Turner 1979

80. K.R. Dark and Dark 1996

81. Insofar as a correlation can be made on the basis of radiocarbon dates

82. P.J. Casey 1993

83. Day 1991, 1993

84. Waton 1982

85. S.P. Dark 1996

86. The overall sequence is discusssed in Hodges 1989a, 1989b

87. Dyer 1995; C. Lewis *et al.* 1996

88. Platt 1978

89. Some areas of medieval woodland overlie Roman sites, as has been demonstrated by Williamson (1984) in Essex. In most cases the period of origin of the woodland is uncertain, but at Sidlings Copse in Oxfordshire, regeneration has been dated to the late Saxon or early medieval periods, giving rise to the large area of woodland that became the medieval Royal Forest of Shotover and Stowood (Day 1990, 1993)

90. Wacher 1995, pp. 266–7

91. Morris 1989, p. 102

92. For example, there are some instances where medieval ridge and furrow seems to overlie, and be aligned with, Roman ditches (C. Taylor and Fowler 1978)

93. Leech 1982

94. On the shifting character of Anglo-Saxon settlement see Hamerow 1991. On the west see K.R. Dark 1996b

95. Dyer 1995; C. Lewis *et al.* 1996

96. K.R. Dark 1994a, pp. 218–33

97. Contra Hoskins 1955, p.11

98. See Wacher 1995

99. K.R. Dark 1994a, p. 35 for a map of these centres

BIBLIOGRAPHY

Only places of publication other than London are cited.

Addison, K., Edge, M.J. and Watkins, R. (eds) 1990. *North Wales Field Guide*, Coventry, Quaternary Research Association

Akeroyd, A.V. 1972. 'Archaeological and Historical Evidence for Subsidence in Southern Britain', *Philosophical Transactions of the Royal Society of London Series A*, **272**, 151–69

Aldsworth, F. and Rudling, D. 1996. 'Excavations at Bignor Roman Villa, West Sussex 1985–90', *Sussex Archaeological Collections* **133** (1995), 103–88

Allen, J.R.L. and Fulford, M.G. 1986. 'The Wentlooge Level: a Romano-British Saltmarsh Reclamation in Southeast Wales', *Britannia*, **17**, 91–117

—— 1987. 'Romano-British Settlement and Industry on the Wetlands of the Severn Estuary', *The Antiquaries Journal*, **67**, 237–74

—— 1992. 'Romano-British and Later Geoarchaeology at Oldbury Flats: Reclamation and Settlement on the Changeable Coast of the Severn Estuary', *Archaeological Journal*, **149**, 82–123

—— 1996. 'The Distribution of South-East Dorset Black Burnished Category I Pottery in South-West Britain', *Britannia*, **27**, 223–81

Allen, M.J. 1992. 'Products of Erosion and the Prehistoric Land-use of the Wessex Chalk' in Bell and Boardman, pp. 37–52

Allen, T.G., Darvill, T.C., Green, L.S. and Jones, M.U. 1993. *Excavations at Roughground Farm, Lechlade, Gloucestershire: a Prehistoric and Roman Landscape*, Oxford, Oxford University Committee for Archaeology

Anderson, J.D. 1992. *Roman Military Supply in North-east England: an Analysis of and an Alternative to the Piercebridge Formula*, Oxford, British Archaeological Reports (BAR) British Series, no. 224

Annells, A.E. and Burnham, B.C. 1986. *Dolaucothi Gold Mines*, National Trust

Anon. 1995. 'Rare Bronze Age and Roman Finds in Thanet', *British Archaeology*, no. 9, 4

Applebaum, S. 1966. 'Peasant Economy and Types of Agriculture' in C. Thomas (ed.) 1966b, pp. 99–107

—— 1972. 'Roman Britain' in Finberg (ed.) 1972, pp. 5–277

ApSimon, A.M. 1965. 'The Roman Temple on Brean Down, Somerset', *Proceedings of the University of Bristol Speleological Society*, **10**, 195–258

Apted, M.R., Gilyard-Beer, R. and Saunders, A.D. (eds) 1977. *Ancient Monuments and their Interpretation*, HMSO

Armitage, P.L., Locker, A. and Straker, V. 1987. 'Environmental Archaeology in London: a Review' in Keeley, pp. 252–331

Armitage, P.L., West, B. and Steedman, K. 1984. 'New Evidence of Black Rat in Roman London', *London Archaeologist*, **4**, 375–83

Aston, M., Austin, D. and Dyer, C. (eds) 1989. *The Rural Settlements of Medieval England*, Oxford, Blackwell

Aston, M. and Burrow, I. (eds) 1982. *The Archaeology of Somerset*, Somerset County Council

Atherden, M.A. 1976. 'Late Quaternary Vegetational History of the North York Moors. III. Fen Bogs', *Journal of Biogeography*, **3**, 115–24

Avent, R. 1973. 'Excavations at Llangynog II 1972', *Carmarthenshire Antiquary*, **9**, 33–52

—— 1975. 'Excavations at Llangynog II 1974', *Carmarthenshire Antiquary*, **11**, 21–54

Baillie, M.G.L. 1994. 'Dendrochronology Raises Questions about the Nature of the AD 536 Dust-veil Event', *The Holocene*, **4**, 212–17

—— 1995. *A Slice Through Time*, Batsford

Baillie, M.G.L. and Munro, M.A.R. 1988. 'Irish Tree Rings, Santorini and Volcanic Dust Veils', *Nature*, **332**, 344–6

Balaam, N.D. *et al.* (eds) 1987. *Studies in Palaeoeconomy and Environment in South West England*, Oxford, BAR British Series, no. 181

Bammesberger, A. and Wollmann, A. (eds) 1990. *Britain, 400–600: Language and History*, Heidelberg, Carl Winter

Barber, K.E. 1981. *Peat Stratigraphy and Climatic Change*, Rotterdam, A.A. Balkema

—— 1982. 'Peat-bog Stratigraphy as a Proxy Climate Record' in Harding, pp. 103–13.

Barber, K.E., Chambers, F.M., Dumayne, L., Haslam, C.J., Maddy, D. and Stoneman, R.E. 1994. 'Climatic Change and Human Impact in North Cumbria: Peat Stratigraphic and Pollen Evidence from Bolton Fell Moss and Walton Moss' in Boardman and Walden, pp. 20–49

Barker, P. 1986. *Understanding Archaeological Excavation*, Batsford

—— (ed.) 1990. *From Roman Viroconium to Medieval Wroxeter*, Worcester, West Mercian Archaeological Consultants Ltd

Barrett, J.C., Fitzpatrick, A.P., Macinnes, L. (eds) 1989. *Barbarians and Romans in North-west Europe*, Oxford, BAR International Series, no. 471

Bartley, D.D., Chambers, C. and Hart-Jones, B. 1976. 'The Vegetational History of Parts of South and East Durham', *New Phytologist*, **77**, 437–68

Bassett, S. 1990. 'The Roman and Medieval Landscape of Wroxeter' in Barker (ed.) 1990, pp. 10–12

—— 1992. 'Church and Diocese in the West Midlands: the Transition from British to Anglo-Saxon Control' in Blair and Sharpe, pp. 13–40

Beagrie, N. 1989. 'The Romano-British Pewter Industry', *Britannia*, **20**, 169–91

Beales, P.W. 1980. 'The Late Devensian and Flandrian Vegetational History of Crose Mere, Shropshire', *New Phytologist*, **85**, 133–61

Bell, M.G. 1976a. 'The Excavation of an Early Romano-British Site and Pleistocene Landforms at Newhaven, Sussex', *Sussex Archaeological Collections*, **114**, 218–305

—— 1976b. 'Further Excavations on Rookery Hill, Bishopstone, East Sussex', *Bulletin of the Institute of Archaeology*, **13**, 66–74

—— 1977. 'Excavations at Bishopstone', *Sussex Archaeological Collections*, **115**, 1–299

—— 1989. 'Environmental Archaeology as an Index of Continuity and Change in the Medieval Landscape' in Aston *et al.*, pp. 269–86

—— 1992. 'The Prehistory of Soil Erosion' in Bell and Boardman, pp. 21–35

Bell, M.G. and Boardman, J. (eds) 1992. *Past and Present Soil Erosion: Archaeological and Geographical Perspectives*, Oxford, Oxbow Monograph, no. 22

Bellhouse, R.L. 1989. 'Roman Sites on the Cumberland Coast; a New Schedule of Coastal Sites', *Kendal, Cumberland and Westmorland Antiquarian and Archaeological Society Research Series*, no. 3

Bennett, C.M. 1962. 'Cox Green Roman Villa', *Berkshire Archaeological Journal*, **60**, 62–91

Bennett, J. 1983. 'The Examination of Turret 10A and the Wall and Vallum at Throckley, Tyne and Wear, 1980', *Archaeologia Aeliana*, 5th series, **11**, 27–60

Benson, D. and Miles, D. 1974. *The Upper Thames Valley: an Archaeological Survey of the River Gravels*, Oxford, Oxfordshire Archaeological Unit

Benson, D.G., Evans, J.G. and Williams, G.H. 1990. 'Excavations at Stackpole Warren, Dyfed', *Proceedings of the Prehistoric Society*, **56**, 179–245

Bewley, R.H. 1994. *Prehistoric and Romano-British Settlement in the Solway Plain, Cumbria*, Oxford, Oxbow Monograph, no. 36

Bick, D.E. 1988. 'An Ancient Leat near Dolaucothi Gold Mine', *Archaeology in Wales*, **28**, 20–1

Bick, D.E. and Boon, G. 1993. 'Dolaucothi Again', *Britannia*, **24**, 247–9

Biddick, K. 1984. 'Pig Husbandry on the Peterborough Abbey Estate from the Twelfth to the Fourteenth Century AD' in Grigson and Clutton-Brock, pp. 161–77

Bidwell, P.T. 1985. *The Roman Fort of Vindolanda*, Historic Buildings and Monuments Commission for England (HBMCE)

—— 1991. 'Later Roman Barracks in Britain' in Maxfield and Dobson, pp. 9–15

—— 1996. 'The Exterior Decoration of Roman Buildings in Britain' in P. Johnson and Haynes, pp. 19–29

Bidwell, P.T. and Holbrook, N. 1989. *Hadrian's Wall Bridges*, HBMCE

Bidwell, P.T. and Speak, S. 1994. *Excavations at South Shields Roman Fort*, Vol. I, Newcastle, Society of Antiquaries

Bird, D.G. 1987. 'The Romano-British Period in Surrey', in Bird and Bird, pp. 165–96

Bird, J. and Bird, D.G. 1987. *The Archaeology of Surrey to 1540*, Guildford, Surrey Archaeological Society

Birks, H.J.B. and West, R.G. (eds) 1973. *Quaternary Plant Ecology*, Oxford, Blackwell

Birley, A.R. 1979. *The People of Roman Britain*, Batsford

—— 1981a. 'The Economic Effects of Roman Frontier Policy' in King and Henig, pp. 39–53

—— 1981b. *The Fasti of Roman Britain*, Oxford, Clarendon

Birley, E., Dobson, B. and Jarrett, M.G. (eds) 1974. *Roman Frontier Studies 1969*, Cardiff, University of Wales Press

Birley, R. 1977. *Vindolanda: a Roman Frontier Post on Hadrian's Wall*, Thames and Hudson

Bishop, M.C. and Dore, J.N. 1988. *Roman Corbridge: the Fort and Town*, HBMCE

Bishop, M.W. and Allason-Jones, L. 1988. *Excavations at Corbridge: the Hoard*, HBMCE

Black, E.W. 1982. 'The Roman Villa at Darenth', *Archaeologia Cantiana*, **97** (1981), 159–83

—— 1987a. 'Romano-British Burial Customs and Religious Beliefs in South-East England', *Archaeological Journal*, **143** (1986), 201–39

—— 1987b. *The Roman Villas of South-East England*, Oxford, BAR British Series, no. 171

—— 1994. 'Villa-owners: Romano-British Gentlemen and Officers', *Britannia*, **25**, 99–110

—— 1995. *Cursus Publicus. The Infrastructure of Government in Roman Britain*, Oxford, BAR British Series, no. 241

Blackford, J.J. and Chambers, F.M. 1991. 'Proxy Records of Climate from Blanket Mires: Evidence for a Dark Age (1400 BP) Climatic Deterioration in the British Isles', *The Holocene*, **1**, 63–7

Blagg, T.F.C. 1986. 'Roman Religious Sites in the British Landscape', *Landscape History*, **8**, 15–25

—— 1991. 'Buildings' in R.F.J. Jones (ed.) 1991, pp. 3–14

—— 1996. 'The External Decoration of Romano-British Buildings' in P. Johnson and Haynes, pp. 9–18

Blagg, T.F.C. and King, A. (eds) 1984. *Military and Civilian in Roman Britain*, Oxford, BAR British Series, no. 136

Blagg, T.F.C. and Millett, M. (eds) 1990. *The Early Roman Empire in the West*, Oxford, Oxbow

Blair, J. and Sharpe, R. (eds) 1992. *Pastoral Care Before the Parish*, Leicester, Leicester University Press

Blockley, K. 1991. 'The Romano-British Period' in Manley *et al.*, pp. 117–28

Boardman, J. 1992. 'Current Erosion on the South Downs: Implications for the Past' in Bell and Boardman, pp. 8–19

Boardman, J. and Walden, J. (eds) 1994. *Cumbria Field Guide*, Oxford, Quaternary Research Association

Böhme, H.W. 1986. 'Das Ende der Römerherrschaft in Britannien un die Angelsachsische Besiedlung Englands im 5 Jahrhundert', *Jahrbuch des Römisch-Germanischen Zetralmuseums*, **33**, 469–574

Boon, G.C. 1974. *Silchester: the Roman Town of Calleva*, Newton Abbot, David and Charles

—— 1980. 'Caerleon and the Gwent Levels in Early Historic Times' in Thompson, pp. 24–36

—— 1988. 'Counterfeit Coins in Roman Britain' in Casey and Reece, pp. 102–88

Boon, G.C. and Williams, C. 1966. 'The Dolaucothi Drainage Wheel', *Journal of Roman Studies*, **56**, 122–7

Bowden, M., Ford, S. and Mees, G. 1993. 'The Date of the Ancient Fields on the Berkshire Downs', *Berkshire Archaeological Journal*, **74** (1991–3), 109–33

Bowden, M., Mackay, D. and Topping, P. (eds) 1989. *From Cornwall to Caithness*, Oxford, BAR British Series, no. 209

Bowden, M. and McOmish, D. 1989. 'Little Boxes: More about Hillforts', *Scottish Archaeological Review*, **6**, 12–16

Bowen, H.C. 1961. *Ancient Fields*, British Association for the Advancement of Science

—— 1978. 'Celtic Fields and "Ranch" Boundaries in Wessex' in Limbrey and Evans, pp. 115–23

Bowen, H.C. and Fowler, P.J. 1966. 'Romano-British Rural Settlements in Dorset and Wiltshire' in C. Thomas (ed.) 1966b, pp. 43–67

—— (eds) 1978. *Early Land Allotment*, Oxford, BAR British Series, no. 48

Bowman, A.K. 1994. *Life and Letters on the Roman Frontier*, British Museum Press

Bowman, A.K. and Thomas, J.D. 1983. *Vindolanda: the Latin Writing-tablets*, Britannia Monograph, no. 4

—— 1987. 'New Texts from Vindolanda', *Britannia*, **18**, 125–42

—— 1991. 'A Military Strength Report from Vindolanda', *Journal of Roman Studies*, **81**, 62–73

Bowman, A.K., Thomas, J.D. and Adams, 1990. 'Two Letters from Vindolanda', *Britannia*, **21**, 33–52

Bradley, R. 1984. *The Social Foundations of Prehistoric Britain*, Longman

—— 1991. 'The Patterns of Change in British Prehistory' in Earle, pp. 44–70

Branigan, K. 1971. *Latimer*, Bristol, Chess Valley Archaeological and Historical Society

—— 1973. 'Gauls in Gloucestershire', *Transactions of the Bristol and Gloucestershire Archaeological Society*, **92**, 82–94

—— 1976a. *The Roman Villa in South-west England*, Bradford-on-Avon, Moonraker Press

—— 1976b. 'Villa Settlement in the West Country' in Branigan and Fowler, pp. 120–41

—— (ed.) 1980. *Rome and the Brigantes: the Impact of Rome on Northern England*, Department of Archaeology and Prehistory, University of Sheffield

—— 1982. 'Celtic farm to Roman Villa' in D. Miles (ed.) 1982b, pp. 81–96

—— 1985. *The Catuvellauni*, Gloucester, Alan Sutton

—— 1989. 'Specialisation in Villa Economies' in Branigan and Miles, pp. 42–50

Branigan, K. and Dearne, M.J. (eds) 1992. *Romano-British Cavemen: Cave Use in Roman Britain*, Oxford, Oxbow Monograph, no. 19

Branigan, K. and Fowler, P.J. (eds) 1976. *The Roman West Country*, Newton Abbot, David and Charles

Branigan, K. and Miles, D. (eds) 1989. *The Economies of Romano-British Villas*, Sheffield, J.R. Collis

Breeze, D.J. 1972. 'Excavations at the Roman Fort of Carrawburgh, 1967–1969', *Archaeologia Aeliana*, 4th series, **50**, 81–144

—— 1975. 'The Abandonment of the Antonine Wall: its Date and Implications', *Scottish Archaeological Forum*, **7**, 67–80

—— (ed.) 1979. *Roman Scotland: Some Recent Excavations*, Edinburgh, unpub. typescript

—— 1982. *The Northern Frontiers of Roman Britain*, Batsford

—— 1984. 'Demand and Supply on the Northern Frontier' in Miket and Burgess, pp. 264–86

—— 1985. 'Roman Forces and Native Populations', *Proceedings of the Society of Antiquaries of Scotland*, **115**, 223–8

—— 1989. 'The Northern Frontiers' in Todd (ed.) 1989b, pp. 37–60

—— 1993. 'Cavalry on Frontiers: Hadrian to Honorius' in Clark *et al.*, pp. 19–35

Breeze, D.J. and Dobson, B. 1969. 'Fort Types on Hadrian's Wall', *Archaeologia Aeliana*, 4th series, **47**, 15–32

—— 1974. 'Fort Types as a Guide to Garrisons: a Reconsideration' in E. Birley *et al.*, pp. 13–19

—— 1985. 'Roman Military Deployment in North England', *Britannia*, **16**, 1–19

—— 1987. *Hadrian's Wall*, 3rd edn, Harmondsworth, Penguin

Brewer, R.J. 1991. 'Caerwent – *Venta Silurum*: a Civitas-capital' in Burnham and Davies, pp. 75–85

—— 1993. '*Venta Silurum*: a Civitas capital' in Greep, pp. 56–65

Briggs, G., Cook, J. and Rowley, T. (eds) 1986. *The Archaeology of the Oxford Region*, Oxford University Department of External Studies

Britnell, W. 1989. 'The Collfryn Hillslope Enclosure, Llansantffraid Deuddwr, Powys: Excavation 1980–1982', *Proceedings of the Prehistoric Society*, **55**, 89–134

Britnell, W. and Musson, C. 1985. 'Rescue Excavation of a Romano-British Double-ditched Enclosure at Arddleen, Llandrinio, northern Powys', *Archaeologia Cambrensis* (1984), **133**, 91–9

Brodribb, A.C.C., Hands, A.R. and Walker, D.R. 1968. *Excavations at Shakenoak Farm, near Wilcote, Oxfordshire Part I: sites A & D*, Oxford, privately published

—— 1971. *Excavations at Shakenoak Farm, near Wilcote, Oxfordshire Part II: Sites B & H*, Oxford, privately published

—— 1972. *Excavations at Shakenoak Farm, near Wilcote, Oxfordshire Part III: Site F*, Oxford, privately published

—— 1973. *Excavations at Shakenoak Farm, near Wilcote, Oxfordshire Part IV: Site C*, Oxford, privately published

—— 1978. *Excavations at Shakenoak Farm, near Wilcote, Oxfordshire Part V: Sites K and E*, Oxford, BAR

Bromwich, J. 1970. 'Freshwater Flooding along the Fen Margins South of the Isle of Ely during the Roman Period' in Phillips, pp. 114–26

Brooks, D.A. 1986. 'A Review of the Evidence for Continuity in British Towns in the Fifth and Sixth Centuries', *Oxford Journal of Archaeology*, **5**, 77–102

—— 1988. 'The Case for Continuity in Fifth Century Canterbury Re-examined', *Oxford Journal of Archaeology*, **7**, 99–114

Brooks, H. and Bedwin, O. 1989. *Archaeology at the Airport. The Stansted Archaeological Project 1985–89*, Chelmsford, Essex County Council

Brown, A.E. (ed.) 1995. *Roman Small Towns in Eastern England and Beyond*, Oxford, Oxbow Monograph, no. 52

Brown, A.P. 1977. 'Late-Devensian and Flandrian Vegetational History of Bodmin Moor, Cornwall', *Philosophical Transactions of the Royal Society B*, **276**, 251–320

Bruce, J.C. 1978. *Handbook to the Roman Wall*, 13th edn, C.M. Daniels (ed.), Newcastle-upon-Tyne, Frank Graham

Brun, P., van der Leeuw, S. and Whittaker, C. (eds.) 1993. *Frontieres d'Empire: Nature et Signification des Frontieres Romaines*, Nemours, Mémoires du Musée de Prehistoire d'Ile-de-France, no. 5

Buckland, P.C. 1976. *The Environmental Evidence from the Church Street Roman Sewer System*, Council for British Archaeology (CBA)

Burgess, C.B., 1980. 'The Bronze Age in Wales' in J.A. Taylor, pp. 243–86

Burl, A. (ed.) 1988. *From Roman Town to Norman Castle: Essays in Honour of Philip Barker*, Birmingham, University of Birmingham

Burnham, B.C. 1989. 'A Survey of Building Types in Romano-British "Small Towns"', *Journal of the British Archaeological Association*, **141** (1988), 35–59

Burnham, B.C. and Burnham, H. 1993. 'Survey and Excavation on the Line of the Annell Leat at Dolaucothi', *Archaeology in Wales*, **33**, 16–19

Burnham, B.C., Burnham, H. and Walker, M.J.C. 1992. 'Excavations Across the Annell and Gwenlais Leats, Near Dolaucothi, in 1990', *Archaeology in Wales*, **32**, 2–8

Burnham, B.C. and Davies, J.L. (eds) 1991. *Conquest, Co-existence and Change: Recent Archaeological Work in Roman Wales*, Trivium, no. **25** (1990)

Burnham, B.C. and Johnson, H.B. (eds) 1979. *Invasion and Response: the Case of Roman Britain*, Oxford, BAR British Series, no. 73

Burnham, B.C. and Wacher, J. 1990. *The Small Towns of Roman Britain*, Batsford

Burnham, C.P. 1989. 'The Coast of South-east England in Roman Times' in Maxfield (ed.) 1989, pp. 12–17

Burrow, I.G.C. 1979. 'Roman Material in Hillforts' in Casey (ed.) 1979, pp. 219–29

—— 1981. *Hillfort and Hill-top Settlement in Somerset in the First to Eighth Centuries AD*, Oxford, BAR British Series, no. 91

Buteux, S. 1990. *Romans in Shepton Mallet*, Birmingham University Field Archaeology Unit

Carson, R.A.G. and Kraay, C.M. (eds.) 1978. *Scripta Nummaria Romana: Essays Presented to Humphrey Sutherland*, Spink

Carver, M.O.H. 1992. *The Age of Sutton Hoo*, Woodbridge, Boydell Press

Caseldine, A.E. 1986. 'The Environmental Context of the Meare Lake Villages', *Somerset Levels Papers*, **12**, 73–96

—— 1988. 'A Reinterpretation of the Pollen Sequence from Meare', *Somerset Levels Papers*, **14**, 53–6

Casey, P.J. (ed.) 1979. *The End of Roman Britain*, Oxford, BAR British Series, no. 71

—— 1982. 'Civilians and Soldiers – Friends, Romans, Countrymen?' in Clack and Haselgrove, pp. 123–32

—— 1993. 'The End of Garrisons on Hadrian's Wall: an Historico-environmental Model' in Clark *et al.*, pp. 69–80

Casey, P.J. and Davies, J.L. 1993. *Excavations at Segontium (Caernarfon) Roman Fort 1975–79*, CBA Research Report, no. 90

Casey, P.J. and Reece, R. (eds) 1988. *Coins and the Archaeologist*, 2nd edn, Seaby

Chambers, F.M. 1983. 'The Palaeoecological Setting of Cefn Gwernffrwd – a Prehistoric Complex in Mid-Wales', *Proceedings of the Prehistoric Society*, **49**, 303–16

—— 1989. 'The Evidence for Early Rye Cultivation in North West Europe' in Milles *et al.*, pp. 165–75

—— 1993. *Climate Change and Human Impact on the Landscape*, Chapman and Hall

Chambers, F.M. and Lageard, J.G.A. 1993. 'Vegetational History and Environmental Setting of Crawcwellt, Gwynedd', *Archaeology in Wales*, **33**, 23–5

Chambers, F.M. and Price, S.-M. 1988. 'The Environmental Setting of Erw-wen and Moel y Gerddi: Prehistoric Enclosures in Upland Ardudwy, North Wales', *Proceedings of the Prehistoric Society*, **54**, 93–100

Chambers, R.A. 1976. 'A Romano-British Settlement Site and Seventh Century Burial, Ducklington, Oxon, 1974', *Oxoniensia*, **40**, 171–200

Champion, T. 1994. 'Socio-economic Development in Eastern England in the First Millennium BC' in Kristiansen and Jensen, pp. 125–44

Champion, T. and Collis, J. (eds) 1995. *Recent Trends in the Archaeology of Iron Age Britain*, Sheffield, J.R. Collis

Champion, T.C. and Megaw, J.V.S. (eds) 1985. *Settlement and Society. Aspects of West European Prehistory in the First Millennium BC*, Leicester, Leicester University Press

Chapman, J.C. and Mytum, H. (eds) 1983. *Settlement in North Britain 1000 BC–AD 1000*, Oxford, BAR British Series, no. 118

Charlesworth, D. 1977. 'The Turrets on Hadrian's Wall' in Apted *et al.*, pp. 13–26

Charlton, B. and Mitcheson, M. 1984. 'The Roman Cemetery at Petty Knowes, Rochester, Northumberland', *Archaeologia Aeliana*, 5th Series, **12**, 1–31

Charlton, D.B. and Day, J.C. 1978. 'Excavation and Field Survey in Upper Redesdale', *Archaeologia Aeliana*, 5th Series, **6**, 61–86

Chevallier, R. 1976. *Roman Roads*, Batsford

Christie, P.M.L. 1978. 'The Excavation of an Iron Age Souterrain and Settlement at Carn Euny, Sancreed, Cornwall', *Proceedings of the Prehistoric Society*, **44**, 309–433

—— 1993. *Chysauster and Carn Euny*, English Heritage

Churchill, D.M. 1970. 'Post-Neolithic to Romano-British Sedimentation in the Southern Fenlands of Cambridgeshire and Norfolk' in Phillips, pp. 132–46

Clack, P.A.G. 1982. 'The Northern Frontiers: Farmers in the Military Zone' in D. Miles (ed.) 1982b, pp. 377–402

Clack, P.A.G. and Haselgrove, S. 1982. *Rural Settlement in the Roman North*, Durham, CBA Research Report, no. 3

Clark, D.F., Roxan, M.M. and Wilkes, J.J. (eds) 1993. *The Later Roman Empire Today*, Institute of Archaeology

Clarke, D.L. 1972a. 'A Provisional Model of an Iron Age Society and its Settlement System' in D.L. Clarke (ed.) 1972b, pp. 801–69

—— (ed.) 1972b. *Models in Archaeology*, Methuen

Clarke, G. 1982. 'The Roman Villa at Woodchester', *Britannia*, **13**, 197–228

Clarke, S. 1990. 'The Social Significance of Villa Architecture in Celtic Northwest Europe', *Oxford Journal of Archaeology*, **9**, 337–53

Clay, P. 1985. 'A Survey of Two Cropmark Sites in Lockington–Hemington Parish, Leicestershire', *Transactions of the Leicestershire Archaeology and History Society*, **59** (1984–85), 17–26

Cleere, H. 1974. 'The Roman Iron Industry of the Weald and its Connexions with the Classis Britannica', *Archaeological Journal*, **131**, 171–99

Cleere, H. and Crossley, D.W. 1986. *The Iron Industry of the Weald*, Leicester, Leicester University Press

Clifford, E.M. 1954. 'The Roman Villa, Witcombe', *Transactions of the Bristol and Gloucestershire Archaeological Society*, **73**, 5–69

—— 1961. *Bagendon: a Belgic Oppidum, Excavations 1954–1956*, Cambridge, Heffer

Cocks, A.H. 1921. 'A Romano-British Homestead in the Hambleden Valley, Bucks', *Archaeologia*, **71**, 141–98

Coggins, D and Fairless, K.J. 1980. 'Excavations at the Early Settlement Site of Forcegarth Pasture North, 1972–4', *Transactions of the Architecture and Archaeology Society of Durham and Northumberland*, 2nd series, **5**, 31–8

Cole, G.H. 1994. *Archaeological Rescue Excavations at No. 42 London Road, Bagshot, Surrey. Interim Report 1992–1994*, Surrey Heath Archaeological and Heritage Trust

Coles, J.M. 1987. 'Meare Village East', *Somerset Levels Papers*, **3**

Coles, J.M., Caseldine, A.E. and Morgan, R.A. 1982. 'The Eclipse Track 1980', *Somerset Levels Papers*, **8**, 26–39

Coles, J.M. and Minnitt, S. 1995. *'Industrious and Fairly Civilized' the Glastonbury Lake Village*, Somerset Levels Project/Somerset County Council Museums Service

Coles, J.M. and Orme, B.J. 1977. 'Neolithic Hurdles from Walton Heath, Somerset', *Somerset Levels Papers*, **3**, 6–29

—— 1978. 'Structures South of Meare Island', *Somerset Levels Papers*, **4**, 91–106

Collingwood, R.G. and Richmond, I.A. 1969. *The Archaeology of Roman Britain*, 2nd edn, Methuen

Collingwood, R.G. and Wright, R.P. 1965. *The Roman Inscriptions of Britain, 1. Inscriptions on Stone*, Oxford, Clarendon Press

Collingwood, W.G. 1908. 'Report of an Exploration of the Romano-British Settlement at Ewe Close, Crosby Ravensworth', *Transactions of the Cumberland and Westmorland Antiquarian and Archaeological Society*, 2nd Series, **8**, 355–68

—— 1909. 'Report on a Further Exploration of the Romano-British Settlement at Ewe Close, Crosby Ravensworth', *Cumberland and Westmorland Archaeological and Antiquarian Society*, 2nd Series, **9**, 295–309

Collis, J.R. 1984. *Oppida: Earliest Towns North of the Alps*, Department of Archaeology and Prehistory, University of Sheffield

—— 1994. 'The Iron Age' in Vyner (ed.) 1994, pp. 123–48

Corder, P. and Kirk, J.L. 1932. *A Roman Villa at Langton, near Malton, East Yorkshire*, Leeds, Yorkshire Archaeological Society

Cottam, S., Dungworth, D., Scott, S. and Taylor, J. 1994. *TRAC 1994*, Oxford, Oxbow

Coulston, J.C.N. (ed.) 1988. *Military Equipment and the Identity of Roman Soldiers*, Oxford, BAR International Series, no. 394

Cowan, C. 1992. 'A Possible Mansio in Roman Southwark: Excavations at 15–23 Southwark Street, 1980–86', *Transactions of the London and Middlesex Archaeological Society*, **43**, 3–191

Craddock, P.T. and Hughes, M.J. (eds) 1985. *Furnaces and Smelting Technology in Antiquity*, British Museum

Creighton, J. 1995. 'Visions of Power: Imagery and Symbols in Late Iron Age Britain', *Britannia*, **26**, 285–301

Crew, P. 1983. 'Bryn y Castell, Ffestiniog', *Archaeology in Wales*, **23**, 17–19

—— 1984a. 'Bryn y Castell, Ffestiniog', *Archaeology in Wales*, **24**, 37–40

—— 1984b. 'Rectilinear Settlements in Gwynedd', *Bulletin of the Board of Celtic Studies*, **31**, 320–1

—— 1989. 'Excavations at Crawcwellt West, Merioneth, 1986–1989: A Late Prehistoric Upland Iron-working Settlement', *Archaeology in Wales*, **29**, 11–16

—— 1991a. 'Crawcwellt West, Trawsfynnydd', *Archaeology in Wales*, **31**, 7

—— 1991b. 'Late Iron Age and Roman Iron Production in North-west Wales' in Burnham and Davies, pp. 150–60

Crossley, D.W. 1981a. 'Medieval Ironsmelting' in Crossley (ed.) 1981b, pp. 29–41

—— (ed.) 1981b. *Medieval Industry*, CBA Research Report, no. 40

Crow, J. 1995 *Housesteads*, Batsford/English Heritage

Crumley, C.L. 1974. *Celtic Social Structure: the Generation of Archaeologically Testable Hypotheses from Literary Evidence*, University of Michigan, Museum of Anthropology

Crummy, P. 1980. 'The Temples of Roman Colchester' in Rodwell (ed.) 1980b, pp. 243–83

—— 1982. 'The Origins of Some Major Romano-British Towns', *Britannia*, **13**, 125–34

—— 1992. 'Royal Graves', *Colchester Archaeologist*, **5** (1991–2), 1–5

—— 1993. 'The Development of Roman Colchester' in Greep, pp. 34–45

Cunliffe, B.W. 1971a. *Excavations at Fishbourne 1961–1969, Vol. I: the Site*, Leeds, Report of the Research Committee of the Society of Antiquaries of London, no. 26

—— 1971b. *Excavations at Fishbourne 1961–1969, Vol. II: the Finds*, Leeds, Report of the Research Committee of the Society of Antiquaries of London, no. 27

—— 1973. *The Regni*, Duckworth

—— 1977. 'The Romano-British Village at Chalton, Hants', *Proceedings of the Hampshire Field Club and Archaeological Society*, **33**, 45–67

—— 1984a. *Danebury: an Iron Age Hillfort in Hampshire Vol. 1: the Excavations, 1969–1978: the Site*, CBA Research Report, no. 52

—— 1984b. *Danebury: an Iron Age Hillfort in Hampshire Vol. 2: the Excavations, 1969–1978: the Finds*, CBA Research Report, no. 52

—— 1984c. 'Iron Age Wessex: Continuity and Change' in Cunliffe and Miles, pp. 12–45

—— 1987. *Hengistbury Head, Dorset, Vol. 1: The Prehistoric and Roman Settlement, 3500 BC–AD 500*, Oxford University Committee for Archaeology

—— 1988. *Mount Batten, Plymouth: a Prehistoric and Roman Port*, Oxford University Committee for Archaeology

—— 1991. *Iron Age Communities in Britain*, 3rd edn, Routledge

—— 1994a. 'After hillforts', *Oxford Journal of Archaeology*, **13**, 71–84

—— 1994b. *Fishbourne Roman Palace*, Sussex Archaeological Society

Cunliffe, B.W. and Miles, D. (eds) 1984. *Aspects of the Iron Age in Central Southern Britain*, Oxford University Committee for Archaeology Monograph, no. 2

Cunliffe, B.W. and Poole, C. 1991a. *Danebury: an Iron Age Hillfort in Hampshire, Vol. 4: the Excavations 1969–1978*, CBA Research Report, no. 73

—— 1991b. *Danebury: an Iron Age Hillfort in Hampshire, Vol. 5: the Excavations 1979–1988*, CBA Research Report, no. 73

Curwen, E.C. 1933. 'Excavations on Thundersbarrow Hill, Sussex', *Antiquaries Journal*, **13**, 109–33

Daniels, C.M. 1980. 'Excavations at Wallsend and the Fourth-Century Barracks on Hadrian's Wall' in Hanson and Keppie, pp. 173–93

—— 1989. 'The Flavian and Trajanic Northern Frontier' in Todd (ed.) 1989b, pp. 31–5

—— 1990. 'How many Miles on the Cumberland Coast?', *Britannia*, **21**, 401–6

—— 1991. 'The Antonine Abandonment of Scotland' in Maxfield and Dobson, pp. 48–51

Daniels, C.M. and Jones, G.D.B. 1969. 'The Roman Camps on Llandrindod Common', *Archaeologia Cambrensis*, **20**, 124–33

Dannell, G.B. and Wild, J.P. 1987. *Longthorpe II: the Military Works Depot*, Britannia Monograph, no. **8**

Dark, K.R. 1983. 'Celtic Monastic Archaeology: Fifth to Eighth Centuries', *Monastic Studies*, **14**, 17–29

—— 1990. *Brawdy Hillfort Excavation. Interim Report 1990*, Brawdy Research Project

—— 1992. 'A Sub-Roman Redefence of Hadrian's Wall?', *Britannia*, **23**, 111–20

—— 1993a. 'Roman-period Activity at Prehistoric Ritual Monuments in Britain and in the Armorican Peninsula' in Scott (ed.) 1993b, pp. 133–46

—— 1993b. 'St Patrick's *Uillula* and the Fifth-century Occupation of Romano-British Villas' in Dumville *et al.*, pp. 19–24

—— 1994a. *Civitas to Kingdom. British Political Continuity 300–800*, Leicester University Press

—— 1994b. *Discovery by Design. The Identification of Secular Elite Settlements in Western Britain AD 400–700*, Oxford, BAR British Series, no. 237

—— 1995. *Theoretical Archaeology*, Duckworth

—— 1996a. 'Proto-industrialisation and the End of the Roman Economy' in K.R. Dark (ed.) 1996c, pp. 1–21

—— 1996b. 'Pottery and Local Production at the End of Roman Britain' in K.R. Dark (ed.) 1996c, pp. 53–65

—— (ed.) 1996c. *External Contacts and the Economy of Late Roman and Post-Roman Britain*, Woodbridge, Boydell Press

Dark, K.R. and Dark, S.P. 1996. 'New Archaeological and Palynological Evidence for a Sub-Roman Reoccupation of Hadrian's Wall', *Archaeologia Aeliana*, 5th Series, **24**, 57–72

Dark, S.P. 1996. 'Palaeoecological Evidence for Landscape Continuity and Change in Britain *ca*. AD 400–800' in K.R. Dark (ed.) 1996c, pp. 23–51

Darvill, T.C. and Gerrard, C. (eds) 1994. *Cirencester: Town and Landscape*, Cirencester, Cotswold Archaeological Trust

Davies, G. and Turner, J. 1979. 'Pollen Diagrams from Northumberland', *New Phytologist*, **82**, 783–804

Davies, J.L. 1980. 'Roman Military Deployments in Wales and the Marches from Claudius to the Antonines' in Hanson and Keppie, pp. 255–77

—— 1984. 'Soldiers, Peasants and Markets in Wales and the Marches' in Blagg and King, pp. 93–127

—— 1991a. 'Military *Vici*: Recent Research and its Significance' in Burnham and Davies, pp. 65–74

—— 1991b. 'Roman Military Deployment in Wales and the Marches from Pius I to Theodosius I' in Maxfield and Dobson, pp. 52–7

Davies, S.M., Stacey, L.C. and Woodward, P.J. 1985. 'Excavations at Allington Avenue, Fordington, Dorchester, 1984/5: Interim Report', *Proceedings of the Dorset Natural History and Archaeological Society*, **107**, 101–10

Davies, W. 1982. *Wales in the Early Middle Ages*, Leicester University Press

Dawson, M. 1994. *A Late Roman Cemetery at Bletsoe*, Bedfordshire Archaeology Monograph, no. 1

Day, S.P. 1990. *History and Palaeoecology of Woodlands in the Oxford Region*, unpublished D.Phil. thesis, University of Oxford

—— 1991. 'Post-glacial Vegetational History of the Oxford Region', *New Phytologist*, **119**, 445–70

—— 1993. 'Woodland Origin and "Ancient Woodland Indicators": a Case-study from Sidlings Copse, Oxfordshire, UK', *The Holocene*, **3**, 45–53

De la Bédoyère, G. 1991. *The Buildings of Roman Britain*, Batsford

Denison, S. 1994. 'Iron Age Origin Suspected for Roman Town', *British Archaeological News*, no. 18, 2

Dennis, M.G. 1978. '1–7 St Thomas Street', in Southwark and Lambeth Archaeological Excavation Committee, pp. 291–422

Dent, J.S. 1982. 'Cemeteries and Settlement Patterns of the Iron Age on the Yorkshire Wolds', *Proceedings of the Prehistoric Society*, **48**, 437–58

—— 1983a. 'The Impact of Roman Rule on Native Society in the Territory of the Parisi', *Britannia*, **14**, 35–44

—— 1983b. 'Weapons, Wounds and War in the Iron Age', *The Archaeological Journal*, **140**, 120–8

Detsicas, A.P. (ed.) 1973. *Current Research in Romano-British Coarse Pottery*, CBA Research Report, no. 10

—— 1983. *The Cantiaci*, Gloucester, Alan Sutton

Devoy, R.J.N. 1979. 'Flandrian Sea-level Changes and Vegetational History of the Lower Thames Estuary', *Philosophical Transactions of the Royal Society of London B*, **285**, 355–407

Dickinson, W. 1975. 'Recurrence Surfaces in Rusland Moss, Cumbria (Formerly North Lancashire)', *Journal of Ecology*, **63**, 913–35

Didsbury, P. 1988. 'Evidence for Romano-British Settlement in Hull and the Lower Humber Valley' in J. Price and Wilson, pp. 21–35

Dix, B. 1981. 'The Romano-British Farmstead at Odell and its Setting: some Reflections on the Roman Landscape of the SE Midlands', *Landscape History*, **3**, 17–26

Dixon, P.H. 1993. 'The Anglo-Saxon Settlement at Mucking: an Interpretation' in Filmer-Sankey, pp. 125–47

Dixon, P.W. 1982. 'How Saxon is the Saxon House?' in Drury, pp. 175–88

—— 1988. 'Life after Wroxeter: the Final Phases of Roman Towns' in Burl (ed.) 1988, pp. 30–9

—— 1992. 'The Cities are not Populated as once they were' in Rich, pp. 145–60

Dobson, B. (ed.) 1979. *The Tenth Pilgrimage of Hadrian's Wall*, Kendal, Cumberland and Westmorland Antiquarian and Archaeological Society

Donaldson, A.M. and Turner, J. 1977. 'A Pollen Diagram from Hallowell Moss, near Durham City, U.K.', *Journal of Biogeography*, **4**, 25–33

Donaldson, G.H. 1986. 'Roman Military Signalling on the North British Frontiers', *Archaeologia Aeliana*, 5th series, **13**, 19–24

—— 1988. 'Signalling Communications and the Roman Imperial Army', *Britannia*, **19**, 349–56

Dore, J. and Greene, K. (eds) 1977. *Roman Pottery Studies in Britain and Beyond*, Oxford, BAR International Series, no. 30

Douglas, I. and Hagedorm, J. (eds) 1993. *Geomorphology and Geoecology: Fluvial Geomorphology*. Zeitschrift fur Geomorphologie, Suppl. **88**

Down, A. 1979. *Chichester Excavations IV. The Roman Villas at Chilgrove and Upmarden*, Chichester, Phillimore

Downey, R., King, A. and Soffe, G. 1980. 'The Hayling Island Temple and Religious Connections across the Channel' in Rodwell (ed.) 1980b, pp. 289–304

Drewett, P.L. 1978. 'Field Systems and Land Allotment in Sussex 3rd Millennium BC to 4th Century AD' in Bowen and Fowler (eds.) 1978, pp. 67–80

—— 1982. *The Archaeology of Bullock Down, Eastbourne, East Sussex: the Development of a Landscape*, Lewes, Sussex Archaeological Society

Drewett, P.L., Rudling, D. and Gardiner, M. 1988. *The South-east to AD 1000*, Longman

Drinkwater, J.F. 1981. 'Money Rents and Food-renders in Gallic Funerary Reliefs' in King and Henig, pp. 215–33

Drury, P.J. 1980. 'Non-classical Religious Buildings in Iron Age and Roman Britain: a Review' in Rodwell (ed.) 1980b, pp. 45–78

—— (ed.) 1982. *Structural Reconstruction*, Oxford, BAR British Series, no. 110

Dudley, D. 1967. 'Excavations on Nor'nour in the Isles of Scilly, 1962–6', *Archaeological Journal*, **124**, 1–64

Dugmore, A.J., Larsen, G. and Newton, A.J. 1995. 'Seven Tephra Isochrones in Scotland', *The Holocene*, **5**, 257–66

Dumayne, L. and Barber, K.E. 1994. 'The Impact of the Romans on the Environment of Northern England: Pollen Data from Three Sites Close to Hadrian's Wall', *The Holocene*, **4**, 165–7

Dumayne, L., Stoneman, R., Barber, K. and Harkness, D. 1995. 'Problems Associated with Correlating Calibrated Radiocarbon-dated Pollen Diagrams with Historical Events', *The Holocene*, **5**, 118–23

Dumville, D.N. *et al.* 1993. *Saint Patrick, AD 493–1993*, Woodbridge, Boydell Press

Duncan-Jones, R.P. 1982. *The Economy of the Roman Empire*, Cambridge, Cambridge University Press

Dunnett, R. 1975. *The Trinovantes*, Duckworth

Dunning, G.C. 1949. 'The Purbeck Marble Industry in Roman Britain', *Archaeological News Letter*, **1**, 15

Dyer, C. 1995. 'On the Trail of the Village Revolution', *British Archaeology*, **5**, 8–9

Eagles, B.N. and Swan, V.G. 1972. 'The Chessalls, a Romano-British Settlement at Kingscote', *Transactions of the Bristol and Gloucestershire Archaeological Society*, **91**, 60–91

Earle, T. (ed.) 1991. *Chiefdoms: Power, Economy and Ideology*, Cambridge University Press

Edwards, N. and Lane, A. (eds) 1988. *Early Medieval Settlements in Wales AD 400–1100*, University College of North Wales, Bangor University College, Cardiff

—— 1992a. 'The Archaeology of the Early Church in Wales: an Introduction' in Edwards and Lane, pp. 1–11

—— 1992b. *The Early Church in Wales and the West*, Oxford, Oxbow Monograph, no. 16

Ehrenreich, R. 1985. *Trade, Technology, and the Ironworking Community in the Iron Age of Southern Britain*, Oxford, BAR British Series, no. 144

—— 1994. 'Ironworking in Iron Age Wessex' in Fitzpatrick and Morris, pp. 16–18

Elkington, H.D.H. 1976. 'The Mendip Lead Industry' in Branigan and Fowler, pp. 183–99

Ellis, P. 1984. *Catsgore 1979*, Bristol, Western Archaeological Trust

Ellis, P., Evans, J., Hannaford, H., Hughes, G. and Jones, A. 1994. 'Excavations in the Wroxeter Hinterland 1988–1990: the Archaeology of the A5/A49 Shrewsbury Bypass', *Transactions of the Shropshire Archaeological and Historical Society*, **69**, 1–119

Elner, J.K. and Happey-Wood, C.M. 1980. 'The History of Two Linked but Contrasting Lakes in North Wales from a Study of Pollen, Diatoms and Chemistry in Sediment Cores', *Journal of Ecology*, **68**, 95–121

Entwistle, R., Fulford, M. and Raymond, F. 1994. *Salisbury Plain Project 1993–4 Interim Report*, Reading, University of Reading

Esmonde Cleary, A.S. 1987. *Extra-Mural Areas of Romano-British Towns*, Oxford, BAR British Series, no. 169

—— 1989. *The Ending of Roman Britain*, Batsford

Evans, J. 1987. 'Graffiti and the Evidence of Literacy and Pottery Use in Roman Britain', *Archaeological Journal*, **144**, 191–204

Evans, J.G., Limbrey, S. and Cleere, H. (eds) 1975. *The Effect of Man on the Landscape: the Highland Zone*, CBA Research Report, no. 11

Farrar, R.A.H. 1973. 'The Techniques and Sources of Romano-British Black-burnished Ware' in Detsicas (ed.) 1973, pp. 67–103

Farwell, D.E. and Molleson, T.I. 1993. *Excavations at Poundbury 1966–80, Vol 2: the Cemeteries*, Dorchester, Dorset Natural History and Archaeological Society

Faull, M.L. and Moorhouse, S.A. (eds) 1981. *West Yorkshire: an Archaeological Survey to AD 1500*, Wakefield, W. Yorkshire Metropolitan County Council

Fawn, A.J., Evans, K.A., McMaster, I. and Davies, G.M.R. 1990. *The Red Hills of Essex*, Colchester Archaeology Group

Field, N.H. 1965. 'Romano-British Settlement at Studland, Dorset', *Proceedings of the Dorset Natural History and Archaeology Society*, **87**, 142–207

Figueiral, I. 1992. 'The Charcoals' in Fulford and Allen 1992, pp. 188–91

Filmer-Sankey, W. (ed.) 1993. *Anglo-Saxon Studies in Archaeology and History*, **6**, Oxford University Committee for Archaeology

Finberg, H.P.R. 1955. *Roman and Saxon Withington*, Occasional Paper, no. 8, Department of Local History, University of Leicester

—— (ed.) 1972. *The Agrarian History of England and Wales, Vol. 1 part 2*, Cambridge University Press

Fitzpatrick, A.P. 1984. 'The Deposition of La Tène Iron Age Metalwork in Watery Contexts in Southern England' in Cunliffe and Miles, pp. 178–90

—— 1985. 'The Distribution of Dressel 1 Amphorae in North-West Europe', *Oxford Journal of Archaeology*, **4**, 305–40

—— 1986. 'Camulodunum and the Early Occupation of South-East England: Some Reconsiderations' in Unz, pp. 35–41

—— 1991. 'Celtic (Iron Age) Religion – Traditional and Timeless?', *Scottish Archaeological Review*, **8**, 123–8

Fitzpatrick, A.P. and Morris, E. (eds) 1994. *The Iron Age in Wessex: Recent Work*, Salisbury, Association Francaise D'Etude de L'Age du Fer/Trust for Wessex Archaeology

Fleming, A. 1988. *The Dartmoor Reaves*, Batsford

Fleuriot, L. 1982. *Les Origines de la Bretagne*, Paris, Payot

Ford, S. 1982. 'Linear Earthworks on the Berkshire Downs', *Berkshire Archaeological Journal*, **71** (1981–2), 1–20

Ford, S., Bowden, M., Mees, G. and Gaffney, V. 1988. 'The Date of the "Celtic" Field-Systems on the Berkshire Downs', *Britannia*, **19**, 401–4

Fowler, P.J. 1962. 'A Native Homestead of the Roman Period at Porth Godrevy, Gwithian', *Cornish Archaeology*, **1**, 61–84

—— 1967. 'The Archaeology of Fyfield and Overton Downs, Wiltshire: Third Interim Report', *Wiltshire Archaeology and Natural History Magazine*, **62**, 16–32

—— 1968. 'Excavation of a Romano-British Settlement at Row of Ashes Farm, Butcombe, North Somerset: Interim Report, 1966–7', *Proceedings of the University of Bristol Speleological Society*, **11**, 209–36

—— 1970. 'Fieldwork and Excavation in the Butcombe Area, North Somerset', *Proceedings of the University of Bristol Speleological Society*, **12**, 169–94

—— 1976. 'Farms and Fields in the Roman West Country' in Branigan and Fowler, pp. 162–82

—— 1978. 'The Abingdon Ard-share' in Parrington, pp. 83–8

—— 1983. *The Farming of Prehistoric Britain*, Cambridge University Press

—— 1986. 'The Roman Field System in Barnsley Park' in G. Webster *et al.*, pp. 77–82

Fox, A., Radford, C.A.R. and Shorter, A.H. 1950. 'Report on the Excavations at Milber Down, 1937–8', *Proceedings of the Devon Archaeological Exploration Society*, **4** (1949–50), 27–66

Fox, A. and Ravenhill, W.L.D. 1966. 'Early Roman Outposts on the North Devon Coast, Old Burrow and Martinhoe', *Proceedings of the Devon Archaeological Society*, **24**, 3–39

—— 1972. 'The Roman Fort at Nanstallon, Cornwall', *Britannia*, **3**, 56–111

France, N.E. and Gobel, B.M. 1985. *The Romano-British Temple at Harlow, Essex*, Gloucester, Alan Sutton

French, C.N. and Moore, P.D. 1986. 'Deforestation, *Cannabis* Cultivation and Schwingmoor Formation at Cors Llyn (Llyn Mire), Central Wales', *New Phytologist*, **102**, 469–82

Frere, S.S. 1982. 'The Bignor Villa', *Britannia*, **13**, 135–96

—— 1984. 'Roman Britain in 1983: Sites Explored', *Britannia*, **15**, 266–332

—— 1986. 'Roman Britain in 1985: Sites Explored', *Britannia*, **17**, 363–427

—— 1987. *Britannia: a History of Roman Britain*, 3rd edn, Routledge/Kegan Paul

—— 1988. 'Roman Britain in 1987: Sites Explored', *Britannia*, **19**, 416–84

Frere, S.S. and St Joseph, J.K.S. 1983. *Roman Britain from the Air*, Cambridge University Press

Fulford, M.G. 1975. *New Forest Roman Pottery: Manufacture and Distribution, with a Corpus of the Pottery Types*, Oxford, BAR British Series, no. 17

—— 1977. 'Pottery and Britain's Foreign Trade in the Later Roman Period' in Peacock (ed.) 1977, pp. 35–84

—— 1982. 'Town and Country in Roman Britain – a Parasitical Relationship?' in D. Miles (ed.) 1982b, pp. 403–19

—— 1984. 'Demonstrating Britannia's Economic Dependence in the First and Second Centuries' in Blagg and King, pp. 129–42

—— 1985. 'Roman Material in Barbarian Society *c.* 200 BC–*c.* AD 400' in Champion and Megaw, pp. 96–108

—— 1989. 'The Economy of Roman Britain' in Todd (ed.) 1989b, pp. 175–201

—— 1991. 'Britain and the Roman Empire: the Evidence for Regional and Long Distance Trade' in R.F.J. Jones (ed.) 1991, pp. 35–47

—— 1992. 'Iron Age to Roman: a Period of Radical Change on the Gravels' in Fulford and Nichols, pp. 23–38

—— 1993. 'Silchester: the Early Development of a Civitas Capital' in Greep, pp. 16–33

Fulford, M.G. and Allen, J.R.L. 1992. 'Iron-making at the Chesters Villa, Woolaston, Gloucestershire: Survey and Excavation 1987–91', *Britannia*, **23**, 159–215

Fulford, M.G., Allen, J.R.L. and Rippon, S.J. 1994. 'The Settlement and Drainage of the Wentlooge Level, Gwent: Excavation and Survey at Rumney Great Wharf 1992', *Britannia*, **25**, 175–211

Fulford, M.G. and Bird, J. 1975. 'Imported Pottery from Germany in Late Roman Britain', *Britannia*, **6**, 171–81

Fulford, M.G. and Hodder, I.R. 1975. 'A Regression Analysis of some Late Romano-British Pottery: a Case Study', *Oxoniensia*, **39**, 26–33

Fulford, M.G. and Huddleston, F. 1991. *The Current State of Romano-British Pottery Studies*, English Heritage

Fulford, M.G. and Nichols, E. (eds) 1992. *The Archaeology of the British Gravels: a Review*, Society of Antiquaries

Fulford, M.G. and Rippon, S. 1994. *Excavations at Pevensey Castle 1994. Interim Report*, Department of Archaeology, University of Reading

—— 1995. *Excavations at Pevensey Castle 1995. Interim Report*, Department of Archaeology, University of Reading

Gaffney, V. and Tingle, M. 1989. *The Maddle Farm Project: an Integrated Survey of Prehistoric and Roman Landscapes on the Berkshire Downs*, Oxford, BAR British Series, no. 200

Gardiner, M. 1991. 'The Archaeology of the Weald – a Survey and a Review', *Sussex Archaeological Collections*, **128** (1990), 33–53

Gardner, W. and Savory, H.N. 1964. *Dinorben: a Hill-fort Occupied in Early Iron Age and Roman Times*, Cardiff, National Museum of Wales

Garton, D. 1988. 'Dunston's Clump and the Brickwork Plan Field Systems at Babworth, Nottinghamshire: Excavations 1981', *Transactions of the Thoroton Society of Nottinghamshire*, **91** (1987), 16–73

Garwood, P. *et al.* 1991. *Sacred and Profane*, Oxford University Committee for Archaeology

Gascoigne, P.E. 1970. 'Clear Cupboard Villa, Farmington, Gloucestershire', *Transactions of the Bristol and Gloucestershire Archaeological Society*, **88**, 34–67

Gelling, M. 1988. *Signposts to the Past*, 2nd edn, Phillimore

Gibson, D. and Geselowitz, M. (eds) 1988. *Tribe and Polity in Late Prehistoric Europe*, New York, Plenum Press

Gillam, J.P. 1970. *Types of Roman Coarse Pottery Vessels in Northern Britain*, Newcastle upon Tyne, Oriel Press

—— 1975. 'Possible Changes in Plan in the Course of Construction of the Antonine Wall', *Scottish Archaeological Forum*, **7**, 51–6

Gillam, J.P. and Daniels, C.M. 1961. 'The Roman Mausoleum on Shorden Brae, Beaufront, Corbridge, Northumberland', *Archaeologia Aeliana*, 4th series, **39**, 37–61

Gillam, J.P., Harrison, R.M. and Newman, T.G. 1973. 'Interim Report on Excavations at the Roman Fort of Rudchester, 1972' *Archaeologia Aeliana*, 5th series, **1**, 81–5

Girling, M. and Staker, V. 1993. 'Plant Macrofossils, Arthropods, and Charcoal' in Woodward and Leach, pp. 250–3

Godwin, H. 1943. 'Coastal Peat-beds of the British Isles and North Sea', *Journal of Ecology*, **31**, 199–247

—— 1967. 'Pollen-analytical Evidence for the Cultivation of *Cannabis* in England', *Review of Palaeobotany and Palynology*, **4**, 71–80

—— 1975. *History of the British Flora*, 2nd edn, Cambridge University Press

—— 1978. *Fenland: its Ancient Past and Uncertain Future*, Cambridge University Press

Goodall, I.H. 1972. 'Industrial Evidence from the Villa at Langton, East Yorkshire', *Yorkshire Archaeological Journal*, **44**, 32–7

Goodburn, D. 1991. 'A Roman Timber Framed Building Tradition', *Archaeological Journal*, **148**, 182–204

Goodburn, R. 1978. 'Winterton: Some Villa Problems' in Todd 1978b, pp. 93–102

—— 1981. *Chedworth Roman Villa*, National Trust

Goodwin, K. and Huntley, J.P. 1991. 'The Waterlogged Plant Remains' in McCarthy 1991, pp. 54–60

Gracie, H.S. 1971. 'Frocester Court Roman Villa; First Report', *Transactions of the Bristol and Gloucestershire Archaeological Society*, **89** (1970), 15–86

Gracie, H.S. and Price, E.G. 1980. 'Frocester Court Roman Villa: Second Report', *Transactions of the Bristol and Gloucestershire Archaeological Society*, **97** (1979), 9–64

Graham, A.H. 1978. 'The Geology of North Southwark and its Topographical Development in the Post-Pleistocene Period', in Southwark and Lambeth Archaeological Excavation Committee, pp. 501–17

Grant, A. 1981. 'The Significance of Deer Remains at Occupation Sites of the Iron Age to the Anglo-Saxon Period' in M. Jones and Dimbleby, pp. 205–13

—— 1989. 'Animals in Roman Britain' in Todd (ed.) 1989b, pp. 135–46

Grant, E. (ed.) 1986. *Central Places, Archaeology and History*, Sheffield, Department of Archaeology and Prehistory, University of Sheffield

Gray, H. St G. 1930. 'Excavations at Kingsdown Camp, near Mells, Somerset', *Archaeologia*, **80**, 59–96

Grealey, S. and Jones, G.D.B. 1972. 'Excavations at Castell Cogan 1971: an Interim Report', *Carmarthenshire Antiquary*, **8**, 17–26

Green, C.S. 1987. *Excavations at Poundbury, Dorchester, Dorset 1966–1982, Vol. I: the Settlements* (ed. by S.M. Davies and A. Ellison), Dorchester, Dorset Natural History and Archaeological Society

Green, M.J. 1978. *A Corpus of Small Cult-objects from the Military Areas of Roman Britain*, Oxford, BAR British Series, no. 52

Greene, K. 1986. *The Archaeology of the Roman Economy*, Batsford

Greenwood, P. and Maloney, C. 1995. 'London Fieldwork and Publication Round-up 1994', *London Archaeologist*, **7**, 343

Greep, S.J. (ed.) 1993. *Roman Towns: the Wheeler Inheritance*, York, CBA Research Report, no. 93

Greig, J. 1976. 'The Plant Remains' in Buckland, pp. 23–8

—— 1988. 'Some Evidence of the Development of Grassland Plant Communities' in M. Jones 1988, pp. 39–54

—— 1991. 'The British Isles' in Zeist *et al.*, pp. 299–334

Grew, F.O. and Hobley, B. (eds) 1985. *Roman Urban Topography in Britain and the Western Empire*, CBA Research Report, no. 59

Griffith, F.M. 1984. 'Roman Military Sites in Devon: Some Recent Discoveries', *Proceedings of the Devon Archaeological Society*, **42**, 11–32

Griffiths, K.E. 1989. 'Marketing of Roman Pottery in Second-century Northamptonshire and the Milton Keynes Area', *Journal of Roman Pottery Studies*, **2**, 67–76

Grigson, C. and Clutton-Brock, J. (eds) 1984. *Animals and Archaeology, 4: Husbandry in Europe*, Oxford, BAR International Series, no. 227

Grimes, W.F. 1930. *Holt, Denbighshire: the Works-depot of the Twentieth Legion at Castle Lyons*, Y Cymmrodor, 41

Groves, C. 1991. 'Absolute Dating' in McCarthy 1991, pp. 50–3

Guthrie, A. 1969. 'Excavation of a Settlement at Goldherring, Sancreed, 1958–1961', *Cornish Archaeology*, **8**, 5–39

Hadman, J. 1978. 'Aisled Buildings in Roman Britain' in Todd (ed.) 1978b, pp. 187–95

Haigh, D. and Savage, M. 1988. 'Sewingshields', *Archaeologia Aeliana*, 5th Series, **12**, 33–147

Hall, A.R. and Kenward, H.K. 1990. *Environmental Evidence from the Colonia: General Accident and Rougier Street*, CBA

—— (eds) 1994. *Urban-rural Connexions: Perspectives from Environmental Archaeology*, Oxford, Oxbow Monograph, no. 47

Hall, A.R., Kenward, H.K. and Williams, D. 1980. *Environmental Evidence from Roman Deposits in Skeldergate*, CBA

Hall, D. and Coles, J. 1994. *Fenland Survey: An Essay in Landscape and Persistence*, English Heritage

Hallam, S.J. 1964. 'Villages in Roman Britain: Some Evidence', *Antiquaries Journal*, **44**, 19–32

—— 1970. 'Settlement Around the Wash' in Phillips, pp. 22–113

Hamerow, H.F. 1991. 'Settlement Mobility and the "Middle Saxon Shift": Rural Settlements and Settlement Patterns in Anglo-Saxon England', *Anglo-Saxon England*, **20**, 1–17

Hands, A.R. 1993. *The Romano-British Roadside Settlement at Wilcote, Oxfordshire I*, Oxford, BAR British Series, no. 232

Hanley, R. 1987. *Villages in Roman Britain*, Princes Risborough, Shire

Hanson, W.S. 1978a. 'The Organisation of Roman Military Timber-Supply', *Britannia*, **9**, 293–305

—— 1978b. 'Roman Campaigns North of the Forth–Clyde Isthmus: the Evidence of the Temporary Camps', *Proceedings of the Society of Antiquaries of Scotland*, **109**, 140–50

—— 1979. 'Croy Hill' in Breeze (ed.) 1979, pp. 19–20

—— 1989. 'The Nature and Function of Roman Frontiers' in Barrett *et al.*, pp. 55–63

—— 1994. 'Dealing with Barbarians: the Romanisation of Britain' in Vyner (ed.) 1994, pp. 149–63

Hanson, W.S. and Campbell, D.B. 1986. 'The Brigantes: from Clientage to Conquest', *Britannia*, **17**, 73–89

Hanson, W.S. and Keppie, L.J.F. (eds) 1980. *Roman Frontier Studies 1979*, Oxford, BAR International Series, no. 71

Hanson, W.S. and Macinnes, L. 1991. 'Soldiers and Settlement in Wales and Scotland' in R.F.J. Jones (ed.) 1991, pp. 85–92

Hanson, W.S. and Maxwell, G.S. 1983. *Rome's North-west Frontier: the Antonine Wall*, Edinburgh University Press

Hanson, W.S., Daniels, C.M., Dore, J.N. and Gillam, J.P. 1979. 'The Agricolan Supply Base at Red House, Corbridge', *Archaeologia Aeliana*, 5th Series, **7**, 1–98

Hanworth, R. 1968. 'The Roman Villa at Rapsley, Ewhurst', *Surrey Archaeological Collections*, **65**, 1–70

Harding, A.F. (ed.) 1982. *Climatic Change in Later Prehistory*, Edinburgh University Press

Härke, H. 1995. 'Finding Britons in Anglo-Saxon Graves', *British Archaeology*, no. 10, 7

Harris, D. 1980. 'Excavation of a Romano-British Round at Shortlanesend, Kenwyn, Truro', *Cornish Archaeology*, **19**, 63–75

Hartley, B.R. 1972. 'The Roman Occupation of Scotland: the Evidence of Samian Ware', *Britannia*, **3**, 1–55

—— 1980. 'The Brigantes and the Roman Army' in Branigan (ed.) 1980, pp. 2–7

Hartley, B.R. and Fitts, R.L. 1988. *The Brigantes*, Gloucester, Alan Sutton

Hartridge, R. 1978. 'Excavations at the Prehistoric and Romano-British Site on Slonk Hill, Shoreham, Sussex', *Sussex Archaeological Collections*, **116**, 69–141

Haselgrove, C.C. 1982. 'Wealth, Prestige and Power: the Dynamics of Late Iron Age Political Centralization in South East England' in Renfrew and Shennan, pp. 79–88

—— 1984. 'Romanization Before the Conquest: Gaulish Precedents and British Consequences' in Blagg and King, pp. 5–63

—— 1986. 'An Iron Age Community and its Hillfort. The Excavations at Danebury 1969–79: a Review', *Archaeological Journal*, **143**, 363–67

—— 1987a. *Iron Age Coinage in South-east England: the Archaeological Context*, Oxford, BAR British Series, no. 174

—— 1987b. 'Culture Process on the Periphery: Belgic Gaul and Rome During the Late Republic and Early Empire' in Rowlands *et al.*, pp. 4–24

—— 1988. 'Coinage and Complexity: Archaeological Analysis of Socio-political Change in Britain and Non-Mediterranean Europe during the Late Iron Age' in Gibson and Geselowitz, pp. 69–96

—— 1993. 'The Development of British Iron Age Coinage', *Numismatic Chronicle for 1993*, 31–64

Haselgrove, C.C., Lowther, P.C. and Turnbull, P. 1991. 'Stanwick, North Yorkshire, Part 3: Excavations on Earthworks Sites 1981–86', *The Archaeological Journal*, **147** (1990), 37–90

Haselgrove, C.C., Turnbull, P. and Fitts, R.L. 1991. 'Stanwick, North Yorkshire, Part 1: Recent Research and Previous Archaeological Investigations', *The Archaeological Journal*, **147** (1990), 1–15

Hassall, M. 1987. 'Romans and Non-Romans' in Wacher (ed.) 1987, pp. 685–700

Hawkes, S.C. (ed.) 1989. *Weapons and Warfare in Anglo-Saxon England*, Oxford University Committee for Archaeology

Hayes, R.H. 1988. *North-east Yorkshire Studies: Archaeological Papers*, (ed. by P.R. Wilson), Leeds, Yorkshire Archaeological Society

Hayfield, C. 1988. 'The Origins of the Roman Landscape around Wharram Percy, East Yorkshire' in Price and Wilson, pp. 99–122

Hayward, L.C. 1953. 'The Roman Villa at Lufton, near Yeovil', *Proceedings of the Somersetshire Archaeological and Natural History Society*, **97** (1952), 91–112

—— 1972. 'The Roman Villa at Lufton, near Yeovil', *Proceedings of the Somerset Archaeology and Natural History Society*, **116** (1971–72), 59–77

Henderson, J. 1992. 'Industrial Specialization in Late Iron Age Britain and Europe', *Archaeological Journal*, **148** (1991), 104–48

Henig, M.E. 1984a. *Religion in Roman Britain*, Batsford

—— 1984b. 'Seasonal Feasts in Roman Britain', *Oxford Journal of Archaeology*, **3**, 213–23

Hibbert, F.A. 1980. 'Possible Evidence for Sea-level Change in the Somerset Levels' in F.H. Thompson (ed.) 1980, pp. 103–5

Hicks, S.P. 1971. 'Pollen-analytical Evidence for the Effect of Prehistoric Agriculture on the Vegetation of North Derbyshire', *New Phytologist*, **70**, 647–67

Higham, N.J. 1978. 'Early Field Survival in North Cumbria' in Bowen and Fowler (eds.) 1978, pp. 119–25

—— 1982. ' "Native" Settlements on the North Slopes of the Lake District', *Transactions of the Cumberland and Westmorland Antiquarian and Archaeological Society*, **82**, 29–33

—— 1983. 'A Romano-British Farm Site and Field System at Yanwath Wood, near Penrith', *Transactions of the Cumberland and Westmorland Antiquarian and Archaeological Society*, **83**, 49–58

—— 1986. *The Northern Counties to AD 1000*, Longman

—— 1989. 'Roman and Native in England North of the Tees: Acculturation and its Limitations' in Barrett *et al.*, pp. 153–74

—— 1992. *Rome, Britain and the Anglo-Saxons*, Seaby

Higham, N.J. and Jones, G.D.B. 1976. 'Frontiers, Forts and Farmers: Cumbrian Aerial Survey, 1974–5', *Archaeological Journal*, **132** (1975), 16–53

—— 1983. 'The Excavation of Two Romano-British Farm Sites in North Cumbria', *Britannia*, **14**, 45–72

—— 1985. *The Carvetii*, Gloucester, Alan Sutton

Hill, J.D. 1995a. 'How Should We Understand Iron Age Societies and Hillforts? A Contextual Study from Southern Britain' in Hill and Cumberpatch, pp. 45–66

—— 1995b. 'The Pre-Roman Iron Age in Britain and Ireland (*ca.* 800 BC to AD 100): an Overview', *Journal of World Prehistory*, **9**, 47–98

Hill, J.D. and Cumberpatch, C. (eds) 1995. *Different Iron Ages: Studies on the Iron Age in Temperate Europe*, Oxford, BAR International Series, no. 602

Hill, P. 1987. *Whithorn 2. Excavations 1987*, Whithorn, privately published

—— 1988. *Whithorn 1988 Supplement*, Whithorn, privately published

Hillam, J. and Morgan, R. 1986. 'Tree-ring Analysis of the Roman Timbers' in Miller *et al.*, pp. 75–85

Hillman, G. 1981. 'Reconstructing Crop Husbandry Practices from Charred Remains of Crops' in Mercer, pp. 123–61

Hinchliffe, J. and Thomas, R. 1980. 'Archaeological Investigations at Appleford', *Oxoniensia*, **45**, 9–111

Hinchliffe, J., Williams, J.H. and Williams, F. 1992. *Roman Warrington. Excavations at Wilderspool, 1966–9 and 1976*, Brigantia Monograph, no. 2, Department of Archaeology, University of Manchester

Hines, J. 1984. *The Scandinavian Character of Anglian England in the Pre-Viking Period*, Oxford, BAR British Series, no. 124

—— 1990. 'Philology, Archaeology, and the *Adventus Saxonum vel Anglorum*' in Bammesberger and Wollmann, pp. 17–36

—— 1992. 'The Scandinavian Character of Anglian England: an Update' in Carver, pp. 315–29

Hingley, R. 1982. 'Recent Discoveries of the Roman Period at the Noah's Ark Inn, Frilford, South Oxfordshire', *Britannia*, **13**, 305–9

—— 1985. 'Location, Function and Status: a Romano-British "Religious Complex" at the Noah's Ark Inn, Frilford, Oxfordshire', *Oxford Journal of Archaeology*, **4**, 201–14

—— 1988. 'The Influence of Roman on Indigenous Social Groups in the Upper Thames Valley' in R.F. Jones *et al.* (eds) 1988, pp. 73–97

—— 1989. *Rural Settlement in Roman Britain*, Seaby

—— 1990. 'Iron Age "Currency Bars": the Archaeological and Social Context', *The Archaeological Journal*, **147**, 91–117

—— 1991. 'The Romano-British Countryside: the Significance of Rural Settlement Forms' in R.F.J. Jones (ed.) 1991, pp. 75–80

Hinton, P. (ed.) 1988. *Excavations in Southwark 1973–76 Lambeth 1973–79*, London and Middlesex Archaeological Society and Surrey Archaeological Society

Hodder, I.R. 1972. 'Locational Models and the Study of Romano-British Settlement' in D.L. Clarke (ed.) 1972b, pp. 887–907

—— 1974. 'Some Marketing Models for Romano-British Coarse Pottery', *Britannia*, **5**, 340–59

—— 1979. 'Pre-Roman and Romano-British Tribal Economies' in Burnham and Johnson, pp. 189–96

Hodder, I.R. and Hassall, M.W.C. 1971. 'The Non-random Spacing of Romano-British Walled Towns', *Man*, **6**, 391–407

Hodder, I.R. and Millett, M. 1980. 'Romano-British Villas and Towns: a Systematic Analysis', *World Archaeology*, **12**, 69–76

Hodges, R. 1989a. *Dark Age Economics*, 2nd edn, Duckworth

—— 1989b. *The Anglo-Saxon Achievement*, Duckworth

—— 1991. *Wall-to-Wall History. The Story of Roystone Grange*, Duckworth

Hodgkinson, J.S. and Tebbutt, C.F. 1985. 'A Fieldwork Study of the Romano-British Iron Industry in the Weald of Southern England' in Craddock and Hughes, pp. 169–74

Hodgson, G.W. and Smith, C. 1985. 'The Animal Remains' in Bidwell 1985, microfiche VIII

Hogg, A.H.A. 1966. 'Native Settlement in Wales' in C. Thomas (ed.) 1966b, pp. 28–38

—— 1975. *Hill-forts of Britain*, Hart-Davis, MacGibbon

—— 1979. *British Hill-forts – an Index*, Oxford, BAR British Series, no. 62

Holgate, R. (ed.) 1995. *Archaeology of the Chilterns*, Dunstable, The Book Castle

Holleyman, G.A. 1935. 'Romano-British Site on Wolstonbury Hill', *Sussex Archaeological Collections*, **76**, 35–45

Hope, W.H. St. J. 1903. 'Excavations on the Site of the Roman City at Silchester, Hants, in 1902', *Archaeologia*, **58**, 413–28

Horne, P.D. 1981. 'Romano-Celtic Temples in the Third Century' in King and Henig, pp. 21–6

Horne, P.D. and King, A.C. 1980. 'Romano-Celtic Temples in Continental Europe: a Gazetteer of those Sites with Known Plans' in Rodwell (ed.) 1980b, pp. 369–555

Hoskins, W.G. 1955. *The Making of the English Landscape*, Harmondsworth, Penguin

Housley, R.A. 1988. 'The Environmental Context of Glastonbury Lake Village', *Somerset Levels Papers*, **14**, 63–82

Huckerby, E., Wells, C. and Middleton, R.H. 1992. 'Recent Palaeoecological and Archaeological Fieldwork in Over Wyre, Lancashire' in R.H. Middleton (ed.) 1992, pp. 9–18

Hunn, J. 1992. 'The Verulamium Oppidum and its Landscape in the Late Iron Age', *Archaeological Journal*, **149**, 39–68

Huntley, J.P. 1991. 'Woodland Management Studies' in McCarthy 1991, pp. 60–4

Inman, R. 1988. 'Romano-British Settlement in the South Tees Basin' in Price and Wilson, pp. 219–34

Isserlin, R. 1994. 'An Archaeology of Brief Time: Monuments and Seasonality in Roman Britain' in Cottam *et al.*, pp. 45–56

Jackson, D.A. and Tylecote, R.F. 1988. 'Two New Romano-British Iron-Working Sites in Northamptonshire', *Britannia*, **19**, 275–98

James, H.J. 1990. 'Carmarthen-Moridunum', *Trivium*, **25**, 86–93

—— 1992. 'Early Medieval Cemeteries in Wales' in Edwards and Lane 1992b, pp. 90–104

—— 1993. 'Roman Carmarthen' in Greep, pp. 93–8

James, H.J. and Williams, G. 1982. 'Rural Settlement in Roman Dyfed' in D. Miles (ed.) 1982b, pp. 289–312

James, S.T. 1984. 'Britain and the Late Roman Army' in Blagg and King, pp. 161–86

—— 1988. 'The Fabricae: State Arms Factories of the Later Roman Empire' in Coulston, pp. 257–331

James, S.T., Marshall, A. and Millett, M. 1984. 'An Early Medieval Building Tradition', *Archaeological Journal*, **141**, 182–215

Jarrett, M.G. 1976. *Maryport, Cumbria: a Roman Fort and its Garrison*, Kendal, Cumberland and Westmorland Archaeological and Antiquarian Society

Jarrett, M.G. and Wrathmell, S. 1981. *Whitton: an Iron Age and Roman Farmstead in South Glamorgan*, Cardiff, University of Wales Press

Jessup, R.F. 1962. 'Roman Barrows in Britain', *Latomus*, **58**, 853–67

Jewitt, L. 1851. 'On Roman Remains Recently Discovered at Headington, near Oxford, *Journal of the British Archaeological Association*, **6**, 52–67

Jobey, G. 1959. 'Excavations at the Native Settlement at Huckhoe, Northumberland 1955–7', *Archaeologia Aeliana*, 4th series, **37**, 217–78

—— 1960. 'Some Rectilinear Settlements of the Roman Period in Northumberland', *Archaeologia Aeliana*, 4th series, **38**, 1–38

—— 1963. 'Additional Rectilinear Settlements in Northumberland', *Archaeologia Aeliana*, 4th series, **41**, 211–15

—— 1964. 'Romano-British Enclosed Stone-built Settlements', *Archaeologia Aeliana*, 4th series, **42**, 41–64

—— 1965. 'Hill-forts and Settlements in Northumberland', *Archaeologia Aeliana*, 4th series, **43**, 21–64

—— 1970. 'An Iron Age Settlement and Homestead at Burradon, Northumberland', *Archaeologia Aeliana*, 4th series, **48**, 51–95

—— 1973. 'A Native Settlement at Hartburn and the Devil's Causeway, Northumberland', *Archaeologia Aeliana*, 5th series, **1**, 11–53

—— 1974. 'Notes on Some Population Problems in the Area Between the Two Roman Walls', *Archaeologia Aeliana*, 5th series, **2**, 17–26

—— 1977. 'Iron Age and Later Farmsteads on Belling Law, Northumberland', *Archaeologia Aeliana*, 5th series, **5**, 5–38

—— 1978a. 'Burnswark Hill, Dumfriesshire', *Transactions of the Dumfries and Galloway Natural History and Antiquarian Society*, 3rd series, **53**, 57–104

—— 1978b. 'Iron Age and Romano-British Settlements on Kennel Hall Knowe, North Tynedale, Northumberland', *Archaeologia Aeliana*, 5th series, **6**, 1–28

—— 1981. 'Excavations at the Romano-British Settlement at Middle Gunnar Peak, Barrasford, Northumberland', *Archaeologia Aeliana*, 5th series, **9**, 51–74

—— 1982a. 'Between Tyne and Forth: Some Problems' in Clack and Haselgrove, pp. 7–20

—— 1982b. 'The Settlement at Doubstead and Romano-British Settlement on the Coastal Plain Between Tyne and Forth', *Archaeologia Aeliana*, 5th series, **10**, 1–23

Johnson, N. and Rose, P. 1982. 'Defended Settlement in Cornwall – an Illustrated Discussion' in D. Miles (ed.) 1982b, pp. 151–207

Johnson, P. 1993. 'Town Mosaics and Urban Officinae' in Greep, pp. 147–65

Johnson, P. and Haynes, I. (ed.) 1996. *Architecture in Roman Britain*, York, CBA Research Report, no. 94

Johnson, P. and Walters, B. 1988. 'Exploratory Excavations of Roman Buildings at Cherhill and Manningford Bruce', *Wiltshire Archaeological and Natural History Magazine*, **82**, 77–91

Johnson, S. 1983. *Late Roman Fortifications*, Batsford

—— 1989. *Hadrian's Wall*, Batsford

Johnston, D.E. 1978. 'Villas of Hampshire and the Isle of Wight' in Todd (ed.) 1978b, pp. 71–92

—— 1988. *Roman Villas*, 3rd edn, Princes Risborough, Shire

Jones, A.H.M. 1964. *The Later Roman Empire, 284–602 AD, Vol. II*, Oxford, Blackwell

Jones, B. and Mattingly, D. 1990. *An Atlas of Roman Britain*, Oxford, Blackwell

Jones, G. 1984. 'Interpretation of Archaeological Plant Remains: Ethnographic Models from Greece' in Zeist and Casparie, pp. 43–61

—— 1987. 'A Statistical Approach to the Archaeological Identification of Crop Processing', *Journal of Archaeological Science*, **14**, 311–23

Jones, G. and Milles, A. 1989. 'Iron Age, Romano-British and Medieval Plant Remains' in Britnell, microfiche 3.5

Jones, G.D.B. 1976. 'The Western Extension of Hadrian's Wall: Bowness to Cardurnock', *Britannia*, **7**, 236–43

—— 1979. 'The Development of the Coastal Frontier' in Dobson, pp. 28–9

—— 1982. 'The Solway Frontier: an Interim Report 1976–81', *Britannia*, **13**, 283–5

—— 1984. '"Becoming Different Without Knowing it": the Role and Development of *Vici*' in Blagg and King, pp. 75–91

—— 1991. 'The Emergence of the Tyne-Solway Frontier' in Maxfield and Dobson, pp. 98–107

Jones, G.D.B. and Lewis, P.R. 1971. 'The Dolaucothi Gold-mines', *Bonner Jahrbuch*, **171**, 288–300

Jones, G.D.B. and Maude, K. 1991a. 'Dating and Dolaucothi', *Britannia*, **22**, 210–11

—— 1991b. 'Dolaucothi: the Dating Problem' in Burnham and Davies, pp. 169–71

Jones, M. 1978. 'The Plant Remains' in Parrington, pp. 93–110

—— 1981. 'The Development of Crop Husbandry' in M. Jones and Dimbleby, pp. 95–128

—— 1984. 'The Plant Remains' in Cunliffe 1984b, pp. 483–95

—— 1986. 'Towards a Model of the Villa Estate' in D. Miles (ed.) 1986, pp. 38–42

—— (ed.) 1988. *Archaeology and the Flora of the British Isles*, Oxford University Committee for Archaeology

—— 1989. 'Agriculture in Roman Britain: the Dynamics of Change' in Todd (ed.) 1989b, pp. 127–34

Jones, M. and Dimbleby, G. (eds) 1981. *The Environment of Man: the Iron Age to the Anglo-Saxon Period*, Oxford, BAR British Series, no. 87

Jones, M. and Robinson, M. 1986. 'The Crop Plants' in D. Miles (ed.) 1986, microfiche, Chapter 9

Jones, M.J. 1985. 'New Streets for Old: the Topography of Roman Lincoln' in Grew and Hobley, pp. 86–93

—— 1993. 'The Latter Days of Roman Lincoln' in Vince, pp. 14–28

—— 1994. 'St Paul-in-the-Bail, Lincoln: Britain in Europe?' in Painter, pp. 325–47

Jones, R., Benson-Evans, K. and Chambers, F.M. 1985. 'Human Influence upon Sedimentation in Llangorse Lake, Wales', *Earth Surface Processes and Landforms*, **10**, 227–35

Jones, R.F.J. 1975. 'The Romano-British Farmstead and its Cemetery at Lynch Farm, near Peterborough', *Northamptonshire Archaeology*, **10**, 94–137

—— 1984. 'Urbanisation in the Roman North' in P.R. Wilson *et al.*, pp. 87–8

—— 1987a. 'Burial in Roman and the Western Provinces' in Wacher (ed.) 1987, pp. 812–37

—— 1987b. '"A False Start?" The Roman Urbanisation of Western Europe', *World Archaeology*, **19**, 48–57

—— (ed.) 1991. *Roman Britain: Recent Trends*, University of Sheffield/J.R. Collis

Jones, R.F.J., Bloemers, J.H.F., Dyson, S.L. and Biddle, M. (eds) 1988. *First Millennium Papers: Western Europe in the First Millennium AD*, Oxford, BAR International Series, no. 401

Karlen, W. 1991. 'Glacier Fluctuations in Scandinavia During the Last 9000 Years' in Starkel *et al.*, pp. 395–412

Keeley, H.C.M. (ed.) 1987. *Environmental Archaeology: a Regional Review*, HBMCE

Keevill, G.D. 1996. 'The Reconstruction of the Romano-British Villa at Redlands Farm, Northamptonshire' in P. Johnson and Haynes, pp. 44–55

Kelly, R.S. 1988. 'Two Late Prehistoric Circular Enclosures near Harlech, Gwynedd', *Proceedings of the Prehistoric Society*, **54**, 101–51

—— 1991. 'Recent Research on the Hut Group Settlements of Northwest Wales' in Burnham and Davies, pp. 102–11

Kenward, H.K. 1979. 'The Insect Remains' in Kenward and Williams, pp. 62–75

Kenward, H.K. and Williams, D. 1979. *Biological Evidence from the Roman Warehouses in Coney Street*, CBA

Keppie, L.F.J. 1975. 'The Building of the Antonine Wall: Archaeological and Epigraphic Evidence', *Proceedings of the Society of Antiquaries of Scotland*, **105** (1972–4), 151–65

—— 1989. 'Beyond the Northern Frontier: Roman and Native in Scotland' in Todd (ed.) 1989b, pp. 61–73

Keppie, L.F.J. and Walker, J.J. 1981. 'Fortlets on the Antonine Wall at Seabegs Wood, Kinneil and Cleddans', *Britannia*, **12**, 143–62

Kilbride-Jones, H.E. 1938. 'The Excavation of a Native Settlement at Milking Gap, High Shield, Northumberland', *Archaeologia Aeliana*, 4th series, **15**, 303–50

King, A.C. 1978. 'A Comparative Survey of Bone Assemblages from Roman Sites in Britain', *Institute of Archaeology Bulletin*, **15**, 207–32

—— 1984. 'Animal Bones and the Dietary Identity of Military and Civilian Groups in Roman Britain, Germany and Gaul' in Blagg and King, pp. 187–218

—— 1986. 'Romano-British Farms and Farmers in Craven, North Yorkshire' in Manby and Turnbull, pp. 181–93

—— 1989. 'Villas and Animal Bones' in Branigan and Miles, pp. 51–9

—— 1990. 'The Emergence of Roman-Celtic Religion' in Blagg and Millett, pp. 220–41

—— 1991. 'Food Production and Consumption – Meat' in R.F.J. Jones (ed.) 1991, pp. 15–20

—— 1996. 'The South-east Façade of Meonstoke Aisled Building' in P. Johnson and Haynes, pp. 56–69

King, A.C. and Henig, M. (eds), 1981. *The Roman West in the Third Century*, Oxford, BAR International Series, no. 109

King, A.C. and Potter, T.W. 1990. 'A New Domestic Building Façade from Roman Britain', *Journal of Roman Archaeology*, **3**, 195–204

King, A.C. and Soffe, G. 1991. 'Hayling Island' in R.F.J. Jones (ed.) 1991, pp. 111–13

Kristiansen, K. and Jensen, J. (eds) 1994. *Europe in the First Millennium BC*, Sheffield, J.R. Collis

Lamb, H.H. 1981. 'Climate from 1000 BC to 1000 AD' in M. Jones and Dimbleby, pp. 53–66

—— 1995. *Climate, History and the Modern World*, 2nd edn, Routledge

Lambrick, G. 1990. 'Ritual and Burial in the Thames Valley', *Current Archaeology*, **121**, 6–13

—— 1992. 'The Development of Late Prehistoric and Roman Farming on the Thames Gravels' in Fulford and Nichols, pp. 78–105

Lambrick, G. and Robinson, M. (eds) 1979. *Iron Age and Roman Riverside Settlements at Farmoor, Oxfordshire*, Oxford Archaeological Unit/CBA

—— 1988. 'The Development of Floodplain Grassland in the Upper Thames Valley' in M. Jones (ed.) 1988, pp. 55–75

Leach, P. 1991a. 'The Roman Site at Fosse Lane, Shepton Mallet: an Interim Report of the 1990 Archaeological Investigations', *Somerset Archaeology and Natural History*, **134** (1990), 47–56

—— 1991b. *Shepton Mallet: Romano-Britons and Early Christians in Somerset*, Birmingham University Field Archaeology Unit and Showering Ltd

Leech, R.H. 1976. 'Larger Agricultural Settlements in the West Country' in Branigan and Fowler, pp. 142–61

—— 1977. 'Iron Age and Romano-British Briquetage Sites at Quarrylands Lane, Badgeworth, Weare', *Proceedings of the Somerset Archaeology and Natural History Society*, **121**, 89–96

—— 1981. 'The Excavation of a Romano-British Farmstead and Cemetery on Bradley Hill, Somerton, Somerset', *Britannia*, **12**, 177–252

—— 1982a. *Excavations at Catsgore 1970–1973. A Romano-British Village*, Bristol, Western Archaeological Trust

—— 1982b. 'The Roman Interlude in the South-west: the Dynamics of Economic and Social Change in Romano-British South Somerset and North Dorset' in D. Miles (ed.) 1982b, pp. 209–67

Leech, R.H. and Leach, P. 1982. 'Roman Town and Countryside 43–450 AD' in Aston and Burrow, pp. 63–82

Leemann, A. and Niessen, F. 1994. 'Holocene Glacial Activity and Climatic Variations in the Swiss Alps: Reconstructing a Continuous Record from Proglacial Lake Sediments', *The Holocene*, **4**, 259–68

Lewis, C., Mitchell-Fox, P. and Dyer, C. 1996. *Village, Hamlet and Field*, Manchester University Press

Lewis, M.J.T. 1966. *Temples in Roman Britain*, Cambridge, Cambridge University Press

Lewit, T. 1991. *Agricultural Production in the Roman Economy AD 200–400*, Oxford, BAR International Series, no. 568

Limbrey, S. and Evans, J.G. (eds) 1978. *The Effect of Man on the Landscape: the Lowland Zone*, CBA

Ling, R. 1993. 'Wall-painting since Wheeler' in Greep, pp. 166–70

Liversidge, J. 1955. *Furniture in Roman Britain*, Alec Tiranti

—— 1969. 'Furniture and Interior Decoration' in Rivet (ed.) 1969b, pp. 127–72

Lloyd-Jones, M. 1984. *Society and Settlement in Wales and the Marches*, Oxford, BAR British Series, no. 121

Longley, D. 1988. 'Bryn Eryr', *Archaeology in Wales*, **28**, 57

Lowther, A.W.G. 1930. 'Excavations at Ashtead, Surrey. Third Report (1929)', *Surrey Archaeological Collections*, **38**, 132–48

Lucas, R.N. 1993. *The Romano-British Villa at Halstock, Dorset. Excavations 1967–85*, Dorchester, Dorset Natural History and Archaeological Society

Luff, R.-M. 1982. *A Zooarchaeological Study of the Roman North-western Provinces*, Oxford, BAR International Series, no. 137

Lyne, M.A.B. and Jefferies, R.S. 1979. *The Alice Holt/Farnham Roman Pottery Industry*, CBA Research Report, no. 30

McCarthy, M.R. 1986. 'Woodland and Roman Forts', *Britannia*, **17**, 339–43

—— 1991. *The Structural Sequence and Environmental Remains from Castle Street, Carlisle: Excavations 1981–2*, Kendal, Cumberland and Westmorland Antiquarian and Archaeological Society

—— 1995. 'Archaeological and Environmental Evidence for the Roman Impact on Vegetation near Carlisle, Cumbria', *The Holocene*, **5**, 491–5

McDonald, A. 1988. 'Changes in the Flora of Port Meadow and Picksey Mead, Oxford' in M. Jones (ed.) 1988, pp. 76–85

Mackay, A.W. and Tallis, J.H. 1994. 'The Recent Vegetational History of the Forest of Bowland, Lancashire, UK', *New Phytologist*, **128**, 571–84

McKinley, J.I. and Heaton, M. 1996. 'A Romano-British Farmstead and Associated Burials at Maddington Farm, Shrewton', *Wiltshire Archaeological and Natural History Magazine*, **89**, 44–72

Macklin, M.G. and Lewin, J. 1993. 'Holocene River Alluviation in Britain' in Douglas and Hagedorm, pp. 109–22

Macklin, M.G. and Needham, S. 1992. 'Studies in British Alluvial Archaeology: Potential and Prospect' in Needham and Macklin, pp. 9–23

Mackreth, D.F. 1978. 'Orton Hall Farm, Peterborough: a Roman and Saxon Settlement' in Todd (ed.) 1978b, pp. 209–28

—— 1984. 'Castor', *Durobrivae*, **9**, 22–5

—— 1987. 'Roman Public Building' in Schofield and Leech, pp. 133–46

—— 1988. 'Excavation of an Iron Age and Roman Enclosure at Werrington, Cambridgeshire', *Britannia*, **19**, 59–151

McOmish, D. 1993. 'Salisbury Plain', *Current Archaeology*, **135**, 110–13

Macphail, R.I. 1994. 'The Reworking of Urban Stratigraphy by Human and Natural Processes' in Hall and Kenward (eds.) 1994, pp. 13–43

Macready, S. and Thompson, F.H. (eds) 1984. *Cross-channel Trade between Gaul and Britain in the Pre-Roman Iron Age*, Society of Antiquaries of London

McWhirr, A.D. (ed.) 1976. *Studies in the Archaeology and History of Cirencester*, Oxford, BAR British Series, no. 30

—— 1979a. 'Tile-kilns in Roman Britain' in McWhirr (ed.) 1979b, pp. 97–189

—— (ed.) 1979b. *Roman Brick and Tile. Studies in Marketing, Distribution and Volume in the Western Empire*, Oxford, BAR International Series, no. 68

—— 1986a. *Houses in Roman Cirencester*, Cirencester Excavation Committee

—— 1986b. *Roman Gloucestershire*, Gloucester, Alan Sutton/Gloucestershire County Library

McWhirr, A.D. and Viner, D. 1978. 'The Production and Distribution of Tiles in Roman Britain with Particular Reference to the Cirencester Region', *Britannia* **9**, 357–77

Maltby, M. 1981. 'Iron Age, Romano-British and Anglo-Saxon Animal Husbandry – a Review of the Faunal Evidence' in M. Jones and Dimbleby, pp. 155–203

—— 1994. 'The Meat Supply in Roman Dorchester and Winchester' in Hall and Kenward (eds.) 1994, pp. 85–102

Manby, T.G. and Turnbull, P. (eds) 1986. *Archaeology in the Pennines*, Oxford, BAR British Series, no. 158

Manley, J., Grenter, S. and Gale, F. (eds) 1991. *The Archaeology of Clwyd*, Clwyd County Council

Mann, J.C. 1988. 'A History of the Antonine Wall: a Reappraisal', *Proceedings of the Society of Antiquaries of Scotland*, **118**, 131–7

Manning, W.H. 1975. 'Economic Influences on Land Use in the Military Areas of the Highland Zone During the Roman Period' in Evans *et al.*, pp. 112–16

—— 1979. 'The Native and Roman Contribution to the Development of Metal Industries in Britain' in Burnham and Johnson, pp. 111–22

—— 1988. *Early Roman Campaigns in the South-west of Britain*, Cardiff, National Museum of Wales

Margary, I.D. 1973. *Roman Roads in Britain*, 3rd edn, John Baker

Masson Phillips, E.N. 1966. 'Excavation of a Romano-British Site at Lower Well Farm, Stoke Gabriel, Devon', *Proceedings of the Devon Archaeological Exploration Society*, **23**, 3–34

Matthews, J.A. and Karlen, W. 1992. 'Asynchronous Neoglaciation and Holocene Climatic Change Reconstructed from Norwegian Glaciolacustrine Sedimentary Sequences', *Geology*, **20**, 991–4

Mawer, C.F. 1995. *Evidence for Christianity in Roman Britain*, Oxford, BAR British Series, no. 243

Maxfield, V.A. 1980. 'The Roman Military Occupation of South-west England: Further Light and Fresh Problems' in Hanson and Keppie, pp. 297–310

—— (ed.) 1989. *The Saxon Shore: a Handbook*, Department of History and Archaeology, University of Exeter

—— 1995. *Soldier and Civilian: Life Beyond the Ramparts*, Cardiff, National Museum of Wales

Maxfield, V.A. and Dobson, M.J. (eds) 1991. *Roman Frontier Studies 1989*, University of Exeter Press

Maxwell, G.S. 1980. 'Agricola's Campaigns: the Evidence of the Temporary Camps', *Scottish Archaeological Forum*, **12**, 25–54

—— 1983a. 'Roman Settlement in Scotland' in Chapman and Mytum, pp. 233–62

—— (ed.) 1983b. *The Impacts of Aerial Reconnaissance on Archaeology*, CBA Research Report, no. 49

—— 1985. 'Fortlets and Distance Slabs on the Antonine Wall', *Britannia*, **16**, 25–8

—— 1989. *The Romans in Scotland*, Edinburgh, J. Thin

May, J. 1996. *Dragonby*, Oxford, Oxbow Monograph, no. 61

Mays, S. 1993. 'Infanticide in Roman Britain', *Antiquity*, **67**, 883–8

Meadows, I. 1996. 'Wollaston: the Nene Valley, a British Moselle?', *Current Archaeology*, **150**, 212–15

Meates, G.W. 1979. *The Roman Villa at Lullingstone, Vol. I: the Site*, Maidstone, Kent Archaeological Society Monograph, no. 1

Meiggs, R. 1982. *Trees and Timber in the Ancient Mediterranean World*, Oxford, Clarendon Press

Mercer, R. (ed.) 1981. *Farming Practice in British Prehistory*, Edinburgh University Press

Middleton, P. 1979. 'Army Supply in Roman Gaul: an Hypothesis for Roman Britain' in Burnham and Johnson, pp. 81–97

Middleton, R.H. (ed.) 1992. *North West Wetlands Survey Annual Report 1992*, Lancaster University Archaeological Unit

Mighall, T.M. and Chambers, F.M. 1989. 'The Environmental Impact of Iron-working at Bryn y Castell Hillfort, Merioneth', *Archaeology in Wales*, **29**, 17–21

—— 1995. 'Holocene Vegetation History and Human Impact at Bryn y Castell, Snowdonia, North Wales', *New Phytologist*, **130**, 299–321

Miket, R. and Burgess, C. (eds) 1984. *Between and Beyond the Walls*, Edinburgh, John Donald

Miles, D. 1982a. 'Confusion in the Countryside: some Comments from the Upper Thames Region' in D. Miles (ed.) 1982b, pp. 53–79

—— (ed.) 1982b. *The Romano-British Countryside: Studies in Rural Settlement and Economy*, Oxford, BAR British Series, no. 103

—— 1983. 'An Integrated Approach to Ancient Landscape: the Claydon Pike Project' in Maxwell (ed.) 1983b, pp. 74–84

—— 1984. 'Romano-British Settlement in the Gloucestershire Thames Valley' in Saville, pp. 191–211

—— (ed.) 1986. *Archaeology at Barton Court Farm, Abingdon, Oxon*, Oxford/London, Oxford Archaeological Unit/CBA

—— 1989. 'The Romano-British Countryside' in Todd (ed.) 1989b, pp. 115–26

Miles, D. and Palmer, S. 1982. *Figures in a Landscape: Archaeological Investigations at Claydon Pike, Fairford/Lechlade, Gloucestershire: an Interim Report 1979–1982*, Oxford Archaeological Unit

—— 1990. 'Claydon Pike and Thornhill Farm', *Current Archaeology*, **121**, 19–23

—— 1995. 'White Horse Hill', *Current Archaeology*, **142**, 372–8

Miles, H. and Miles, T. 1973. 'Excavations at Trethurgy, St Austell: Interim Report', *Cornish Archaeology*, **12**, 25–30

—— 1974. 'Trethurgy', *Current Archaeology*, **40**, 142–6

Miles, J. 1988. 'Vegetation and Soil Change in the Uplands' in Usher and Thompson, pp. 57–70

Miller, L., Schofield, J. and Rhodes, M. 1986. *The Roman Quay at St Magnus House, London*, Museum of London/London and Middlesex Archaeological Society

Milles, A., Williams, D. and Gardner, N. (eds) 1989. *The Beginnings of Agriculture*, Oxford, BAR International Series, no. 496

Millett, M. 1986. 'Central Places in a Decentralised Roman Britain' in E. Grant, pp. 45–7

—— 1990. *The Romanization of Britain: an Essay in Archaeological Interpretation*, Cambridge University Press

—— 1991. 'Roman Towns and their Territories: an Archaeological Perspective' in Rich and Wallace Hadrill, pp. 169–90

—— 1995. *Roman Britain*, Batsford/English Heritage

Milne, G. 1985. *The Port of Roman London*, Batsford

—— 1993. 'The Rise and Fall of Roman London' in Greep, pp. 11–15

Milne, G., Battarbee, R.W., Straker, V. and Yule, B. 1983. 'The River Thames in London in the Mid 1st Century AD', *Transactions of the London and Middlesex Archaeological Society*, **34**, 19–30

Monaghan, J. 1987. *Upchurch and Thameside Roman Pottery: a Ceramic Typology for Northern Kent, First to Third Centuries AD*, Oxford, BAR British Series, no. 173

Money, J.H. 1977. 'The Iron Age Hill-fort and Romano-British Iron-working Settlement at Garden Hill, Sussex: Interim Report on Excavations, 1968–76', *Britannia*, **8**, 339–50

Moore, P.D. 1968. 'Human Influence upon Vegetational History in North Cardiganshire', *Nature*, **217**, 1006–7

—— 1993. 'The Origin of Blanket Mire, Revisited' in Chambers (ed.) 1993, pp. 217–24

Moore, P.D., Webb, J.A. and Collinson, M.E. 1991. *Pollen Analysis*, 2nd edn, Oxford, Blackwell

Morris, E. 1994a. 'The Organization of Pottery Production and Distribution in Iron Age Wessex' in Fitzpatrick and Morris, pp. 26–9

—— 1994b. 'Production and Distribution of Pottery and Salt in Iron Age Britain: a Review', *Proceedings of the Prehistoric Society*, **60**, 1–23

Morris, P. 1979. *Agricultural Buildings in Roman Britain*, Oxford, BAR British Series, no. 70

Morris, R. 1989. *Churches in the Landscape*, Dent

Morris, R. and Roxan, J. 1980. 'Churches on Roman Buildings' in Rodwell (ed.) 1980b, pp. 175–209

Morrison, I. 1985. *Landscape with Lake Dwellings: the Crannogs of Scotland*, Edinburgh University Press

Murphy, K. 1985. 'Excavation at Penycoed, Llangynog, Dyfed, 1983', *Carmarthenshire Antiquary*, **21**, 75–112

Musson, C.R. 1981. 'Prehistoric and Romano-British Settlement in Northern Powys and Western Shropshire', *Archaeological Journal*, **138**, 5–7

Musson, C.R., with Britnell, W.J. and Smith, A.G. 1991. *The Breiddin Hillfort*, CBA Research Report, no. 76

Mynard, D.C. (ed.) 1987. *Roman Milton Keynes: Excavations and Fieldwork 1971–82*, Aylesbury, Buckinghamshire Archaeological Society

Mytum, H.C. 1982. 'Rural Settlement of the Roman Period in North and East Wales' in D. Miles (ed.) 1982b, pp. 313–35

Nash-Williams, V.E. 1969. *The Roman Frontier in Wales*, 2nd edn (by M.G. Jarrett), Cardiff, University of Wales Press

Neal, D.S. 1970. 'The Roman Villa at Boxmoor: Interim Report', *Britannia*, **1**, 156–62

—— 1974. *The Excavation of the Roman Villa in Gadebridge Park, Hemel Hempstead 1963–8*, Reports of the Research Committee of the Society of Antiquaries of London, no. 31

—— 1976. 'Northchurch, Boxmoor and Hemel Hempstead Station: the Excavation of Three Roman Buildings in the Bulbourne Valley', *Hertfordshire Archaeology*, **4**, 1–135

—— 1989. 'The Stanwick Villa, Northants: an Interim Report on the Excavations of 1984-88', *Britannia*, **20**, 149–68

Neal, D.S., Wardle, A. and Hunn, J. 1990. *Excavation of the Iron Age, Roman and Medieval Settlement at Gorhambury, St Albans*, HBMCE

Needham, S. and Macklin, M.G. (eds) 1992. *Alluvial Archaeology in Britain*, Oxford, Oxbow Monograph, no. 27

Niblett, R. 1992. 'A Catuvellaunian Chieftain's Burial from St Albans', *Antiquity*, **66**, 917–29

—— 1993. 'Verulamium since the Wheelers' in Greep, pp. 78–92

Noddle, B.A. 1984. 'A Comparison of the Bones of Cattle, Sheep, and Pigs from Ten Iron Age and Romano-British Sites' in Grigson and Clutton-Brock, pp. 105–23

—— 1986. 'The Animal Bones' in G. Webster *et al.* 1986, pp. 82–97

Nye, S. and Jones, M. 1987. 'The Carbonised Plant Remains' in Cunliffe 1987, pp. 323–8

Olson, L. 1989. *Early Monasteries in Cornwall*, Woodbridge, Boydell Press

O'Neil, B.H. St J. 1937. 'Excavations at Breiddin Hill Camp, Montgomeryshire, 1933–35', *Archaeologia Cambrensis*, **92**, 86–128

Ordnance Survey, 1969. *The Antonine Wall*, Southampton

—— 1989. *Hadrian's Wall*, Southampton

Oswald, A. 1937. 'A Roman Fortified Villa at Norton Disney, Lincs', *Antiquaries Journal*, **17**, 138–78

—— 1949. 'A Re-excavation of the Roman Villa at Mansfield Woodhouse, Nottinghamshire, 1936–39', *Transactions of the Thoroton Society*, **53**, 1–14

Ottaway, P. 1993. *Roman York*, Batsford/English Heritage

Painter, K. (ed.) 1994. *Churches Built in Ancient Times: Recent Studies in Early Christian Archaeology*, Society of Antiquaries

Parrington, M. 1978. *The Excavation of an Iron Age Settlement, Bronze Age Ring-ditches and Roman Features at Ashville Trading Estate, Abingdon (Oxfordshire) 1974–76*, Oxford Archaeological Unit/CBA

Peacock, D.P.S. 1969. 'A Romano-British Salt Working Site at Trebarveth, St Keverne', *Cornish Archaeology*, **8**, 47–65

—— (ed.) 1977. *Pottery and Early Commerce*, Academic Press

—— 1982. *Pottery in the Roman World: an Ethnoarchaeological Approach*, Longman

—— 1987. 'Iron Age and Roman Quern Production at Lodsworth, West Sussex', *Antiquaries Journal*, **67**, 61–85

Pearce, S.M. 1982. *The Early Church in Western Britain and Ireland*, Oxford, BAR British Series, no. 102

Pearson, E. and Giorgi, J. 1992. 'The Plant Remains' in Cowan, pp. 165–70

Percival, J. 1976. *The Roman Villa: an Historical Introduction*, Batsford

—— 1982. 'Recent Work on Roman Villas in Britain', *Caesarodunum*, **17**, 305–20

—— 1988. *The Roman Villa: an Historical Introduction*, 2nd edn, Batsford

Perring, D. 1987. 'Domestic Buildings in Romano-British Towns' in Schofield and Leech, pp. 147–55

—— 1991a. 'The Buildings' in Perring and Roskams, pp. 67–107

—— 1991b. *Roman London*, Seaby

Perring, D. and Roskams, S. 1991. *The Archaeology of Roman London, Vol. 2: Early Development of Roman London West of the Walbrook*, Museum of London/CBA

Phillips, C.W. (ed.) 1970. *The Fenland in Roman Times*, The Royal Geographical Society

Philp, B.J. 1968. *Excavations at Faversham, 1965: the Royal Abbey, Roman Villa and Belgic Farmstead*, First Research Report of the Kent Archaeological Research Groups' Council

—— 1973. *Excavations in West Kent 1960–70*, Dover, Kent Archaeological Rescue Unit

—— 1984. *Excavations in the Darent Valley, Kent*, Dover, Kent Archaeological Rescue Unit

—— 1996. *The Roman Villa Site at Orpington, Kent*, Dover, Kent Archaeological Rescue Unit

Philp, B.J., Parfitt, K., Willson, J., Dutto, M. and Williams, W. 1991. *The Roman Villa Site at Keston, Kent. First Report (Excavations 1968–1978)*, Dover, Kent Archaeological Rescue Unit

Philpott, R. 1991. *Burial Practices in Roman Britain*, Oxford, BAR British Series, no. 219

Pilcher, J.R. and Hall, V.A. 1996. 'Tephrochronological Studies in Northern England', *The Holocene*, **6**, 100–5

Platt, C. 1978. *Medieval England*, Routledge and Kegan Paul

Pollard, S.M.H. 1974. 'A Late Iron Age Settlement and a Romano-British Villa at Holcombe, near Uplyme, Devon', *Proceedings of the Devon Archaeological Society*, **32**, 59–161

Potter, T.W. 1979. 'The Cumbrian Coast Defences and Ravenglass' in Dobson, pp. 24–8

—— 1980. 'The Roman Frontier in Cumbria' in Hanson and Keppie, pp. 195–200

—— 1981. 'The Roman Occupation of the Central Fenland', *Britannia*, **12**, 79–133

—— 1989. 'The Roman Fenland: a Review of Recent Work' in Todd (ed.) 1989b, pp. 147–73

—— 1996. 'The Roman Stone Building at Stonea, Cambridgeshire' in P. Johnson and Haynes, pp. 70–4

Potter, T.W. and Johns, C. 1992. *Roman Britain*, British Museum Press

Potter, T.W. and Potter, C.F. 1980. 'A Romano-British Village at Grandford, March', *Proceedings of the Cambridge Antiquarian Society*, **70**, 75–111

—— 1982. *A Romano-British Village at Grandford, March, Cambridgeshire*, British Museum Occasional Paper, no. 35

Powlesland, D. 1988. 'Approaches to the Excavation and Interpretation of the Romano-British Landscape in the Vale of Pickering' in Price and Wilson, pp. 139–50

Price, E.G. 1993. 'Frocester Court Excavations 1993', *Glevensis*, **27**, 40–1

Price, J. and Wilson, P.R. (eds) 1988. *Recent Research in Roman Yorkshire*, Oxford, BAR British Series, no. 193

Pryor, F. 1984. *Excavation at Fengate, Peterborough, England: the Fourth Report*, Toronto/Northampton, Royal Ontario Museum Archaeology/Northamptonshire Archaeological Society

Qualmann, K.E. 1993. 'Roman Winchester' in Greep, pp. 66–77

Quinnell, H. 1986. 'Cornwall During the Iron Age and Roman Period', *Cornish Archaeology*, **25**, 111–34

—— 1993. 'A Sense of Identity: Distinctive Cornish Stone Artefacts in the Roman and Post-Roman periods', *Cornish Archaeology*, **32**, 29–46

Quinnell, H. *et al.* 1991. 'The Villa and Temple at Cosgrove, Northamptonshire', *Northamptonshire Archaeology*, **23**, 4–65

Rackham, J. 1979. '*Rattus rattus*: the Introduction of the Black Rat into Britain', *Antiquity*, **53**, 112–20

Rackham, O. 1977. 'Neolithic Woodland Management in the Somerset Levels: Garvin's, Walton Heath and Rowland's Tracks', *Somerset Levels Papers*, **3**, 65–71

—— 1990. *Trees and Woodland in the British Landscape*, rev. edn, Dent

Radford, C.A.R. 1936. 'The Roman Villa at Ditchley, Oxon', *Oxoniensia*, **1**, 24–69

Rahtz, P.A. 1951. 'The Roman Temple at Pagan's Hill, Chew Stoke, North Somerset', *Proceedings of the Somerset Archaeological and Natural History Society*, **96**, 112–42

Rahtz, P.A. and Greenfield, E. 1977. *Excavations at Chew Valley Lake, Somerset*, HMSO

Rahtz, P.A. and Watts, L. 1979. 'The End of Roman Temples in the West of Britain' in Casey (ed.) 1979, pp. 183–201

Raistrick, A. and Holmes, P.F. 1962. 'The Archaeology of Malham Moor', *Field Studies*, **1**, 73–100

Ramm, H. 1978. *The Parisi*, Duckworth

—— 1980. 'Native Settlements East of the Pennines' in Branigan (ed.) 1980, pp. 28–40

—— 1988. 'Aspects of the Roman Countryside in East Yorkshire' in Price and Wilson, pp. 81–8

Randsborg, K. 1991. *The First Millennium AD in Europe and the Mediterranean*, Cambridge University Press

Rawes, B. 1981. 'The Romano-British Site at Brockworth, Glos', *Britannia*, **12**, 45–77

—— 1983. 'Gloucester Severn Valley Ware', *Transactions of the Bristol and Gloucestershire Archaeological Society*, **100** (1982), 33–46

—— 1985. 'The Romano-British Site on the Portway, near Gloucester', *Transactions of the Bristol and Gloucestershire Archaeological Society*, **102** (1984), 23–72

—— 1992. 'A Prehistoric and Romano-British Settlement at Vineyards Farm Charlton Kings, Gloucestershire', *Transactions of the Bristol and Gloucestershire Archaeological Society*, **109** (1991), 25–89

Rawlings, M. and Fitzpatrick, A.P. 1996. 'Prehistoric Sites and a Romano-British Settlement at Butterfield Down, Amesbury', *Wiltshire Archaeological and Natural History Magazine*, **89**, 1–43

Reece, R. 1980. 'Town and Country: the End of Roman Britain', *World Archaeology*, **12**, 77–92

—— 1988. *My Roman Britain*, Cirencester, Cotswold Studies

Rees, S.E. 1979. *Agricultural Implements in Prehistoric and Roman Britain*, Oxford, BAR British Series, no. 69, 2 vols

Reid, C. 1903. 'Notes on the Plant Remains of Roman Silchester' in Hope, pp. 425–8

Renfrew, C. and Shennan, S. 1982. *Ranking, Resource and Exchange*, Cambridge University Press

Reynolds, P.J. 1979. *Iron-Age Farm: The Butser Experiment*, British Museum

—— 1981. 'Deadstock and Livestock' in Mercer, pp. 97–122

Rich, J. (ed.)1992. *The City in Late Antiquity*, Routledge

Rich, J. and Wallace Hadrill, A. (eds) 1991. *City and Country in the Ancient World*, Routledge

Richmond, I.A. 1966. 'Industry in Roman Britain' in Wacher, pp. 76–86

—— 1969. 'The Plans of Roman Villas in Britain' in Rivet (ed.) 1969b, pp. 49–70

Richmond, I.A. and Gillam, J.P. 1951. 'The Temple of Mithras at Carrawburgh', *Archaeologia Aeliana*, 4th series, **29**, 1–92

Riley, D.N. 1978. 'An Early System of Land Division in South Yorkshire and North Nottinghamshire' in Bowen and Fowler (eds) 1978, pp. 103–9

—— 1980. *Early Landscapes from the Air*, Department of Prehistory and Archaeology, University of Sheffield

Rippengal, R. 1993. 'Villas as a Key to Social Structure? Some Comments on Recent Approaches to the Romano-British Villa and Some Suggestions Toward an Alternative' in Scott (ed.) 1993, pp. 79–101

Rippon, S. 1996. *Gwent Levels: The Evolution of a Wetland Landscape*, York, CBA

Rivet, A.L.F. 1964. *Town and Country in Roman Britain*, 2nd edn, Hutchinson

—— 1969a. 'Social and Economic Aspects' in Rivet (ed.) 1969b, pp. 173–216

—— (ed.) 1969b. *The Roman Villa in Britain*, Routledge/Kegan Paul

Rivet, A.L.F. and Smith, C. 1979. *The Place-names of Roman Britain*, Batsford

Roberts, B.K., Turner, J. and Ward, P.F. 1973. 'Recent Forest History and Land Use in Weardale, Northern England' in Birks and West, pp. 207–21

Robertson, A.S. 1970. 'Roman Finds from Non-Roman Sites in Scotland', *Britannia*, **1**, 198–226

—— 1975. 'The Romans in North Britain: the Coin Evidence' in Temporini and Haase, pp. 364–426

—— 1978. 'The Circulation of Roman Coins in North Britain: the Evidence of Hoards and Site Finds from Scotland' in Carson and Kraay, pp. 186–219

—— 1979. *The Antonine Wall*, 3rd edn, Glasgow, Glasgow Archaeological Society

—— 1983. 'Roman Coins Found in Scotland, 1971–82', *Proceedings of the Society of Antiquaries of Scotland*, **113**, 424–6

Robinson, M. 1986. 'Waterlogged Plant and Invertebrate Evidence' in D. Miles (ed.) 1986, microfiche, chapter 8

Rodwell, W.J. 1980a. 'Wells: the Cathedral and City', *Current Archaeology*, no. **73**, 38–44

—— 1980b. *Temples, Churches, and Religion: Recent Research in Roman Britain with a Gazetteer of Romano-Celtic Temples in Continental Europe*, Oxford, BAR British Series, no. 77

—— 1982. 'From Mausoleum to Minster: the Early Development of Wells Cathedral' in Pearce, pp. 49–59

Rowell, T.K. and Turner, J. 1985. 'Litho-, Humic- and Pollen Stratigraphy at Quick Moss, Northumberland', *Journal of Ecology*, **73**, 11–25

Rowlands, M., Larsen, M. and Kristiansen, K. (eds) 1987. *Centre and Periphery in the Ancient World*, Cambridge University Press

Royal Commission on Ancient and Historical Monuments in Wales. 1976. *Glamorgan, Vol. I Part II: The Iron Age and the Roman Occupation*, Cardiff, HMSO

Royal Commission on Ancient and Historical Monuments in Wales and Monmouthshire. 1937. *An Inventory of the Ancient Monuments in Anglesey*, HMSO

Royal Commission on Historical Monuments (England). 1976. *Iron Age and Romano-British Monuments in the Gloucestershire Cotswolds*, HMSO

—— 1984. 'West Park Roman Villa, Rockbourne, Hampshire', *Archaeological Journal*, **140** (1983), 129–50

Rudling, D.R. 1982a. 'The Romano-British Farm on Bullock Down' in Drewett, pp. 97–142

—— 1982b. 'Rural Settlement in Late Iron Age and Roman Sussex', in D. Miles (ed.) 1982b, pp. 269–88

—— 1986. 'The Excavation of a Roman Tilery on Great Cansiron Farm, Hartfield, East Sussex', *Britannia*, **17**, 191–230

Rush, P. 1995. *Theoretical Roman Archaeology: Second Conference Proceedings*, Aldershot, Avebury

Salway, P. 1970. 'The Roman Fenland' in Phillips, pp.1–21

—— 1980. 'The *Vici*: Urbanisation in the North' in Branigan (ed.) 1980, pp. 8–17

—— 1993. *The Oxford Illustrated History of Roman Britain*, Book Club Associates

Saunders, A. 1962. 'Excavations at Park Street, 1954–7', *Archaeological Journal*, **118** (1961), 100–35

Saunders, A. and Harris, D. 1982. 'Excavations at Castle Gotha, St Austell', *Cornish Archaeology*, **21**, 109–53

Saunders, C. 1972. 'The Excavations at Grambla, Wendron, 1972', *Cornish Archaeology*, **11**, 50–2

Saville, A. (ed.) 1984. *Archaeology in Gloucestershire*, Cheltenham Art Gallery and Museums/Bristol and Gloucestershire Archaeological Society

Savory, H.N. 1961. 'Excavations at Dinas Emrys, Beddgelert (Caern), 1954–56', *Archaeologia Cambrensis*, **109** (1960), 13–77

Scarre, C. and Healy, F. (eds) 1993. *Trade and Exchange in Prehistoric Europe*, Oxford, Oxbow

Schofield, J. and Leech, R. (eds) 1987. *Urban Archaeology in Britain*, CBA Research Report, no. 61

Scott, E. 1990. 'A Critical Review of the Interpretation of Infant Burials in Roman Britain, with Particular Reference to Villas', *Journal of Theoretical Archaeology*, **1**, 30–46

—— 1991. 'Animal and Infant Burials in Romano-British Villas: a Revitalisation Movement' in Garwood *et al.*, pp. 115–21

—— 1993a. *A Gazetteer of Roman Villas in Britain*, Leicester University Archaeological Research Centre

—— (ed.) 1993b. *Theoretical Roman Archaeology: First Conference Proceedings*, Aldershot, Avebury

Scull, C. 1992. 'Before Sutton Hoo: Structures of Power and Society in Early East Anglia' in Carver, pp. 3–23

—— 1993. 'Archaeology, Early Anglo-Saxon Society and the Origins of Anglo-Saxon Kingdoms' in Filmer-Sankey, pp. 65–82

Sealey, P.R. 1995. 'New Light on the Salt Industry and Red Hills of Prehistoric and Roman Essex', *Essex Archaeology and History*, **26**, 65–81

Seaward, M.R.D. 1993. 'Environmental Evidence' in Van Driel-Murray *et al.*, pp. 91–119

Sedgley, J.P. 1975. *The Roman Milestones of Britain*, Oxford, BAR British Series, no. 18

Selkirk, R. 1983. *The Piercebridge Formula: a Dramatic New View of Roman History*, Cambridge, Patrick Stevens

Sellwood, L. 1984. 'Tribal Boundaries Viewed from the Perspective of Numismatic Evidence' in Cunliffe and Miles, pp. 191–204

Sharples, N.M. 1991a. *Maiden Castle: Excavations and Field Survey 1985–86*, English Heritage

—— 1991b. 'Warfare in the Iron Age of Wessex', *Scottish Archaeological Review*, **8**, 79–89

Shennan, I. 1986. 'Flandrian Sea-level Changes in the Fenland. II: Tendencies of Sea-level Movement, Altitudinal Changes, and Local and Regional Factors', *Journal of Quaternary Science*, **1**, 155–79

Simco, A. 1984. *The Roman Period in Bedfordshire*, Bedford, Bedfordshire County Council/Royal Commission on Historical Monuments (England)

Simmons, B.B. 1979. 'The Lincolnshire Car Dyke: Navigation or Drainage?', *Britannia*, **10**, 183–96

—— 1985. 'Sapperton', *Archaeology in Lincolnshire* 1984–5, 16–20

Simmons, I.G. and Cundill, P.R. 1974. 'Late Quaternary Vegetational History of the North York Moors I. Pollen Analyses of Blanket Peats', *Journal of Biogeography*, **1**, 159–69

Simmons, I.G., Rand, J.I. and Crabtree, K. 1983. 'A Further Pollen Analytical Study of the Blacklane Peat Section on Dartmoor, England', *New Phytologist*, **94**, 655–67

—— 1987. 'Dozmary Pool, Bodmin Moor, Cornwall: a New Radiocarbon Dated Pollen Profile' in Balaam *et al.*, pp. 125–33

Simmons, I.G., Atherden, M., Cloutman, E.W., Cundill, P.R., Innes, J.B. and Jones, R.L. 1993. 'Prehistoric Environments' in Spratt, pp. 15–50

Simpson, S.J., Griffith, F.M. and Holbrook, N. 1989. 'The Prehistoric, Roman, and Early Post-Roman Site at Hayes Farm, Clyst Honiton', *Proceedings of the Devon Archaeological Society*, **47**, 1–28

Simpson, W.G. 1966. 'Romano-British Settlement on the Welland Gravels' in C. Thomas (ed.) 1966b, pp. 15–25

Sims, R.E. 1978. 'Man and Vegetation in Norfolk' in Limbrey and Evans, pp. 57–62

Smith, C.A. 1974. 'A Morphological Analysis of Late Prehistoric and Romano-British Settlements in North-west Wales', *Proceedings of the Prehistoric Society*, **40**, 157–69

—— 1977. 'Late Prehistoric and Romano-British Enclosed Homesteads in North-west Wales: an Interpretation of their Morphology', *Archaeologia Cambrensis*, **126**, 38–52

—— 1986. 'Excavations at the Ty Mawr Hut-circles, Holyhead, Anglesey. Part II', *Archaeologia Cambrensis*, **134** (1985), 11–52

—— 1987. 'Excavations at the Ty Mawr Hut-circles, Holyhead, Anglesey. Part III. The Finds', *Archaeologia Cambrensis*, **135** (1986), 12–80

—— 1988. 'Excavations at the Ty Mawr Hut-circles, Holyhead, Anglesey. Part IV. Chronology and Discussion', *Archaeologia Cambrensis*, **136** (1987), 20–38

Smith, J.T. 1963. 'Romano-British Aisled Houses', *Archaeological Journal*, **120**, 1–30

—— 1964. 'The Roman Villa at Denton', *Reports and Papers of the Lincolnshire Architecture and Archaeology Society*, **10**, 75

—— 1978a. 'Halls or Yards? A Problem of Villa Interpretation', *Britannia*, **9**, 351–8
—— 1978b. 'Villas as a Key to Social Structure' in Todd (ed.) 1978b, pp. 149–85
—— 1982. 'Villas, Plans and Social Structure in Britain and Gaul', *Caesarodunum*, **17**, 321–36
—— 1985. 'Barnsley Park Villa: its Interpretation and Implications', *Oxford Journal of Archaeology*, **4**, 341–51
—— 1987. 'The Social Structure of a Roman Villa: Marshfield – Ironmongers Piece', *Oxford Journal of Archaeology*, **6**, 243–55
Smith, K., Coppen, J., Wainwright, G.J. and Beckett, S. 1981. 'The Shaugh Moor Project: Third Report – Settlement and Environmental Investigations', *Proceedings of the Prehistoric Society*, **47**, 205–73
Smith, N.A.F. 1978. 'Roman Canals', *Transactions Newcomen Society*, **49** (1977–8), 75–86
Smith, R.F. 1981. 'Hibaldstow', *Current Archaeology*, **77**, 168–71
—— 1987. *Roadside Settlements in Lowland Roman Britain*, Oxford, BAR British Series, no. 157
Snape, M.E. 1991. 'Roman and Native: Vici on the North British Frontier' in Maxfield and Dobson, pp. 468–71
Soffe, G., Nicholls, J. and Moore, G. 1989. 'The Roman Tilery and Aisled Building at Crookhorn, Hants, Excavations, 1974–5', *Proceedings of the Hampshire Field Club and Archaeological Society*, **45**, 43–112
Sommer, C.S. 1984. *The Military Vici in Roman Britain*, Oxford, BAR British Series, no. 129
Southwark and Lambeth Archaeological Excavation Committee (SLAEC) (ed.) 1978. *Southwark Excavations 1972–1974*, London and Middlesex Archaeological Society/Surrey Archaeological Society
Southern, P. and Dixon, K.R. 1996. *The Late Roman Army*, Batsford
Spain, R.J. 1985. 'Romano-British Watermills', *Archaeologia Cantiana*, **100** (1984), 101–28
Speidel, M.P. 1987. 'The Chattan War, the Brigantian Revolt and the Loss of the Antonine Wall', *Britannia*, **18**, 233–7
Spratt, D.A. (ed.) 1993. *Prehistoric and Roman Archaeology of North-East Yorkshire*, rev. edn, CBA
Spratt, D.A. and Hartley, B.R. 1993. 'The Roman Period (AD 70–410)' in Spratt, pp. 155–66
Starkel, L., Gregory, K.J. and Thornes, K.B. (eds) 1991. *Temperate Palaeohydrology*, Chichester, John Wiley
Stead, I.M. 1972. 'Beadlam Roman Villa: an Interim Report', *Yorkshire Archaeological Journal*, **43** (1971), 178–86
—— 1976a. *Excavations at Winterton Roman Villa and other Roman Sites in North Lincolnshire, 1958–1967*, HMSO
—— 1976b. 'La Tène Burials between Burton Fleming and Rudston, North Humberside', *The Antiquaries Journal*, **56**, 217–26
—— 1980. *Rudston Roman Villa*, Leeds, Yorkshire Archaeological Society
Stephens, G.R. 1985a. 'Civic Aqueducts in Britain', *Britannia*, **16**, 197–208
—— 1985b. 'Military Aqueducts in Roman Britain', *Archaeological Journal*, **142**, 216–36
Stevens, C.E. 1966. 'The Social and Economic Aspects of Rural Settlement' in C. Thomas (ed.) 1966b, pp. 108–28
Stewart, P.C.N. 1995. 'Inventing Britain: the Roman Creation and Adaptation of an Image', *Britannia*, **26**, 1–10
Stirland, A. and Waldron, T. 1990. 'The Earliest Cases of Tuberculosis in Britain', *Journal of Archaeological Science*, **17**, 221–30
Stopford, J. 1988. 'Danebury: an Alternative View', *Scottish Archaeological Review*, **4**, 70–5
Straker, V. 1984. 'First and Second Century Carbonised Cereal Grain from Roman London' in Zeist and Casparie, pp. 323–29
Strickland, T. 1995. *The Romans at Wilderspool*, Warrington, The Greenalls Group
Stuiver, M. and Pearson, G.W. 1993. 'High Precision Bidecadal Calibration of the Radiocarbon Time Scale, AD 1950–500 BC and 2500–6000 BC', *Radiocarbon*, **35**, 1–23
Sumpter, A. 1988. 'Iron Age and Roman at Dalton Parlours' in J. Price and Wilson, pp. 171–96
Swan, V.G. 1984. *The Pottery Kilns of Roman Britain*, HMSO
—— 1988. *Pottery in Roman Britain*, Princes Risborough, Shire
Taylor, C. 1983. *Village and Farmstead: a History of Rural Settlement in England*, George Philip
Taylor, C. and Fowler, P. 1978. 'Roman Fields into Medieval Furlongs?' in Bowen and Fowler (eds) 1978, pp. 159–62
Taylor, J.A. (ed.) 1980. *Culture and Environment in Prehistoric Wales*, Oxford, BAR British Series, no. 76
Temporini, H. and Haase (ed.) 1975. *Aufstieg und Niedergang der Romischen Welt II.3*, Berlin, Walter de Gruyter
Thomas, A. and Holbrook, N. 1996. 'Llandough', *Current Archaeology*, **146**, 73–7
Thomas, C. 1966a. 'The Character and Origins of Roman Dumnonia' in C. Thomas (ed.) 1966b, pp. 74–98
—— 1966b. *Rural Settlement in Roman Britain*, CBA Research Report, no. 7
—— 1981. *Christianity in Roman Britain to AD 500*, Batsford
—— 1985. *Exploration of a Drowned Landscape: Archaeology and History of the Isles of Scilly*, Batsford
Thompson, D.J. 1987. 'Imperial Estates' in Wacher (ed.) 1987, pp. 555–67
Thompson, F.H. (ed.) 1980. *Archaeology and Coastal Change*, The Society of Antiquaries of London
Timby, J. 1990. 'Severn Valley Ware: a Reassessment', *Britannia*, **21**, 243–51
Tinsley, H.M. and Smith, R.T. 1974. 'Surface Pollen Studies Across a Woodland/Heath Transition and their Application to the Interpretation of Pollen Diagrams', *New Phytologist*, **73**, 547–65
Tipping, R. 1995a. 'Holocene Evolution of a Lowland Scottish Landscape: Kirkpatrick Fleming. Part I: Peat- and Pollen-stratigraphic Evidence for Raised Moss Development and Climatic Change', *The Holocene*, **5**, 69–81
—— 1995b. 'Holocene Evolution of a Lowland Scottish Landscape: Kirkpatrick Fleming. Part II: Regional Vegetation and Land-use Change', *The Holocene*, **5**, 83–96
Todd, M. 1973. *The Coritani*, Duckworth
—— 1978a. 'Villas and Romano-British Society' in Todd (ed.) 1978b, pp. 197–208
—— (ed.) 1978b. *Studies in the Romano-British Villa*, Leicester University Press
—— 1984a. 'The Early Roman Phase at Maiden Castle', *Britannia*, **15**, 254–5
—— 1984b. 'Hembury (Devon): Roman Troops in a Hillfort', *Antiquity*, **58**, 171-4
—— 1985. 'Oppida and the Roman Army: a Review of Recent Evidence', *Oxford Journal of Archaeology*, **4**, 187–99

—— 1987. *The South-west to AD 1000*, Longman

—— 1989a. 'Villa and Fundus' in Branigan and Miles, pp. 14–20

—— (ed.) 1989b. *Research on Roman Britain: 1960–89*, Britannia Monograph, no. 11

—— 1994. 'Charterhouse on Mendip: an Interim Report on Survey and Excavation in 1993', *Somerset Archaeology and Natural History*, **137** (1993), 59–68

Tomalin, D.J. 1987. *Roman Wight*, Newport, Isle of Wight County Council

Topping, P. 1989a. 'The Context of Cord Rig Cultivation in Later Prehistoric Northumberland' in Bowden *et al.*, pp. 145–57

—— 1989b. 'Early Cultivation in Northumberland and the Borders', *Proceedings of the Prehistoric Society*, **55**, 161–79

Trow, S.D. 1988. 'Excavations at Ditches Hillfort, North Cerney, Gloucestershire, 1982–3', *Transactions of the Bristol and Gloucestershire Archaeological Society*, **106**, 19–85

—— 1990. 'By the Northern Shores of Ocean: Some Observations on Acculturation Process at the Edge of the Roman World' in Blagg and Millett, pp. 35–41

Trow, S.D. and James, S. 1989. 'Ditches Villa, North Cerney: an Example of Locational Conservatism in the Early Roman Cotswolds' in Branigan and Miles, pp. 83–7

Turner, E.G. 1956. 'A Roman Writing Tablet from Somerset', *Journal of Roman Studies*, **46**, 115–18

Turner, J. 1964. 'The Anthropogenic Factor in Vegetational History. I: Tregaron and Whixall Mosses', *New Phytologist*, **63**, 73–90

—— 1965. 'A Contribution to the History of Forest Clearance', *Proceedings of the Royal Society of London B*, **161**, 343–53

—— 1979. 'The Environment of North-east England During Roman Times as Shown by Pollen Analysis', *Journal of Archaeological Science*, **6** , 285–90

—— 1981. 'The Vegetation' in M. Jones and Dimbleby, pp. 67–73

Turner, R. 1982. *Ivy Chimneys, Witham: an Interim Report*, Chelmsford, Essex County Council

Turner, R.C. and Scaife, R.G. (eds) 1995. *Bog Bodies: New Discoveries and Perspectives*, British Museum

Tyers, I. 1988. 'Environmental Evidence from Southwark and Lambeth' in Hinton, pp. 443–77

Unz, C. (ed.) 1986. *Studien zu den Militärgrenzen Roms III, 13 Internationaler Limeskongress*, Aalen 1983, Stuttgart

Usher, M.B. and Thompson, D.B.A. (eds) 1988. *Ecological Change in the Uplands*, Oxford, Blackwell

Van Arsdell, R. 1989. *Celtic Coinage of Britain*, Spink

Van Driel-Murray, C. 1993. 'The Leatherwork' in Van Driel-Murray *et al.*, pp. 1–75

Van Driel-Murray, C., Wild, J.P., Seaward, M. and Hillam, J. 1993. *Vindolanda, Vol. III: the Early Wooden Forts*, Hexham, Roman Army Museum

Veen, M. van der. 1989. 'Charred Grain Assemblages from Roman-Period Corn Driers in Britain', *Archaeological Journal*, **146**, 302–19

—— 1992. *Crop Husbandry Regimes*, Sheffield, J.R. Collis

Vince, A. (ed.) 1993. *Pre-Viking Lindsey*, Lincoln Archaeological Studies

Vyner, B. (ed.) 1994. *Building on the Past*, Royal Archaeological Institute

—— (ed.) 1995. *Moorland Monuments: Studies in the Archaeology of North-east Yorkshire in Honour of Raymond Hayes and Don Spratt*, CBA Research Report, no. 101

Wacher, J. (ed.) 1966. *The Civitas Capitals of Roman Britain*, Leicester University Press

—— 1974. 'Villae in Urbibus?', *Britannia*, **5**, 251–61

—— 1978. *Roman Britain*, Dent

—— (ed.) 1987. *The Roman World*, Routledge/Kegan Paul

—— 1995. *The Towns of Roman Britain*, 2nd edn, Batsford

Waddelove, A.C. and Waddelove, E. 1990. 'Archaeology and Research into Sea-level during the Roman Era: Towards a Methodology Based on Highest Astronomical Tide', *Britannia*, **21**, 253–66

Wainwright, A. 1990. 'The Mollusc and Seed Remains' in Neal *et al.*, pp. 213–18

Wainwright, G.J. 1967. *Coygan Camp. A Prehistoric, Romano-British and Dark Age Settlement in Carmarthenshire*, Cardiff, Cambrian Archaeological Association

—— 1971. 'The Excavation of Prehistoric and Romano-British Settlements near Durrington Walls, Wiltshire, 1970', *Wiltshire Archaeological Magazine*, **66**, 76–128

—— 1979. *Gussage All Saints: an Iron Age Settlement in Dorset*, DOE

Wainwright, G.J. and Davies, S.M. 1995. *Balksbury Camp, Hampshire*, English Heritage

Wait, G. 1985. *Ritual and Religion in Iron Age Britain*, Oxford, BAR British Series, no. 149

Waller, M. 1994. *The Fenland Project, Number 9: Flandrian Environmental Change in Fenland*, Cambridge, Fenland Project Committee

Walters, B. 1994. *Littlecote Roman Villa*, Roman Research Marketing Ltd

—— 1996. 'Exotic Structures in 4th-century Britain' in P. Johnson and Haynes, pp. 152–62

Walthew, C.V. 1975. 'The Town House and the Villa House in Roman Britain', *Britannia*, **6**, 189–205

Ward, J. 1907. 'Roman Remains at Cwmbrwyn, Carmarthenshire', *Archaeologia Cambrensis*, **7**, 175–212

Ward-Perkins, J.B. 1938. 'The Roman Villa at Lockleys, Welwyn', *Antiquaries Journal*, **18**, 339–76

Watkins, R. 1990. 'The Postglacial Vegetational History of Lowland Gwynedd – Llyn Cororion' in Addison *et al.*, pp. 131–6

Waton, P.V. 1982. 'Man's Impact on the Chalklands: Some New Pollen Evidence' in Bell and Limbrey, pp. 75–91

Webster, D., Webster, H. and Petch, D.F. 1967. 'A Possible Vineyard of the Romano-British Period at North Thoresby, Lincolnshire', *Lincolnshire History and Archaeology*, **2**, 55–61

Webster, G. 1953. 'The Lead Mining Industry in North Wales in Roman Times', *Journal of the Flintshire Historical Society*, **13** (1952–3), 5–33

—— 1980. *The Roman Invasion of Britain*, Batsford

—— 1981. *Rome Against Caratacus: the Roman Campaigns in Britain AD 48–58*, Batsford

—— 1982. 'The Excavation of a Romano-British Rural Establishment at Barnsley Park, Gloucestershire, 1961–79. Part I: *c.* AD 140–360', *Transactions of the Bristol and Gloucestershire Archaeological Society*, **99** (1981), 21–77

—— (ed.) 1988. *Fortress into City: the Consolidation of Roman Britain, First Century AD*, Batsford

—— 1991. *The Cornovii*, rev. edn, Stroud, Alan Sutton

—— 1993. 'The City of Viroconium (Wroxeter): its Military Origins and Expansion under Hadrian' in Greep, pp. 50–5

Webster. G. and Dudley, D.R. 1965. *The Roman Conquest of Britain*, Pan Books

Webster, G., Fowler, P., Noddle, B. and Smith, L. 1986. 'The Excavation of a Romano-British Rural Establishment at Barnsley Park, Gloucestershire, 1961–1979: Part III', *Transactions of the Bristol and Gloucestershire Archaeological Society*, **103** (1985), 73–100

Webster, G. and Smith, L. 1983. 'The Excavation of a Romano-British Rural Establishment at Barnsley Park, Glos. 1961–79: Part II', *Transactions of the Bristol and Gloucestershire Archaeological Society*, **100** (1982), 65–190

Webster, P.V. 1972. 'Severn Valley Ware on Hadrian's Wall', *Archaeologia Aeliana*, 4th series, **50**, 191–203

—— 1977a. 'Severn Valley Ware', *Transactions of the Bristol and Gloucestershire Archaeological Society*, **94** (1976) 18–46

—— 1977b. 'Severn Valley Ware on the Antonine Frontier' in Dore and Greene, pp. 63–76

—— 1987. *Roman Samian Ware: Background Notes*, 3rd edn, Cardiff, Department of Extra-Mural Studies, University College

—— 1991. 'Pottery and Trade in Roman Wales' in Burnham and Davies, pp. 138–49

Webster, R.A. 1972. 'The Excavation of a Romano-British Settlement at Waitby', *Transactions of the Cumberland and Westmorland Archaeological and Antiquarian Society*, **72**, 66–73

Wedlake, W.J. 1982. *The Excavation of the Shrine of Apollo at Nettleton, Wiltshire, 1956–1971*, Research Reports of the Society of Antiquaries of London, no. 40

Welfare, H. and Swan, V. 1995. *Roman Camps in England: the Field Archaeology*, HMSO

Welfare, H., Topping, P., Blood, K. and Ramm, H. 1991. 'Stanwick, North Yorkshire, Part 2: a Summary Description of the Earthworks', *The Archaeological Journal*, **147** (1990), 16–36

Welsby, D.A. 1982. *The Roman Military Defence of the British Province in its Later Phases*, Oxford, BAR British Series, no. 101

West, S. 1976. 'The Roman Site at Icklingham', *East Anglian Archaeology*, **3**, 63–125

Wheeler, R.E.M. 1932. *The Excavation of the Prehistoric, Roman and Post-Roman Site in Lydney Park, Gloucestershire*, Report of the Research Committee of the Society of Antiquaries of London, no. 9

—— 1943. *Maiden Castle, Dorset*, Report of the Research Committee of the Society of Antiquaries of London, no. 12

—— 1954. *The Stanwick Fortifications*, Oxford, Society of Antiquaries of London

Whimster, R. 1977. 'Iron Age Burial in Southern Britain', *Proceedings of the Prehistoric Society*, **43**, 317–27

—— 1981. *Burial Practices in Iron Age Britain*, Oxford, BAR British Series, no. 90

White, K.D. 1977. *Country Life in Classical Times*, Paul Elek

White, R.H. 1988. *Roman and Celtic Objects from Anglo-Saxon Graves*, Oxford, BAR British Series, no. 191

—— 1990. 'Excavations on the Site of the Baths Basilica' in Barker, pp. 3–7

White, S.I. 1981. 'Excavations at Capel Eithin, Gaerwen, Anglesey, 1980: First Interim Report', *Transactions of the Anglesey Antiquarian Society for 1981*, 15–27

—— 1982. 'Capel Eithin' in Youngs and Clark, pp. 226–7

Whittaker, C.R. 1990. 'The Consumer City Revisited: the *Vicus* and the City', *Journal of Roman Archaeology*, **3**, 110–18

Whittick, G.C. 1982. 'The Earliest Roman Lead-mining on Mendip and in North Wales: a Reappraisal', *Britannia*, **13**, 113–23

Whitwell, B. 1988. 'Late Roman Settlement on the Humber and Anglian Beginnings' in J. Price and Wilson, pp. 49–78

Wild, J.P. 1978. 'Villas in the Lower Nene Valley' in Todd (ed.) 1978b, pp. 59–70

Willcox, G.H. 1978. 'Seeds from the Late 2nd-century Pit F28' in Dennis, pp. 411–3

Williams, A.M. 1909. 'The Romano-British Establishment at Stroud, near Petersfield, Hants', *Archaeological Journal*, **66**, 33–52

Williams, D. 1977. 'A Consideration of the Sub-fossil Remains of *Vitis vinifera* L. as Evidence for Viticulture in Roman Britain', *Britannia*, **8**, 327–34

—— 1979. 'The Plant Remains' in Kenward and Williams, pp. 52–62

Williams, G. 1985. *Fighting and Farming in Iron Age West Wales. Excavations at Llawhaden 1980–4*, Carmarthen, Dyfed Archaeological Trust

—— 1988. 'Recent Work on Rural Settlement in Later Prehistoric and Early Historic Dyfed', *Antiquaries Journal*, **68**, 30–54

Williams, R.J., Hart, P.J. and Williams, A.T.L. 1996. *Wavendon Gate: a Late Iron Age and Roman Settlement in Milton Keynes*, Milton Keynes Archaeological Monograph, no. 10

Williamson, T.M. 1984. 'The Roman Countryside: Settlement and Agriculture in N.W. Essex', *Britannia*, **15**, 225–30

—— 1987. 'Early Co-axial Field Systems on the East Anglian Boulder Clays', *Proceedings of the Prehistoric Society*, **53**, 419–31

—— 1993. *The Origins of Norfolk*, Manchester University Press

Wilmot, T. 1995. 'Collapse Theory and the End of Birdoswald' in Rush, pp. 59–69

—— 1996. 'Birdoswald: a Military Case Study' in P. Johnson and Haynes, pp. 93–103

Wilson, B. 1979. 'The Vertebrates' in Lambrick and Robinson, pp. 128–33

Wilson, D.R. 1975. 'Romano-Celtic Temple Architecture', *Journal of the British Archaeological Association*, 3rd series, **38**, 3–27

Wilson, D.R. and Sherlock, D. 1980. *North Leigh Roman Villa, Oxfordshire*, HMSO

Wilson, P.R. (ed.) 1989. *The Crambeck Roman Pottery Industry*, Leeds, Yorkshire Archaeological Society

——— 1995. 'North-east Yorkshire in the Roman Period: Developments and Prospects' in Vyner (ed.) 1995, pp. 69–78

Wilson, P.R., Jones, R.F.J. and Evans, D.M. (eds) 1984. *Settlement and Society in the Roman North*, School of Archaeology, University of Bradford/Yorkshire Archaeological Society

Wingfield, C. 1995. 'The Anglo-Saxon Settlement of Bedfordshire and Hertfordshire: the Archaeological View' in Holgate (ed.) 1995, pp. 31–43

Wise, P. 1991. 'Wasperton', *Current Archaeology*, **126**, 256–9

Wolseley, G.R., Smith, R.A. and Hawley, W. 1927. 'Prehistoric and Roman Settlements on Park Brow', *Archaeologia*, **76**, 1–40

Woodfield, C.C. 1965. 'Six Turrets on Hadrian's Wall', *Archaeologia Aeliana*, 4th series, **43**, 87–200

Wooding, J.M. 1996. 'Cargoes in Trade Along the Western Seaboard' in K.R. Dark (ed.) 1996c, pp. 67–82

Woodiwiss, S. (ed.) 1992. *Iron Age and Roman Salt Production and the Medieval Town of Droitwich*, CBA Research Report, no. 81

Woodward, A. and Leach, P. 1993. *The Uley Shrines: Excavations of a Ritual Complex on West Hill, Uley, Gloucestershire: 1977–9*, English Heritage

Woolf, G. 1992. 'The Unity and Diversity of Romanisation', *Journal of Roman Archaeology*, **5**, 349–52

——— 1993a. 'Rethinking the Oppida', *Oxford Journal of Archaeology*, **12**, 223–34

——— 1993b. 'The Social Significance of Trade in Late Iron Age Europe' in Scarre and Healy, pp. 211–18

——— 1993c. 'European Social Development and Roman Imperialism' in Brun *et al.*, pp. 13–20

Wrathmell, S. and Nicholson, A. (eds) 1990. *Dalton Parlours*, Wakefield, West Yorkshire Archaeology Service

Young, C.J. 1977. *The Roman Pottery Industry of the Oxford Region*, Oxford, BAR British Series, no. 43

——— 1986. 'The Upper Thames Valley in the Roman Period' in Briggs *et al.*, pp. 58–63

Youngs, S.M. and Clark, J. (eds) 1982. 'Medieval Britain in 1981', *Medieval Archaeology*, **26**, 164–227

Yule, B. 1990. 'The "Dark Earth" and Late Roman London', *Antiquity*, **64**, 620–8

Zeist, W. van and Casparie, W.A. (eds) 1984. *Plants and Ancient Man*, Rotterdam, Balkema

Zeist, W. van, Waslikowa, K. and Behre, K.-E. 1991. *Progress in Old World Palaeoethnobotany*, Rotterdam, Balkema

INDEX